Race and Wealth Disparities

(6(00(

A Multidisciplinary Discourse

Edited by
Beverly Moran

Project Funds
Provided by

VANDERBILT®

FORD FOUNDATION

UNIVERSITY PRESS OF AMERICA, ® INC.
Lanham • Boulder • New York • Toronto • Plymouth, UK

Copyright © 2008 by
University Press of America,® Inc.
4501 Forbes Boulevard
Suite 200
Lanham, Maryland 20706
UPA Acquisitions Department (301) 459-3366

Estover Road
Plymouth PL6 7PY
United Kingdom

Library of Congress Control Number: 2007936546
ISBN-13: 978-0-7618-3925-5 (clothbound : alk. paper)
ISBN-10: 0-7618-3925-9 (clothbound : alk. paper)
ISBN-13: 978-0-7618-3926-2 (paperback : alk. paper)
ISBN-10: 0-7618-3926-7 (paperback : alk. paper)

∞™ The paper used in this publication meets the minimum
requirements of American National Standard for Information
Sciences—Permanence of Paper for Printed Library Materials,
ANSI Z39.48—1992

Contents

Preface

This group of essays looks at one important aspect of race: how race in the United States and, to a lesser extent, other parts of the world, influences the wealth of individuals, communities and nations. Because the question of race and wealth disparities is a complicated one, the question is discussed through multidisciplinary lenses. In a day when multidisciplinary work is touted throughout the academy, there are few resources for how researchers, either in groups or as individuals, actually step outside of their fields in order to look at the world with a different perspective. The authors in this work took it upon themselves to model how multidisciplinary conversations take place by actually engaging with one another for two years before sitting down to write their pieces. Working together in private seminars and through public lectures, the authors learned from one another about how each others' disciplines looked at this crucial issue of race and wealth disparities. In the tradition of looking at race from a variety of perspectives, a tradition most notably mined by African-American Studies, the authors in this collection represent a number of social science and humanities perspectives from anthropology, economics, education, history, literature and law, to management, political science, psychology and sociology. Through their many disciplines, the commentators give a broad range of perspectives on race and wealth disparities. In turn, readers receive both a greater and more textured understanding of how race and wealth intersect as well as a deeper appreciation for each author's academic discipline.

This volume is the result of an initiative by the Ford Foundation and Vanderbilt University. The idea was to bring together professors from a broad range of social science and humanities departments, pair them with community activists and let each learn from the other about one of the most pressing issues of our time—the wealth gap between the races in the United States. The group met once a month from 2002 to 2004. At each meeting we discussed an article or book chapter that focused on race and wealth disparities. The group member whose field was represented in the readings would lead the discussion by pointing out both how the work under discussion fit within the discipline and how his or her field studied (or failed to study) race and wealth disparities. The hope was that by meeting together and reading works from a broad range of perspectives, participants would come to understand what drove each others' disciplines and how to speak to one another across the divides that exist in the early 21st century university. In this way we strove to help each other learn how to judge works in other disciplines and how to take advantage of different points of view and research styles.

The two years were filled with controversies that focused our discussions and reminded us that race and wealth disparities are not simply academic questions but, instead, are at the core of our lives. When the time came to study rhetoric, Senator Trent Lott was under attack for saying:

> I want to say this about my state. When Strom Thurmond ran for president, we voted for him. We're proud of it. And if the rest of the country had followed our lead, we wouldn't have had all these problems over all these years either.[1]

Senator Lott's comments, and the troubles that they caused him, gave us a wonderful example of multidisciplinary perspectives as anthropologists, community activists, health care professionals, historians, lawyers, literary theorists, political scientists, rhetoricians and sociologists all jumped into an analysis of how public opinion is shaped and when tipping points develop in public discourse. The ways that our group members looked at the controversy, the factors that they focused on or ignored, helped all of us understand more about the particular event and about how different disciplines understand the world around us.

In fact, that discussion introduced us to one of the most interesting parts of looking at race and wealth from many perspectives, i.e., that we do not even share common definitions of race or wealth. For the medical school people among us, wealth meant health and healthy communities. For the anthropologists, wealth meant the ability to control one's own culture and to determine the cultural meaning of various activities. Even among our economists and management professors wealth was not limited solely to cash but included the ability to work as well as to pass property from generation to generation.

When the time came to discuss economics, a new tax bill had just passed giving substantial benefits to wealthy families in the form of a diminished gift and estate tax. At the same time, the first indications that the personal bankruptcy laws might be tightened at the behest of the credit card industry signaled a step back for the middle class family in trouble from unexpected medical bills or job loss. Having medical school faculty members alongside law professors and economists gave a depth to our conversation that a single disciplinary perspective lacks. It is our hope that at least some of the depth of those multidisciplinary conversations comes through in this work.

This volume is meant to do a number of things. One is to give the reader substantive information about race and wealth disparities particularly (although not exclusively) within the United States. Another is to serve as a model of a conversation that might take place in any American university if people from a variety of disciplines were to come together in order to discuss a critical topic of national importance. In that sense these chapters represent the approaches and insights that might occur in any similar peer group at any number of research universities around the nation. No doubt, the individual voices would sound different notes but the training, expertise, and knowledge systems employed are familiar. In fact, by sticking to one question—the question of race and wealth—but changing the discipline that looks at this topic chapter by chapter, we model a multidisciplinary conversation for use by individuals, classes and seminars seeking to explore either the substantive topic or the methods employed. In this sense, the volume is a demonstration case study of what a cross-disciplinary and multidisciplinary conversation looks like when centered in the capital of knowledge—the modern university.

It is particularly significant that this volume focuses on wealth, rather than income. We learned that for many of our group members, particularly those outside the social sciences, income was the measure of class in the United States. High income individuals were seen as upper middle or upper class and low income individuals were seen as working class or poor. What we did by shifting the focus away from income and toward wealth was to recognize that income is fleeting while wealth endures. As Robert Margo and William Collins point out in their chapter on home ownership, wealth is what protects families in hard times and provides opportunities in good times. Income disappears as soon as a job is lost or the wage earner dies. Wealth remains to pass on generation to generation.

How race and wealth intersect is a particularly urgent question in the American context because, unlike many other peoples, our culture tends to ignore class while obsessing about race. To illustrate: at this very moment, the income gap between nations gets wider and wider as 2 billion people live on $2 or less a day;[2] at this very moment, a middle class American family cannot survive on one income.[3] Personal bankruptcies rise.[4] Personal income falls. In many other countries, these facts would fuel political unrest. But not in the United States.

In the United States, the credit card industry lobbies Congress which, in turn, makes bankruptcy more difficult.[5] Yet, the Americans who most need bankruptcy protection are silent. American families are driven to bankruptcy by events like job loss or illness.[6] Yet, both layoffs and outsourcing increase and medical costs soar while Medicare is prohibited from negotiating volume discounts on drugs and elderly Americans are prohibited from purchasing cheap Canadian substitutes.[7] Instead of engaging in class struggle, middle class Americans actively support legislation that favors the rich more than themselves: from the middle class opposition to the gift and estate tax (a tax that leaves the middle class virtually untouched) to the middle class support for tax cuts that gave them very little while giving the rich a tremendous amount of additional cash. Nor is the middle class alone in voting against its economic interests. Gone are the days when unions made a difference in local and national elections and the poor, who represent almost 15% of the population, remain silent as well.

In matters of class identification, we Americans differ from other nations. We are not like the English who maintain allegiance to their social class even as their personal income (and wealth) rises or falls. We are not like the Chinese or citizens of the former Soviet states who were raised on the rhetoric of class struggle. Instead, because Americans believe that we are all middle class and anyone can be rich, we rarely discuss class inside (or outside) our politics, nor do we discuss race as an aspect of class. Yet, race is clearly an aspect of class in America. Like class in Britain, race in America does not disappear with the rise or fall of prosperity. Like the former socialist states, race in America is understood to pit one group against another. In other societies, class determines where one lives, who one knows and where one is educated. Welcome to race in America. In contrast to class, Americans self consciously base their lives on race. While Americans don't vote their economic class, they most certainly do vote their race and race, even more than class, determines where we live and who we know. The latest trend in urban development might mix economic classes by grouping homes of different costs together, but American housing patterns, like our employment and marriage patterns, remain segregated by race.

As philosophers from outside and inside the United States have commented, race in America is an old story repeated often. As early as *Democracy in America*, de Tocqueville wrote of America's race problem. Almost a century later, W.E.B. Du Bois named the problem of the color line as America's central concern. Half a century after Du Bois, in *American Dilemma,* Gunnar Myrdal documented Du Bois' assertion that racism poisoned all aspects of American life. Twenty years past Gunnar Myrdal white Americans turned fire hoses on their fellow citizens and stood in front of school house doors all to make sure that blacks remained an exploited underclass. Forty years after the attack dogs and fire hoses, we Americans litigate affirmative action and complain about immigration while our prisons house more dark skinned men than our colleges. How can one study class and culture in America without speaking of race?

Race plays an important role in American class and culture but what about wealth as a class marker? Do wealth and race together give us greater insights than either alone or combined with some other factor, for example, education? To some extent we authors selected wealth as our class marker because wealth, like class, is understudied in the United States. Although our cultural blindness to class is certainly one reason for our lack of attention to wealth, other factors also play into our overemphasis on income. First, government statistics often refer to income rather than wealth because income is routinely reported to government through the tax system. Wealth, on the other hand, is not generally reported to government at all or, if reported, only in incomplete ways. For example, local government might know the value of houses located in the county and the state government might know the value of stocks and bonds held by those within its boundaries and the federal government might learn the value of a few estates. But the routine, annual reporting that governments receive on income is not available for wealth.

The government practice of acquiring and reporting information on income also led generations of social scientists to study income instead of wealth. After all, if information on wealth is hard for governments to come by, imagine how much more difficult the task of learning about wealth is for individual researchers. Nevertheless, recent studies of the wealth gap between blacks and whites in this country have consistently shown that the wealth gap is greater than more studied disparities such as income, education or health. Those studies are part of what inspired these essays' focus on wealth. Other reasons for highlighting wealth include wealth's importance in peoples' lives. Wealth is what protects families in hard times. Wealth is what gives people opportunities to study, explore and earn. A family with wealth can survive the illnesses and layoffs that drive less fortunate others to bankruptcy and to avoid the host of social ills that hard times bring.

In the context of race and wealth in the United States, it is also important to remember that race has long determined who has wealth in America. Not so long ago, blacks in this country were property and America's European immigrants grew wealthy from American Indian lands. In fact, one might argue that American slavery and the Indian conquests helped create our modern concept of race because before Europeans dominated the world no one called himself black or white, Latino or Asian but instead identified as Celt, Oneida or Abyssinian.

This volume is multidisciplinary because the multidisciplinary approach allows us to explore a wide range of questions concerning class and culture/race and wealth. As you read through this book you will see that each field brings a different (sometimes radically different) understanding to all four concepts. To illustrate using wealth: we see that Edward Fischer, the volume's cultural anthropologist, uses wealth to mean both economic well being and the ability to control one's own culture and to name its meaning while Kenneth Wong, our political scientist, understands wealth in terms of access to education and the political power to structure education reform to one's benefit.

Race too is open to a variety of interpretations in this volume. As economists, William Collins and Robert Margo take a traditional black/white approach to American race relations and their approach is echoed in the political science chapter. On the other hand, Edward Fischer looks at Native Americans in his meditation on race even though many American Indians see themselves as citizens of sovereign nations rather than members of a race. In addition to Indians, Fischer's chapter discusses Latinos and blacks, thus taking his discussion outside the black/white American race standard. In the management chapter, Bruce Barry and Jason Stansbury look at race as encompassing every nonwhite group inside and outside of Europe and North America not so much to contrast between white and nonwhite as to contrast between poverty and wealth. James Quirin, the group's historian, echoes this theme of alternative views of race by understanding race as power. His work introduces us to a mystery facing scholars of world history—why did the rest of the world fall behind just as Europe flourished? Cecelia Tichi, author of one of the chapters on literary criticism, looks at race as a type of shape shifter and the United States as a nation in the process of turning middle class white Americans into members of a downwardly mobile chain gang.

Thus, if nothing else, the multidisciplinary approach to class and culture/race and wealth gives us a richer and more complete understanding of what class and culture/race and wealth mean over time and across disciplines. But, there is more to the multidisciplinary approach used in this volume because, in addition to writing about class and culture/race and wealth from their own academic perspective, the authors here have committed to considering how their academic discipline shapes their analysis. Thus, as they work through the problem of race and wealth in each essay, the authors invite the reader to look at both the substance of what they present and at how their field shaped that presentation. By exposure to ten different disciplinary perspectives on the same topic, the reader is able to both learn more substantive information on class and culture/race and wealth and to also compare a variety of social science and humanitarian approaches to the study of an important social issue.

Various types of social science methodology grace these pages. Professors Margo and Collins give a historical review of economic studies of wealth and race disparities in the United States that focuses on blacks, whites and home ownership. In their chapter, Margo and Collins first start with the harsh reality that blacks exited slavery with so little wealth that all blacks, both those who were free before the Emancipation and those freed thereafter, owned less than half a penny for every dollar owned by whites. Using home ownership as a substitute for all holdings by race, Collins and Margo then trace how the black/white wealth gap has closed over the last 150 years far less rapidly than gaps in income and education. As a result, even blacks with advanced degrees and high incomes are far less wealthy than their white peers. In addition to providing information about the most significant asset Americans own, the chapter also introduces us to how economists study various assets and asset accumulation.

Bruce Barry and Jason Stansbury use a different type of social science method in order to investigate what business school academics write about race and wealth. By taking us through their survey of the last two decades of academic business literature on poverty, Barry and Stansbury introduce us to an academic culture where poverty is only considered in terms of transforming poor people into consumers or low paid workers. Race, Barry and Stansbury tell us, is also under represented in the business literature except for a few studies of corporate managers and the role that race plays in their climb up the corporate ladder.

For another example of social science theory and method, Tony Brown and Daniel Cornfield introduce us to economic sociology and critical race theory and to how each sub-discipline looks at race and wealth disparities. In economic sociology, Professor Cornfield describes how researchers study individual workers' strategies to increase their income and, perhaps, their wealth, and how race shapes three of these income enhancing approaches: unionization, increases in human capital and self employment. Tony Brown then introduces us to critical race theory and how its emphasis on race and racism as deeply embedded within our culture's structures influences sociological studies.

As Brown and Cornfield explain, their chapter emphasizes two of many sub-disciplines in order to demonstrate that there are many ways to understand problems even within the same field. Their chapter, in combination with Barry's and Stansbury's management chapter and Margo's and Collins' chapter on economics, demonstrate how approach shapes findings. For example: where scholars are not interested in race and poverty, those topics disappear from their work just as when a theory makes race central to its analysis, race is always a factor; when a field is concerned with economic well being, its studies will emphasize tradable assets (like homes); but where a field is concerned with culture, cultural capital (as, for example, cultural sovereignty or the power to control education) receives more attention.

Building on power as a source of wealth, Professor Kenneth Wong demon-strates how one political scientist looks at the power to control education. His analysis of the "No Child Left Behind" Act and its effects on inner city school systems makes a strong statement about power over education as a form of wealth. That chapter also shows that there are many ways to look at legisla-tion. For example, a law review article might discuss the statute's internal structure and legal implications while Professor Wong's political science per-spective places the Act within the context of power plays between schools, school districts and communities.

Roland Mitchell and Reavis Mitchell join in the view that education is a form of wealth and that control over the educational process leads to even greater and more varied forms of wealth. By looking at Historically Black Universities and Colleges (HBCUs), Roland Mitchell and Reavis Mitchell re-veal a paradox that says volumes about America and the American educa-tional system: HBCUs are emblematic of the place of blacks in America in that they are the most under funded institutions in our system of higher edu-cation. Yet these schools with their underpaid faculty and administration and their under maintained physical plants are producing more black doctors, lawyers and Ph.D.'s than our well funded affirmative action driven Ivy League universities. How professors with very little support and students without adequate secondary school training become intellectual and profes-sional leaders through HBCUs is the topic of the Roland Mitchell's and Reavis Mitchell's research.

On the humanities side, we have two works from literary critics, Cecelia Tichi and Dennis Kezar. Tichi confronts a problem echoed by many others in this volume, the American reticence to confront the possibility of white down-ward mobility. In a world where the middle class white population is more and more vulnerable but also unwilling (or unable) to acknowledge the possibility of losing wealth and position, how does modern literature convert this unac-knowledged concern into a compelling narrative? Using *House of Sand and Fog* as an illustrative text, Tichi shows how a story that appears to relate very personal circumstances actually represents broader social issues from the plight of divorced women to the challenges immigrants face in adapting to America. In this way, Tichi shows how *House of Sand and Fog* both reveals American culture and submits to its need for denial while also exposing such American cultural issues as the tensions between whites and nonwhites, native born peoples and immigrants, intact families and those left alone.

Edward Fischer's chapter turns to American advertising in order to con-tinue Cecelia Tichi's theme of mass produced art as a reflection of social and cultural issues. Using advertising, Professor Fischer explores how the Amer-ican attraction to individualism and multi-culturalism is adopted by American business in order to mask the assault on individuality contained in capitalism, industrialization and mass production. For Professor Fischer, America's mass production economy has completely displaced individual craftsmanship and American business' response to a lingering craving for individual expression is to claim that individuality is expressed through consumption.

Dennis Kezar's and James Quirin's essays emphasize how their disciplines understand wealth and race disparities. From the vantage point of world history, Quirin explores how several students of world history have tried to learn how the world economy shifted in the 18th century so that, at the century's beginnings, China and India controlled most of the world's manufacturing yet, at the dawn of the 19th century and until today, Europe became the dominant player in industrial production. That manufacturing shift from Asia to Europe accompanied political and social shifts as well so that now the economies that once dominated the world are seen as emerging nations while Europeans (and their North American children) are seen as the creators of industrialization.

Dennis Kezar continues the process of looking at how his discipline works through issues of race and wealth by exploring how these concepts become tropes in the hands of literary critics. Kezar draws on his work in Renaissance English literature as well as on the works of Zora Neal Hurston and Henry Louis Gates to show an interpretative line from Shakespeare to the Harlem Renaissance.

Returning to the theme of home ownership, Bettie Kirkland and Sheila Peters look at the same information as Margo and Collins but with a decidedly psychological spin. While our economists dwell on the value of housing as an objective fact, our psychologists look at the value of housing as a created fact, created not from an indifferent market economy but from our group psychology that says that: "white is right, let brown step down and if you're black, get back get back get back." The dilemma that Kirkland and Peters present is that the same housing in the same neighborhood will see its value rise and fall depending on whether its residents are black or white, regardless of how well the property is maintained. That the simple fact of the color of an occupant can make housing values go up or down should bring shame to us all.

Although almost every essay touches in some way on law, whether by noting the decline in the union movement because of a decline in legal protections, or the difference in home ownership that is driven in part by government legislation and funding, or the role that law plays in literature as the catalyst for depriving one person of rights or granting rights to another, Stephanie Wildman and Beverly Moran in their chapter on law show that the legal academy has an uneasy relationship with the role of wealth and poverty in our legal system much less the role of race. Bringing the two together is one of the themes of their essay as is the role of critical race theory in its attempt to make race a central part of legal analysis.

Thus, each essay brings something unique to the challenge of wealth and race disparities in the United States and the world. Separately, each tells a story of the author's personal vision and the way that his or her vision is shaped by a discipline. Together, they give the reader the chance to learn more about the subject and about the disciplines they use to study race and wealth, class and culture.

NOTES

1. David M. Halbfinger, *Lott Apologizes But Won't Yield Leadership Post*, N.Y. Times, December 14, 2002.

2. The World Bank Group, Annual Report 2000, The Poverty Challenge: Where are we today?

3. Elizabeth Warren, The Two Income Trap: Why Middle Class Mothers and Fathers are Going Broke, Basic Books 2003.

4. Mary Williams Walsh, *Storm Victims May Face Curbs on Bankruptcy*, N.Y. Times, September 27, 2005.

5. Louise Witt, *When Entrepeneurs Risk it All and Lose*, N.Y. Times, July 7, 2005.

6. Josh Fischman, *Medical bills lead to personal bankruptcy*, US News and World Reports Best Health, February 2, 2005.

7. Jennifer Barrett, *Millions of seniors are expected to miss the enrollment deadline for Medicare Part D. What happens now?*, Newsweek, May 15, 2006.

Introduction

The difference in per capita gross national product between the richest and poorest nations is 400 to one. The richest countries are populated by peoples of European ancestry. The poorest nations' citizens are of markedly darker hue.[1] In this multidisciplinary discourse on race and wealth disparities the authors employ different methods in order to introduce readers to both the subject and their disciplines. Yet, although each chapter looks at race and wealth disparities through a different lens, some common themes emerge including: what wealth is; why wealth is important; what factors hinder studies of wealth and race disparities; what explains the wealth and race gap; strategies for reducing the gap and historical reasons for why the gap exists.

WHAT IS WEALTH?

The authors most reflect their discipline in their definitions of wealth. The economists look at cash and property.[2] The social psychologists look at social standing in the intersection of skin color and home value.[3] The political scientist examines wealth through the prism of community control over institutions and local government, particularly elementary and secondary education.[4] The anthropologist understands wealth as the power to control cultural images.[5]

What comes out of all these perspectives is the realization that wealth perpetuates its owner's authority and power. Material wealth helps build strong communities which, in turn, protect against crime and provide healthy environments. Healthy, safe citizens with control over the institutions that structure their lives and a sense of ownership over their culture and cultural images experience a full range of the benefits known as wealth.

WHY WEALTH IS IMPORTANT

Even in the most advanced societies, wealth provides more protection than income or government programs. Wealth has private and public impact. When the wage earner falls ill, when the crop fails, when the business market declines, when the tenant leaves in the middle of the night, wealth ensures that the medical bills are paid, food is on the table, children are educated, babies are cared for, homes are heated and wealth can pass to the younger generation. Wealth leads to more stable marriages, healthier children and adults, and better informed citizens.

WHAT FACTORS HINDER STUDIES OF WEALTH ALONE AS WELL AS STUDIES OF RACE AND WEALTH DISPARITIES?

Given wealth's importance to well being, why do scholars study wealth less frequently than income and educational attainment? The simple answer is that scholars are less likely to study wealth because there is less available information about wealth. Governments keep statistics on educational attainment and several forms of income but information on wealth is not as centrally located or as neatly packaged. Because researchers need information in order to complete their studies, they tend to use easily gathered statistics over harder to find information.

For example, Collins and Margo use homeownership as a proxy for wealth in their history of race and wealth disparities in the United States and Kirkland and Peters use homeownership as a proxy for wealth in their study of the link between home values and homeowner's race.[6] Researchers often use homeownership as a proxy for wealth because of the data on homeownership's ready availability and because most Americans put most of their investment into their homes.

Salary is used as a proxy for income in some of the studies reported by Barry and Stansbury in Chapter IV because salary data is easier to collect than information on other, more private, forms of income.[7]

In Chapter V, Cornfield tells us that increases in human capital is the wealth enhancement strategy used by 80% of all Americans.[8] Increases in human capital are measured through educational attainment in Chapter VI by Kenneth Wong and in Chapter VII by Roland Mitchell and Reavis Mitchell because we have more information on educational attainment than on other types of human capital.[9]

In addition to the search for appropriate proxies, studies of wealth and race disparities are hampered by the lack of available data across populations. For example, in Chapter IV Barry and Stansbury tell us that there are often so few racial minorities and women in corporate middle management that studies of these groups include everyone who is not white male under one "minority/women" category.

Given the lack of information and the lack of significant populations to study, it is no wonder that there is less written about wealth and race disparities than about income inequality or other more accessible questions.

WHAT EXPLAINS THE RACE AND WEALTH GAP?

A review of *Origins of Global Wealth Disparities: A World History Case Study* by James A. Quirin might lead to speculation that wealth comes from Empire. For example, as recently as 1750, India and China were jointly responsible for more than half of all world manufacturing. In the age of European Empire, wealth distribution shifted rapidly away from Asia. Today the gap between rich and poor mirrors differences in human complexion.

What is the 21st century equivalent of Empire? Arguably the corporation plays that contemporary role. The racialized wealth gap is evident throughout the world and corporations have spread across continents. Although the promise of capitalism is that rising tides lift all boats, corporations don't always provide a lift. Might corporation have something to do with both creating and alleviating the wealth gap? As Barry and Stansbury make clear in Chapter IV, despite the many reasons why Corporate Managers might want to know about the race and wealth gap, Management research is almost completely uninterested in any wealth gap, race or other.[10]

Perhaps critical race theory, a perspective that is reflected in many chapters explains the race and wealth gap. As Tony Brown and Daniel Cornfield explain in Chapter V, critical race theory provides a critique of institutionalized racial subordination as conveyed by five themes: (1) Racism is ordinary, ubiquitous, and reproduced in mundane and extraordinary customs and experiences; (2) The race problem is difficult to comprehend and impossible to remedy because claims of objectivity and meritocracy camouflage whites' self-interest, power, and privilege; (3) Race is both completely a product of our shared culture and psychology and a powerful force; (4) Although experiential knowledge is often discounted in order to support white privilege and power, experiential knowledge is in fact legitimate, appropriate, and insightful; (5) The purpose of critical race theory is to engineer social justice.[11]

Brown tells us in Chapter V that critical race theory's wide application unites scholars from a variety of academic traditions in the shared mission of revealing the many hidden and overt ways that race impacts lifestyles and life chances. This volume is testament to that assertion.

For example, when Kirkland and Peters illustrate in Chapter III how our shared psychology can force market price up or down based on who lives in a property, they illustrate how norms police racial stratification.

When Cornfield tells us in Chapter V that 80% of Americans use increases in human capital for wealth enhancement and Barry and Stansbury tell us in Chapter IV that the techniques that bring white male corporate managers increased human capital do not benefit white women and minorities, both chapters make the critical race theory point that race changes outcomes.

When Wong tells us in Chapter VI that the basis for human capital is strong elementary and secondary education but that the responsible institutions routinely under-serve poor and minority communities, he is making a critical race theory observation that institutions often support racial subordination.

In turn, when Roland Mitchell and Reavis Mitchell tell us that the most successful set of institutions for enhancing black human capital, the Historically Black Colleges and Universities, are starved of support, they too make the critical race theory point in Chapter VII that our institutions support the racialized wealth gap.

STRATEGIES FOR REDUCING THE WEALTH GAP

Many of the chapters critique strategies for reducing the wealth gap. Strategies discussed in this text include home ownership, increased human capital through education, unionization, entrepreneurship, and succeeding in corporate management. Each discussion of wealth enhancing strategies also reveals that what works for white males does not work with equal success for others.

For example, one strategy for wealth enhancement is homeownership. Yet, in Chapter III, Kirkland and Peters trace how a black person can lower home values merely by purchasing a property. In other words, race *in and of itself* increases (or decreases) wealth so that the strategy—buy a home—works far better for whites than for blacks.

Or, to illustrate the other side of the equation: in Chapter VII Roland Mitchell and Reavis Mitchell explain that the most successful institutions for bringing blacks out of poverty and into the middle class are the historically black colleges and universities. Yet, these Historically Black Colleges and Universities (HBCUs) are constantly under threat due to under funding, calls for their elimination in our "race neutral" society, and the black brain drain into white institutions.

SOURCES OF WEALTH DISPARITIES BY RACE

As Collins and Margo explain in Chapter II, most societies manifest unequal distributions of wealth and the United States is no exception.[12] For example, in 1995 the top one percent of Americans held 39% of all private wealth. As one might imagine, that top one percent is almost exclusively white while the bottom twenty percent is disproportionately black, Asian, Indian and Hispanic.

Collins and Margo look at a number of factors that contribute to America's racialized wealth gap starting with the obvious: For most of their history, American blacks were wealth. As a result, after twenty generations slaved to produce wealth for the nation, blacks had no wealth for themselves. Further, while blacks were allowed to live because they brought benefit to the Republic, Indians were forced to die so that whites could take their wealth. Race and Wealth: Tied together from the beginning.

No wonder that, five years after the Civil War, blacks had 2.5 cents for every dollar held by whites. Yet despite this overwhelming gap, blacks soldiered on during Reconstruction and raised their wealth to 6.9 cents for every white dollar. But, as Reconstruction faded, blacks became subject to a web of laws and practices that kept them from growing wealth for the next ten generations.[13] Today, almost 150 years after the Civil War, blacks own approximately 12 cents for every dollar owned by whites.

As a number of chapters make clear, in general, our institutions do not work against the wealth gap. For example, no Management literature systematically studies the higher poverty rates and lower access to resources that afflicts blacks, Latinos and Native Americans within the United States; and, to the extent that Management literature does look at poverty, the theme is less about how business can help reduce poverty and more about how corporations can better exploit the poor either as consumers or as low paid employees.

In Chapter V, Cornfield looks at unionization as a strategy for wealth enhancement. He reveals that, although historically unionized ethnic-racial minorities and women workers have earned more than their non-union counterparts, the union movement is shrinking and one of its challenges is how to work through the strategic importance of non-union ethnic-racial minorities as prospective union members.

Two chapters on education underline the important relationship between human capital and wealth. The first by Kenneth Wong looks at elementary and secondary education while the second, by Roland Mitchell and Reavis Mitchell examines higher education.[14] Each chapter looks at education from a different disciplinary perspective: Wong through the lens of a political scientist and Roland Mitchell and Reavis Mitchell as historians and educators.

Starting with political science, Wong builds on the themes introduced by Kirkland, Peters and Brown by expanding his definition of wealth beyond tangible property and cash. In Chapter VI Wong focuses on the power to control one's children's education and the interrelationship between the local community and the federal government in shaping our educational system.

Roland Mitchell and Reavis Mitchell build on the themes of enhancing human capital, critical race theory and education by looking at HBCUs. In Chapter VII they expose one of the many paradoxes that fill this volume, that while HBCUs are the most under funded and underpaid portion of our higher education system, with low endowments and students from impoverished school systems with inadequate physical plants, they remain the most successful educational institution for increasing blacks' human capital. Far more successful, for example, than Harvard or Yale.

In asking why schools with every advantage achieve much less than HBCUs, Roland Mitchell and Reavis Mitchell start with a historical review of American education that shows that America has always operated a multi track educational system: one track to train whites for leadership; another to contain the Indian population; and yet a third track designed to keep blacks as low paid labor.

RACE AND CULTURE

Chapter VIII, *Wealth Whiteout: Creative Writers Confront Whites' Downward Mobility in America's Newest Gilded Age* by Cecelia Tichi reminds us that whites also live in a racialized world. Drawing on Walter Mosley's *Workin' on a Chain Gang* and Andre Dubus' *Shadows and Fog*, Tichi asks us to look at how whites outside the American wealth system understand their condition. Tichi uses the discourse of nativism and immigrant status that runs through *Shadows and Fog* to show one character's confusion as she experiences the loss of her family home.[15] When the formerly middle class white owner's life plummets without a social safety net, Tichi's analysis beautifully illuminates the text's meditations on native white status in the face of a dark skinned immigrant threat. Add to this Tichi's analysis of Mosley's work on the "white chain gang" and we get a sense of the value of white privilege and its limitations in a world where race alone does not bring wealth.

Returning to Brown's theme in Chapter V that acts that sometimes seem progressive often mask hidden costs, in Chapter IX Edward Fischer takes us through an important review of many of the themes reflected in this work.[16]

First, Fischer starts from a completely different understanding of wealth than expressed in other chapters. Fischer adopts community control over culture as his definition of wealth, unlike Quirin or Collins and Margo (with their emphasis on tangible objects) or Kirkland and Peters and Tichi (with their emphasis on social status) or Wong, the Mitchells, Cornfield, Barry and Stansbury with their focus on enhancements to human capital.

To illustrate the use of culture as wealth as well as the theme that what appears progressive can mask hidden problems, Fischer looks at the television and print media that are filled with non white images from Crying Indians to Hip Hop sneaker salesmen. Although some might say that these images demonstrate that America is becoming ever more accepting and multicultural, Fischer, echoing Brown's critical race theory observation that progress on the surface is not always progress in fact, questions whether large corporations' use of multicultural images to sell products undermines community power.

Denis Kezar adds to the discussion of culture, race and wealth in Chapter X by echoing Tichi's theme of literature as illumination in Chapter VIII.[17] One topic that runs through this volume is the idea of race as a fiction, albeit a powerful fiction. What better discipline for revealing the power of narrative than literary theory? As Tichi showed us the power of text in revealing the inner life of a person in the throws of lost status, Kezar shows us how literary theory helps us appreciate race as a trope and the power of fiction made real. Working through Elaine Scarry's essay, *"The Made Up and the Made Real,"* and Henry Louis Gates' *The Signifying Monkey: A Theory of African-American Literary Criticism,* Kezar takes us through the distinction between the literary "made-up" and the socially "made-real." Kezar demonstrates that, by obscuring the devices we use to construct stories about race, race becomes "made-real" through the power of "illusion."

Many of these chapters look to the role law plays in enforcing wealth and race disparities. For example, Margo and Collins and Kirkland and Peters examine how government financing and housing policies reinforced racial segregation and low property values in black neighborhoods, while Reavis Mitchell and Roland Mitchell and Kenneth Wong look at federal and local educational policy and the laws that perpetuate differences in attainment of human capital by race. In these chapters law is an obvious part of what shapes race and wealth disparities. Yet Stephanie Wildman and Beverly Moran take a different view of law in Chapter XI. As law professors, their chapter deals with how legal workers, whether judges, advisors, litigators, professors, or students, engage in strategies that hide the role law plays in race and wealth, thus allowing law to appear neutral while creating far from neutral results.

CONCLUSION

Both race and wealth deserve multi-disciplinary investigation because each topic, standing alone, has such broad and deep influence over our public and private lives. These authors, who self-consciously address their disciplines and the intersection of race and wealth have created a rich tapestry of fact, philosophy and method. Many common themes emerge in this volume. They include: the central importance of wealth in the lives of communities and individuals; the world wide distribution of wealth by skin color; the omnipresence of racism in public, institutional and private dealings; the need to understand wealth as a multifaceted bundle of rights, privileges and ownerships; and race as a sort of concrete fiction that has no basis in the physical world and yet has tremendous power in a wide range of cultures.

This volume also includes some lovely and unique insights that help demonstrate how different ways of approaching the interface between race and wealth helps illuminate distinct aspects of that interface. For example: the way that literature and literary theory expose the concrete power of fiction helps us to understand how something can be both fictional and powerful at the same time; how social psychology helps us observe shared evaluations of the value of race turning into real world changes in home value; how each of the many different definitions of wealth reveals something about the discipline that uses that definition; and how many questions remain unanswered about race and wealth disparities.

We hope that you are inspired by the wide range of perspectives and methods that we bring to bear on this problem, as well as by the urgency that race and wealth disparities present on their own. The information on the world wide race and wealth gap contained in these chapters are meant to inspire your own thinking and research. Clearly there is much left to learn in this fascinating area.

NOTES

1. See Chapter I: *Origins of Global Wealth Disparities: A World History Case Study* by James A. Quirin.

2. See Chapter II: *Racial Differences in Wealth: A Brief Historical Overview* by William J. Collins and Robert A. Margo.

3. Chapter III: *"Location, Location, Location" Residential Segregation and Wealth Disparity* by M. Elizabeth Kirkland and Sheila R. Peters.

4. Chapter VI: *Federalism and Equity: Evolution of Federal Educational Policy* by Kenneth K. Wong.

5. Chapter IX: *Selling Identities: A Cultural Approach to Race and Identity Politics in the Postmodern Age* by Edward Fischer.

6. See Chapter II: *Racial Differences in Wealth: A Brief Historical Overview* by William J. Collins and Robert A. Margo and Chapter III: *"Location, Location, Location" Residential Segregation and Wealth Disparity* by M. Elizabeth Kirkland and Sheila R. Peters.

7. Chapter IV: *Corporatism and Inequality: The Race to the Bottom (Line)* by Bruce Barry and Jason Stansbury.

8. Chapter V: *A Selective Review of Sociological Perspectives on the Relationship Between Race and Wealth* by Tony N. Brown, Ph.D. and Daniel B. Cornfield, Ph.D.

9. Chapter VI: *Federalism and Equity: Evolution of Federal Educational Policy* by Kenneth K. Wong and Chapter VII: *History and Education Mining the Gap: Historically Black Colleges as Centers of Excellence for Engaging Disparities in Race and Wealth* by Dr. Roland Mitchell and Dr. Reavis Mitchell, Jr.

10. Chapter IV: *Corporatism and Inequality: The Race to the Bottom (Line)* by Bruce Barry and Jason Stansbury.

11. Chapter V: *A Selective Review of Sociological Perspectives on the Relationship Between Race and Wealth* by Tony N. Brown, Ph.D. and Daniel B. Cornfield, Ph.D.

12. Chapter II: *Racial Differences in Wealth: A Brief Historical Overview* by William J. Collins and Robert A. Margo.

13. The policies Collins and Margo identify in Chapter II include:

- Overt discrimination in public schooling prior to at least 1970 that led to less job skills among black workers;
- Labor market discrimination;
- Lower incomes as a result of less effective schooling and job discrimination that prevents savings;
- Less ability to save because of lower incomes;
- A series of federal and state laws that prevented blacks from purchasing housing such as:
  - redlining of black neighborhoods in order to prevent federal funds from being used to purchase housing at the same time that the federal government was encouraging white home ownership;
  - segregated housing patterns; and
  - predatory lending

14. Chapter VI: *Federalism and Equity: Evolution of Federal Educational Policy* by Kenneth K. Wong and Chapter VII: *History and Education Mining the Gap: Historically Black Colleges as Centers of Excellence for Engaging Disparities in Race and Wealth* by Dr. Roland Mitchell and Dr. Reavis Mitchell, Jr.

15. As Collins and Margo explained to us in Chapter II, for most Americans homes are their only wealth. As Kirkland and Peters echoed in even more depth in Chapter III, because of its association with white privilege, home ownership is subsidized for whites and circumscribed for others.

16. Chapter IX: *Selling Identities: A Cultural Approach to Race and Identity Politics in the Postmodern Age* by Edward Fischer.

17. Chapter X: *The "Currency" and "Purchase" of Literary Criticism* by Dennis D. Kezar.

Chapter One

Origins of Global Wealth Disparities: A World History Case Study

James A. Quirin

The nature, methods, and relevance of history as a field of study have been much examined in recent decades.[1] The relevance of historical analysis to current world problems has also become increasingly clear. This chapter emphasizes the necessity for a world historical context in analyzing some of the recent research seeking to explain the historical origins of the global disparities in wealth that have become so striking.

One of the most confusing questions for students about the nature of history is whether it fits into the arts (humanities) or sciences. In truth, history is both an art and a science.[2] History is a science in the sense that "scientists, social scientists and historians are all engaged in different branches of the same study: the study of man and his environment, of the effects of man on his environment and of his environment on man."[3] On the other hand, historical "facts" are often harder to define than scientific "facts" and the writing of history involves the elusive task of trying to communicate "meaning" and "understanding."[4]

Historical schools or approaches to achieve understanding since the nineteenth century when the field emerged as a professional scholarly discipline have varied between some degree of "idealist" or "positivist" emphasis.[5] The positivist and neo-positivist fetish for historical "facts" and written documents is clearly insufficient on several counts. What is a significant historical fact as opposed to something that happened in the past is itself a matter of interpretation and definition by the historian, and facts certainly do not speak for themselves.[6] And, of course, whatever "facts" may be teased out of the past do not all exist in written documents, but must be found by utilizing a variety of methodologies, including archaeology, linguistics, biochemistry and botany, ethnology and the analysis of oral tradition.[7] It has not taken post-colonial and deconstructionist

1

discourse to convince serious historians that sources do not stand alone and that historical analysis is a matter of limited constructed meanings.

On the other hand, history is also not merely interpretation or opinion in blatant disregard of "evidence," however problematic that evidence may be. Practicing historians believe that complete disregard of common sense "factual realities" about actual human societies moves one's scholarship out of history and into literature, philosophy, literary theory or some other discipline.[8]

In recent years, one of the fastest growing fields of history at the high school and college level is world history. The recent book by Patrick Manning, *Navigating World History*, provides the best overview available on the development of this field of study.[9] World history as a field of scholarship breaks some of the canons of traditional historical research, though there have always been people who wrote from the perspective of "metahistory" or universal history. Obviously, no one person can command sufficient fluency in every language required to read all the primary sources in such a field, nor would any one person have the time to do so. Therefore, world history writing and research requires a heavier direct reliance on the findings of other scholars than is traditionally the case. It is also, of course, not nearly so geographically and chronologically restricted as most traditional monographic history.

In Manning's view, "historical study is indeed undergoing a revolution, with world history currently in the lead."[10] According to Manning's analysis, the study of world history has advanced through two types of changes: the internal development of the discipline of history, and the external influence of other fields of study on history which he calls the "scientific-cultural path" to world history. Information from many fields in the natural and social sciences as well as the humanities has been incorporated into new approaches to history, specifically world history.[11]

In general, world history has grown because people feel a need to make sense of an increasingly complex world. An exciting field of research within world history in the last several decades is the crucial issue of the development of "the gap" between the economically wealthier and poorer parts of the world. Measured merely by per capita income (the gross national product divided by the population), the gap is now on the order of 300 or 400 to one in the most extreme cases.[12]

For decades, almost all explanations of this gap approached the question from a unipolar "rise of the West" perspective, taking little account of other parts of the world. This type of analysis sought factors unique to European civilization that predated the fifteenth century, but continued into an account of the origins and development of the industrial revolution from the late eighteenth through the mid-twentieth centuries almost entirely in terms of what Europeans did. In other words, these narratives were almost entirely Europe-centered with such catchy titles as "the rise of the West," the "unbound Prometheus," or the "European miracle," and tended to dismiss or ignore other parts of the world.[13] These narratives sought out factors said to be "unique" to the European cultural and historical experience, such as "rationality" and "progressive cultural evolution," that allowed Europe to be more innovative than any other part of the world "in technology, in social, economic and political institutions" as well as in "science, art and religion."[14]

Such approaches built on earlier traditions of Europe-centered world historical analyses, such as those as old as Voltaire, Hegel, Max Weber and Karl Marx. They all tended to use the rest of the world merely as a foil to the real historical events and the presumed "unique" or "exceptional" cultural, geographic and economic factors associated with western Europe.[15]

European exceptionalism has been critiqued effectively by the geographer, J. M. Blaut. His powerful analyses have effectively undermined the "colonizer's model of the world." Besides his general work, he has focused specifically on "eight Eurocentric historians," including many well-known, respected, and even best-selling authors.[16] Blaut has been thorough in his critique of Eurocentric analysis, but he has been less convincing in developing an alternate explanation for the chronological primacy of western European industrialization.[17]

Blaut argues in the introduction to his book, *Eight Eurocentric Historians*, that "four kinds of Eurocentric theory have been advanced to explain the fact that Europe (or the West) grew richer and more powerful than all other societies. The four are:

1. *Religion*: Europeans (Christians) worship the True God and He guides them forward through history.
2. *Race*: White people have an inherited superiority over the people of other races.
3. *Environment*: The natural environment of Europe is superior to all others.
4. *Culture*: Europeans, long ago, invented a culture that is uniquely progressive and innovative."[18]

As Blaut points out, these arguments have been used in various combinations. The religious and racial approaches were dominant in the nineteenth century. Now both of those have been rejected, but the environmental and cultural explanations are still given. Blaut argues that all four types of argument are based on "false history and bad geography."[19] Many parts of the world have had the environmental and cultural characteristics—not to mention race and religion—that would have allowed industrialization, as the history of the last several decades has demonstrated as various countries and regions with diverse cultural and environmental backgrounds have begun to industrialize. The real problem is that the answer to the origins of global disparities of wealth cannot be obtained by looking only within the West; rather, a global approach is necessary.

In recent decades, while some research as critiqued by Blaut has continued to mine the "rise of the West" approach, other work has contextualized this story methodologically, chronologically, and geographically. Beginning in the 1970s, scholars such as the sociologist, Immanuel Wallerstein, the historian, Leften Stavrianos, and the anthropologist, Eric Wolf contributed to the development of the world-systems approach that took the events of the world outside Europe seriously. This type of dependency, or center-periphery analysis was extended to African and African-American perspectives by Walter Rodney and Manning Marable.[20] Though Wolf's title, *Europe and the People Without History,* was obviously meant ironically, the center-periphery approach did tend to privilege Europeans (specifically western Europeans and later European-derived North Americans) as the main world historical actors, while the rest of the world merely reacted to European initiatives. Some historians, such as Janet Abu-Lughod, broadened world systems analysis chronologically by focusing on interacting world centers of trade in the thirteenth century, long before Europe played a dominant role.[21]

Within the past decade, however, scholars have focused particularly on Asia and somewhat on Africa to broaden the geographic as well as chronological context of world economic development processes. These analyses have emphasized the key economic initiatives taken by various countries and regions, with a strong emphasis on China. A recent forum, introduced by Patrick Manning appeared in the *American Historical Review* (2002),[22] the major journal for historians in the United States. The presentation of this forum in this journal illustrates the on-going paradigm shift that is occurring in efforts to explain the world gap in wealth disparities historically. Manning introduces the work of two of the historians from what has been called the "California school" because of where they teach. The two in this discussion are Kenneth Pomeranz and R. Bin Wong. Other scholars in this group include Andre Gunder Frank (the only one not in California), Jack Goldstone, John E. Wills, Richard von Glahn, Dennis Flynn and Arturo Giraldez. Collectively, they have contributed to a broadening of the framework for this question from a "monopolar" Europe to at least a "bipolar" approach.

All of these works have made important contributions to this topic. In particular, the pioneering work of Dennis Flynn and Arturo Giraldez, has been utilized by other scholars in this group. They have shown that the demand for silver in China between the sixteenth and eighteenth centuries was a major engine for the expansion of the world economy during that time period.[23] In their interpretation, the old view that silver was sent to China as money in order to pay for the Chinese goods desired in Europe such as silk and porcelain is outmoded. The silver was not money because the Chinese did not want gold or copper at this time, only silver. Furthermore there was a lively trade in silver directly across the Pacific after 1571 when Manila became a Spanish port, and there was also trade in silver from Japan to China. Neither of those trades can be explained by a silver-as-money interpretation, but only by taking into account the voracious Chinese appetite for silver itself during these centuries.[24]

Parenthetically, Flynn and Giraldez allude to possible connections between the African trade and this demand for silver in China. They suggest that the Portuguese traded "huge numbers" of African slaves for silver smuggled into Brazil and go on to state: "Since, as we argued, the Spanish enterprise in America was financed by the world silver market (as were the activities of the Portuguese traders), since China was the dominant factor in the global silver market, then it appears that the trans-Atlantic slave trade was heavily, though indirectly, influenced by the monetary and fiscal developments in China."[25] Further research on these suggestions is necessary.

Other accounts of world history from a global trade perspective emphasize the significance of the "Asian Age,"[26] but there are differences of interpretation concerning the role of silver in China, and the relative role of other Asian areas, such as Japan, India or Southeast Asia.[27] On the silver trade, Frank sees the massive silver imports by China as a positive factor in the economic development of China, but Flynn and Giraldez take a more negative view of that impact.[28] All these scholars focus on the key role of China compared to other areas, but also suggest the need for a more comprehensive global view, taking into account the roles of China, Japan, India, the Americas and to a lesser extent Africa.[29]

One of the major issues on this question of the global disparities of wealth is to explain why the industrial revolution did ultimately begin in England instead of China or another country. A truly global approach to the issue realizes that in fact it was not inevitable that the type of self-sustaining economic transformation that was later labeled the "industrial revolution" should have begun in England or, indeed, anywhere in Europe. Many other parts of the world had risen and fallen in relative wealth and power over the centuries.

China especially since the Sung dynasty, particularly the Southern Sung period (1127–1279) had become the most productive and populous country in the world, and also developed into the largest naval power by the early Ming dynasty. By 1400, China had a navy of 3500 ocean-going ships, including 1700 warships and 400 armed grain transports.[30] Its seven major expeditions under admiral Zheng He dominated the Indian Ocean and demonstrated that China had the economic, technological and navigational capability to circumnavigate the globe.[31] Even though the government scuttled its navy after these voyages, China remained the largest economy in the world.

Between the sixteenth and eighteenth century, China went through another period of economic growth. In particular, the Qing dynasty between 1680 and 1780 was in every sense an economic "golden age," comparable to those of England and Holland during the early Industrial revolution era. China under the Qing "should thus stand out as one of the remarkable episodes of economic growth in world history."[32] Indeed, China and India together accounted for more than half of the world's economic production as late as 1750.[33] Thus, a large body of detailed research on China, India, Southeast Asia and Japan have contributed to a more nuanced view of the global economy in this early modern view.

In contrast, however, to this plethora of research on the "Asian Age," scholarship on Africa's global connections has not kept pace. Much African-based research seems to have been ignored or disregarded as insignificant. Even the "Williams thesis" that used to be more generally accepted—that the Atlantic slave trade had an important connection to the rise of England in the late eighteenth century—was later critiqued and increasingly discounted.[34]

With regard to earlier global connections, for example, the path-breaking and influential work of Janet Abu-Lughod essentially left out the well-documented world economic connections of both East and West Africa as early as the twelfth century and later. Her important map, for example, showing the "eight circuits of the thirteenth-century world system" inexplicably omitted both the East African end of the Indian Ocean trade routes, and the trans-Saharan West African connection to the Mediterranean.[35] Evidence for the necessity to include trans-Saharan and the East and Northeast African ends of the Indian Ocean trade networks is multiple, such as the many recent works on the East African Swahili trading role, and both older and newer accounts of the significance of the gold trade from West Africa as early as the European Middle Ages.[36]

Not only Abu-Lughod, but almost all the key works cited above, explaining the role of Asia in stimulating the world economy in the early modern world, hardly mention the prominent role of Africa at the same time, though suggestions on the possible connections of the silver trade and the slave trade, as well as the potential role of the cowrie trade is mentioned by Flynn and Giraldez.[37] Is this ignoring of Africa simply the continuation of longstanding Eurocentric biases, or just a matter of not looking widely enough? As Maghan Keita points out, "race and the writing of history" has long been a theme and often a problem in historical reconstructions.[38] There has been a vibrant tradition among African American scholars and activists going back to the nineteenth century, documenting and arguing for the significance of Africa in world history. This scholarship has often been ignored by more "mainstream" writers, but recent works have demonstrated that in order to move away from merely a monopolar or even bipolar explanation of the rise of the Gap, the Americas and Africa must be brought fully into the story, including the period before the emergence of the Atlantic slave trade in the fifteenth century.

Thus, the period of early Chinese efflorescence during the southern Sung dynasty (1127–1279) was also the period of growth in the East African Swahili city-states that engaged in extensive coastal and overseas trade. The early Ming dynasty in China (from 1368) was the peak of Swahili international engagement according to East African-centered analyses. The recent analysis by Mark Horton and John Middleton shows the contribution to international trade by the Swahili, including the East African goods that reached Europe and Asia.[39] Likewise, for the centuries before the discovery of massive silver deposits in the Americas, the West African gold trade was "absolutely vital for the monetization of the medieval Mediterranean economy and the maintenance of its balance of payments with South Asia."[40]

Finally, for the period of the Atlantic economy and the colonial exploitation of the slave trades from Africa, a recent work by Joseph Inikori, *Africans and the Industrial Revolution in England*, caps a lifetime of research on the significance of the African and American connections to the industrialization of Europe. Though Inikori's work fits in with a long tradition of African-American, Afro-Caribbean and African scholarship on the topic, his research sources and methodology go well beyond such pioneers as W. E. B. Du Bois, Eric Williams and C. L. R. James.[41]

Inikori argues that the Atlantic slave trade in an era of mercantilism not only allowed the creation of capital which was later invested in industry (the "Williams thesis"),[42] but also directly stimulated manufacturing production within England in a time of world competition for cotton textile markets. He thus demonstrates specifically how the colonial trade, in which England exported manufactured textiles to both Africa and the Americas to pay for and then to clothe the enslaved Africans provided the key economic stimulus that allowed England to continue its "efflorescence" by transforming its economy as Jack Goldstone has argued.

Goldstone's analysis is a carefully-argued piece that shows the significance not only of the development of the steam engine as a new energy source, and the fortuitous presence of large coal deposits in England, but also the development of a new attitude in England toward the relationship of science and technology that he calls "engine science." He explains this occurrence as a "rather odd and unusual development" that originated in England, but that was "by no means a necessary and inevitable outcome of a broader 'scientific' revolution or of European craft and mercantile development." Nor is this approach to nature, science and technology restricted or unique to England. Indeed, this perspective has since been adopted by every country that has industrialized regardless of cultural and historical background.[43]

Thus, these articles and books, taken together, allow for the beginning of the development of a nuanced and multipolar appreciation of the many historical conjunctures that led to the creation of the world economic Gap, or the "great divergence" that still characterizes the contemporary world. It appears that the most mainstream or traditional explanations of the development of self-sustaining economic systems would agree that such transformations require a massive capital accumulation and the investment of such capital in manufacturing processes that use inanimate and mobile sources of energy. To institutionalize such changes into the transformation of society has also required a fundamental reorganization of society and the economy, as well as a significant reorientation of attitudes toward science and nature. The works discussed in this chapter which emphasize the necessity for a geographical and historical multipolar approach, elucidating the global economic stimulus provided by China, India, Arabia and East Africa,[44] the specific influence of the Atlantic connection to Africa and the Americas,[45] and the fortuitous and transformative development of new attitudes toward "engine science"[46] together provide the building blocks for a new interpretation of the origins of the global gap in the disparities of wealth. The remaining disagreements among historians provide many opportunities and challenges for continuing historical research within a world framework.

NOTES

1. Philip Curtin, "Depth, Span and Relevance," *American Historical Review* 89 (1984): 1–9.
2. H. Stuart Hughes, *History as Art and as a Science*, New York, 1964.
3. Edward Hallett Carr, *What is History?* New York, 1961, p. 111.
4. Ibid. pp. 3–35. This chapter is entitled "The Historian and His Facts."
5. Hughes, *History*, pp. 7–21.
6. Carr, *What is History*, pp. 15–16.
7. Historians of Africa have pioneered these and other methodologies; see: Jan Vansina. *Oral Tradition*. Chicago, 1965; Creighton Gabel and Norman Bennet, ed. *Reconstructing African Culture History*. Boston, 1967; Joseph Miller, ed. *The African Past Speaks*. Hamden, 1980; the journal *History in Africa* (1974 to present); J. Ki-Zerbo, ed. *General History of Africa, vol. I: Methodology and African Prehistory*. Berkeley, 1981.
8. Much fuller discussions of methodology and the philosophy of history may be found in Carr, *What is History*; Hughes, *History*; Hans Meyerhoff, ed. *The Philosophy of History in Our Time*, Garden City, 1959; Marc Bloch, *The Historian's Craft*, New York, 1953, and many other works.
9. Patrick Manning. *Navigating World History: Historians Create a Global Path*. New York, 2003.
10. Ibid., p. 11.

11. Ibid., pp. 7–15.

12. Robert Marks. *The Origins of the Modern World.*

13. William McNeill. *The Rise of the West.* New York, 1965; David Landes. *The Unbound Prometheus.* Cambridge, 1969; Eric Jones. *The European Miracle.* Cambridge, 1981.

14. J.M. Blaut, *Eight Eurocentric Historians.* New York, 2000, p. 7.

15. Voltaire, *Essai sur les moeurs et l'espirit des nations.* Paris, 1962; G.W. F. Hegel, *The Philosophy of History,* trans. By J. Sibree, in Robert Maynard Hutchins, ed., *Great Books of the Western World.* Vol. 46, Chicago, 1952; Karl Marx, *Capital: A Critique of Political Economy.* New York, 1906; pp. 784–848, Max Weber, *The Protestant Ethic and the Spirit of Capitalism.* New York, 1958. I have also analyzed Eurocentric World History: "Africa and World History," paper presented to the 8th annual conference, World History Association, University of Victoria, Canada, June 24–27, 1999.

16. J. M. Blaut, *Eight Eurocentric Historians* (the eight are Max Weber, Lynn White, Jr., Robert Brenner, Eric L. Jones, Michael Mann, John A. Hall, Jared Diamond and David Landes); J.M. Blaut, *The Colonizers Model of the World: Geographical Diffusionism and Eurocentric History,* New York, 1993.

17. Janet L. Abu-Lughod, "The World-System Perspective in the Construction of Economic History," in Philip Pomper, et al. Eds. *World History: Ideologies, Structures and Identities.* Oxford: Blackwell, 1998, p. 69; Patrick Manning, *Navigating,* p. 99.

18. Blaut, *Eight Eurocentric Historians,* p. 1.

19. Ibid.

20. Immanuel Wallerstein, *The Modern World-System I,* New York, 1974 (vols. 2 and 3 followed in the 1980s); L.S. Stavrianos, *Global Rift: The Third World Comes of Age.* New York, 1981; Eric Wolf, *Europe and the People Without History.* Berkeley, 1982; Walter Rodney, *How Europe Underdeveloped Africa,* Kingston, Jamaica, 1972; Manning Marable, *How Capitalism Underdeveloped Black America.* Boston, 1983.

21. Janet Abu-Lughod, *Before European Hegemony.* New York, 1989. For a thorough survey of several schools of world history interpretations, see Patrick Manning, *Navigating,* pp. 37–105.

22. Patrick Manning, "Asia and Europe in the World Economy: Introduction," *American Historical Review* 107 (2002): 419–24.

23. Dennis O. Flynn and Arturo Giraldez, "Born with a 'Silver Spoon': The Origin of World Trade in 1571," *Journal of World History* 6 (1995): 201–221.

24. Ibid., pp. 214–15.

25. Ibid., pp. 216–17.

26. Andre Gunder Frank, *ReORIENT: Global Economy in the Asian Age.* Berkeley, 1998.

27. On India, see: Rene Barendse, *The Arabian Sea: The Indian Ocean World of the Seventeenth Century.* Armonk, New York, 2001; David Washbrook, "South Asia, the World System and World Capitalism," *Journal of Asian Studies,* 49 (1990): 479–508. On Southeast Asia, see: Anthony Reid, *Southeast Asia in the Age of Commerce, 1450–1650,* vol. 2: *Expansion and Crisis.* New Haven, 1993. On Japan, see Nakai Nobuhiko and James L. McClain, "Commercial Change and Urban Growth in Early Modern Japan," in John Whitmey Hall, ed. *The Cambridge History of Japan,* vol. 4: *Early Modern Japan.* New York, 1991.

28. Flynn and Giraldez, "Cycles of Silver" pp. 419–20.

29. R. Bin Wong, "The Search for European Differences and Domination in the Early Modern World: A View from Asia," *American Historical Review*, 107 (2002): 468; Wong, *China Transformed: Historical Change and the Limits of European Experience*. Ithaca, New York, 1997; Flynn and Giraldez, "Cycles of Silver," pp. 413–20.

30. Abu-Lughod, *Hegemony*, pp. 320–21.

31. Louise Levathes. *When China Ruled the Seas*. New York, 1994.

32. Jack Goldstone, "Efflorescences and Economic Growth in World History: Rethinking the 'Rise of the West' and the Industrial Revolution," *Journal of World History* 13 (2002): 359.

33. Abu-Lughod, *Hegemony*, pp. 316–51; Marks, *Modern World*, pp. 2, 81, 123.

34. Eric Williams. *Capitalism and Slavery*. Chapel Hill, 1944; Roger Anstey, "Capitalism and Slavery: A Critique," *Economic History Review*. 2nd ser. 21 (1968): 307–320.

35. Abu-Lughod, *Hegemony*, map, p. 34.

36. Mark Horton and John Middleton. *The Swahili: The Social Landscape of a Mercantile Society*. Oxford, 2000; Ralph Austen, *African Economic History*. London, 1987; R. Barendse. *Arabian Seas*.

37. Flynn and Giraldez, "Cycles of Silver," p. 418. See the pioneering work on cowrie shells as currency: Marion Johnson, "The Cowrie Currencies of West Africa," *Journal of African History*, 11 (1970): 17–48, 331–53; Jan Hogendorn and Marion Johnson. *The Shell Money of the Slave Trade*. Cambridge, 1986.

38. Maghan Keita, *Race and the Writing of History: Riddling the Sphinx*. Oxford, 2000.

39. Horton and Middleton, *The Swahili*, pp. 72–88. See especially, R. Barendse, *Arabian Seas*.

40. Austen, *African Economic History*, p. 36. Austen cites the following and other works: Timothy Garrard, *Akan Goldweights and the Gold Trade*. London, 1980; John Day, "The Great Bullion Famine of the Fifteenth Century," *Past and Present*, 79 (1979): 3–54.

41. W.E.B. Du Bois, *The Negro*. London, 1970 [orig. ed. 1915]; Du Bois *Africa: Its Place in Modern History*. Girard, Kansas, 1930; Du Bois, *The World and Africa*. New York, 1965 [orig. ed. 1946]; Eric Williams, *Capitalism and Slavery*, Chapel Hill, 1944; C.L.R. James, "The African Slave Trade and Slavery: Some Interpretations of their Significance in the Development of the United States and the Western World," in John A. Williams and Charles F. Harris, eds *Amistad I*. New York, 1970, pp. 119–164.

42. See the extensive discussion and references to Eric Williams' work in Joseph Inikori, *Africans and the Industrial Revolution in England: A Study in International Trade and Economic Development*, Cambridge, 2002, pp. 2–7.

43. Goldstone, "Efflorescences," pp. 373–74, 377.

44. See the works cited above by Pomeranz, Wong, Frank, Flynn and Giraldez, Goldstone, and Barendse.

45. Inikori. *Africans*.

46. Goldstone, "Efflorescences."

Chapter Two

Racial Differences in Wealth: A Brief Historical Overview

William J. Collins and Robert A. Margo

INTRODUCTION

Within the disciplinary framework of economics, the word "wealth" typically is used as shorthand for the net monetary value of land, natural resources, or capital—in short, the value of anything other than labor. Wealth may be "private"—that is, owned by one or more individuals, or by a private-sector business—or "public"—owned by a government.[1] In a modern economy like that of the United States, private wealth can take many forms ("assets"), such as owner-occupied housing, automobiles, jewelry, furniture, stocks and bonds, business equipment, savings and checking accounts, among others. Importantly, wealth is measured at a point in time—what economists call a "stock" variable, as opposed to a "flow" variable (like income) which is measured over a period of time. The value of an asset at a point in time depends on the value of the flow of economic services that the asset is expected to generate in the future. As a macroeconomic rule of thumb, the private wealth of an economy at any point in time tends to be 3 to 4 times larger than the gross national product that the economy generated over the course of the previous year.

Economists are interested in the measurement and analysis of private wealth primarily because such wealth is presumed to contribute directly to the average material well-being of a society, as well as to differences in well-being across people within a society.[2] For example, wealth held in the form of a savings account or a mutual fund provides interest and dividend income that can be used to purchase goods and services. Wealth in the form of owner-occupied housing and furnishings provides shelter and comfort, and by virtue of location may also facilitate access to good schools, recreational facilities, and other local amenities. Indeed, in a hypothetical society in which medical care is allocated entirely within the private sector, having wealth might literally mean the difference between life and death. At extreme (or even not so extreme) levels, wealth may confer political clout or social connections that also directly affect well being.

When individuals live together in a group or "household", the economic benefits of wealth owned by one or more individuals in the group may be shared in some manner among the members of the group. For example, in a household comprised of an adult woman, her spouse, and two children, the house in which the group lives may be owned jointly by the two adults, but the economic benefits are obviously shared with the children. In recognition of this, data on private wealth are often expressed on a "per household" basis. However, for reasons of convenience or because of data limitations, data may sometimes be expressed per person (or "per capita").

A distinguishing feature of wealth in most societies is that it is unequally distributed, typically much more so than the distribution of income. For example, in the United States in 1995, the wealthiest one percent of households held 39 percent of all the private wealth in the country. By contrast, the top five percent of households in terms of income earned only about 20 percent of total income. Some types of inequality in wealth may be difficult to explain, in the sense that they may not be correlated with any observable characteristics of persons or households. However, other differences in wealth may be strongly correlated with observable characteristics and, as we document in this essay, race is one such characteristic. Historically, as well as today, African-Americans hold a relatively small share of the aggregate wealth in the United States, although this share has been slowly rising over time.

ECONOMICS AND THE STUDY OF
RACIAL ECONOMIC DISPARITIES

Economists have long been interested in studying racial economic disparities. This interest has at least three fundamental sources. First, many economists believe that racial inequality in the distribution of economic variables (like income or wealth) is intrinsically worthy of study. This may reflect a variety of underlying concerns, ranging from the morality of such large disparities to their implications for macroeconomic growth and social policy.

Second, race has been, and continues to be, a salient feature of the social, political, and economic history of the United States. It is impossible, for example, to understand the evolution of the Southern economy in the nineteenth and twentieth centuries without understanding the economics of slavery and its aftermath.

Third, given that racial economic disparities have been large and persistent, economists try to understand the combination of behavioral and institutional factors that have prevented faster inter-racial economic convergence. In thinking about such factors, particular attention has been paid to the role of racial discrimination.[3] In any specific economic setting, such discrimination is said to occur whenever an individual receives "unequal treatment" because of her race—for example, if an African-American is paid a lower salary than a white worker even when performing at the same level of ability in the same job. Discrimination in some settings may influence a person's economic standing in other settings—the most obvious example would be the overt discrimination in public schooling that most African-Americans faced prior to (at least) 1970. Economic research has demonstrated that government sanctioned discrimination in public education negatively influenced the set of skills that blacks workers brought to the private labor market after completing their schooling. The additional discrimination encountered in labor markets compounded the disadvantages associated with discriminatory treatment earlier in life.

As a point of departure for a study of racial differences in wealth, it is useful to ask why two individuals or households might have different levels of wealth in the first place. As we noted in the Introduction, wealth is measured at a point in time—a stock variable. Because wealth is a stock variable the level that person holds will depend directly on economic outcomes that have previously occurred. Imagine two individuals: one holds $100,000 in stocks and bonds, whereas the other holds a checking account with a balance of $1,000. How would an economist explain the difference in wealth between these two individuals? Differences in income up to that point in time will almost certainly be one key reason. Individuals who have been earning a high level of income are typically able to save some portion, whereas low income individuals need to spend most or all of their income on food, clothing, shelter, and other necessities. The allocation of wealth across different types of assets is also important: some assets may have paid a high "rate of return" whereas others paid a relative low rate of return.[4] Historically, for example, the average rate of return on stocks and bonds has considerably exceeded the interest paid by banks on checking or savings accounts. Inheritances or "inter-vivos transfers" may also be important. All other things equal, an individual who receives an inheritance or wealth transfer from a relative will hold (and be in a better position to accumulate) more wealth than someone who does not receive such a transfer.[5] Each of these factors might help account for the observed wealth difference, and suggest where to look for deeper causes. For example, if racial disparities in wealth holding could be entirely explained by lifetime differences in labor market earnings then attention should focus on the determinants of labor market earnings.

Within this context, racial discrimination may play an important role in several ways. If African-Americans have lower incomes because of racial discrimination, they will face greater difficulty in saving and thus generating wealth. If African-Americans face discrimination that prevents them from holding their wealth in assets that have a high rate of return, their wealth will be lower. Finally, if African-Americans currently receive smaller inter-vivos transfers or inheritances because previous generations faced discrimination in one form or another, less wealth will be held and accumulated over time.

While economists are interested in the full distribution of wealth—from the poorest to the richest—most studies of racial (or other) disparities concentrate on differences in average (or median) wealth and attempt to account for these differences, using various statistical techniques. Our discussion, as well, concentrates on average (or median) differences.

HISTORICAL AND RECENT EVIDENCE ON WEALTH

At the end of the Civil War, the vast majority of African Americans were former slaves with little more than the clothes on their back. Prior to the War, some free blacks were able to accumulate wealth (for example, land holdings), but most free blacks were poor as well. Thus, the racial gap in wealth, measured in percentage terms, literally could not have been much larger. Since then, as we review here, the racial divide in wealth has narrowed, but the pace of convergence has been remarkably slow.

The 1870 census is the first nationwide survey of wealth that provides representative national evidence by race. This census collected information on real estate wealth and on some components of personal property. According to these data, the black-white ratio of average household wealth in 1870 was approximately 0.025. That is, there were 2.5 cents of wealth per black household for every dollar of wealth held by white households.[6]

The prospects for catching up were not auspicious. Besides the obvious burdens of starting with little physical or financial capital, about 80 percent of adult blacks were illiterate in 1870 (Collins and Margo 2005). More than 90 percent of blacks lived in the South, a regional economy lagging behind the rest of the nation through the late nineteenth century, and one that pursued a brutal course of establishing and enforcing a new system of white supremacy. Finally, labor market discrimination was pervasive in the United States, and therefore movement to the North, especially before World War I, guaranteed neither significant economic advancement nor economic security.

The reports of state auditors for various southern states, such as Georgia and Louisiana, are another useful source of historical information about racial disparities in wealth in the late nineteenth and early twentieth centuries. These documents report taxable wealth by race over the period 1870 to 1915 and have been studied by Higgs (1982) and Margo (1984). Most blacks remained desperately poor compared with whites during the post-bellum period. However, despite poverty and overt racial discrimination, the black-white wealth gap in the South diminished somewhat in the late nineteenth century. For example, in Georgia, the black-white ratio of per capita wealth rose from 0.029 in 1880 to 0.064 in 1910.[7]

Over the following 60 years, the wholesale recasting of social norms regarding discrimination, the widening of economic opportunities and growing political voice for African Americans, and the reversal of government policy regarding race had strong implications for the economic status of African Americans. Unfortunately, the implications for racial differences in wealth are not easily documented, primarily because there is comparatively little nationally representative information on wealth by race category during this period. Clearly, the absolute level of wealth held by African Americans increased greatly between 1910 and 1970. In the aggregate, however, one may be surprised by just how little racial convergence in wealth occurred.

Modern studies (that is, post World War Two) of racial wealth differences are based on a variety of specialized surveys.[8] One such study is the paper by Blau and Graham (1990) that relied on data from the National Longitudinal Survey. Focusing on relatively young families (ages 24 to 34) in the 1970s, Blau and Graham documented that the average black household held wealth equal to 18 percent of the wealth of white households. However, the black-white ratio varied by type of asset. It was much higher for equity in housing or automobiles than for net "liquid" (bank account, stocks and bonds, and so on) and business assets. Indeed, in the sample studied by Blau and Graham, the average black family's holdings of net liquid assets equaled just 2.4 percent of that of white families. Business equity was similarly lopsided; the black-white ratio in the sample was 6.4 percent. These low ratios highlight fundamental racial disparities in how white and black households allocate their wealth; in particular, they suggest that black families are less likely to accumulate financial and business assets.[9]

Using statistical techniques, Blau and Graham also show that most of the racial difference in average wealth cannot be explained by racial differences in such factors as household income or education, nor can the difference be explained by a lower propensity to save on the part of black households.[10] These findings suggest the potential importance of ongoing racial discrimination in labor and financial markets as well as factors that the authors could not observe in the data that they analyzed, in particular, inheritances and inter-vivos transfers.

Wolff (1998, pp. 140–142) provides estimates of the black-white ratio of mean and median wealth from 1983 to 1995 based on the Survey of Consumer Finances conducted by the Federal Reserve. In 1983, the mean wealth ratio was 0.19 while the median ratio was 0.07. The median ratio increased slightly from 1983 to 1995 (to 0.12) while the mean wealth ratio fell slightly (to 0.17). As in Blau and Graham's paper, Wolff documents that racial wealth differences are larger for financial assets than wealth in general. Slightly less than a third of black households over this time period reported either zero or negative net worth, approximately three times the level of white households. Wolff also emphasizes the importance of intergenerational transfers, and in particular, inheritances. Whites in the 1995 sample were more likely to receive inheritances than blacks, and among those who did receive inheritances, whites received much larger sums on average.

Comparisons of economic variables over very long time spans are inherently problematic because of changes in prices and other factors.[11] Still, the available evidence suggests that the black-white wealth ratio has increased by a factor of about 7 since 1870.[12] This pace of convergence is arguably faster than racial convergence in incomes as the black-white ratio of income appears to have increased by a factor of about 2.5 over the same period.[13] However, in terms of levels, the black-white ratio of incomes currently is much higher than the corresponding wealth ratio. Further, the long-term pace of racial convergence in wealth is far slower than that of racial convergence in educational attainment (Collins and Margo 2005). Put another way, African-Americans today are more similar to white Americans in terms of income or educational attainment than in terms of wealth, where the gap remains extremely large in absolute terms.

HOME OWNERSHIP AND HOME VALUES

Although historical information on wealth, broadly defined, is relatively scarce, much more information is available on an important component of wealth—home ownership and the value of owner-occupied housing units. Wolff (1998) documents that housing is a principal component of household wealth in 1995, especially for those outside the top twenty percent of the wealth distribution, and it seems likely that housing was an even greater share of household wealth in earlier decades. Importantly, home ownership is not merely a means of holding one's wealth. Rather, it is typically a highly leveraged investment that is given favorable treatment in the tax code, and home owners may earn significant capital gains if property values rise. In this context, racial disparities in home ownership and home property values and the legacies of past housing market discrimination are especially salient.

The federal census began collecting information on home ownership in 1890. This information is reported in the published census volumes, but it is more convenient and informative to use the "integrated public use micro-data series" (IPUMS, for short), as these provide the information at the level of individuals, along with a host of other individual and household characteristics (Ruggles and Sobek 2003).[14]

Collins and Margo (2001, table 1, p. 73) use the IPUMS data to study the evolution of racial differences in home ownership among male household heads. At the turn of the twentieth century approximately 22 percent of adult black men were classified as homeowners—an impressive figure, in light of what must have been the black home ownership rate a scant three decades earlier (near zero). Still, blacks lagged far behind whites at the time—the white home ownership rate in 1900 was nearly 46 percent. The black home ownership rate did not reach the 46 percent mark until 1970, seventy years after whites. An interesting aspect of this lag is that the great redistribution of African Americans from the rural South to central cities throughout the country, tended to depress rates of black home ownership since a relatively low proportion of central city residents (of either race) owned their homes.

Home ownership rates for both races remained roughly constant from 1900 to 1930, but they declined for both races during the Great Depression. Black household heads succeeded in dramatically increasing the rate of the home ownership between 1940 and 1960 such that, by 1960, the black home ownership was 39 percent, 17 percentage points higher than at the turn of the century. White gains in home ownership, however, outpaced those of blacks over the same period, and so the racial gap was actually larger in 1960 (27 percentage points) than in 1900 (22 percentage points).

The Civil Rights Movement led to the passage of federal anti-discrimination legislation pertaining to the labor and housing markets (1964 and 1968 respectively), to substantial changes in discriminatory sentiment among whites (Schuman et al. 1997), and eventually, to lower levels of residential segregation (Cutler and Glaeser 1999). These and other changes may be partly responsible for a sixteen percentage point jump in the black male home ownership rate between 1960 (39 percent) and 1980 (54 percent), and for a contemporaneous narrowing of the racial ownership gap. In the two decades following 1980, rates of home ownership among adult black male household heads increased modestly, and the racial ownership gap decreased slightly (Collins and Margo 2004a, p. 194). Despite the long-term rise in black homeownership, absolutely and relative to whites, the racial gap in 2000 was still quite large—on the order of 24 percent points.

In a related paper, Collins and Margo (2003a, table 1, p. 260) use the IPUMS to document changes in racial differences in the value of owner-occupied housing from 1940 to 1990. In 1940 the typical black-owned home was valued at 37 percent of the typical white-owned home. This figure increased to 62 percent by 1970, largely because of racial convergence in certain valuable characteristics of housing, such as the number of rooms (or indoor plumbing). Further progress in the 1970s was hampered, however, by a sharp decline in the black-white ratio of housing values in central cities.[15] This decline was particularly severe in cities that were heavily segregated in 1970, and was also greater in cities that experienced a severe riot in the 1960s (Collins and Margo 2003a, 2004). The deterioration in the relative value of black-owned housing in central cities continued in the 1980s but was mitigated somewhat at the national level by a rising value ratio and shift in homeownership towards suburban areas, a trend that continued in the 1990s.

Because the price of a house may be several multiples of annual household income, most households, regardless of race, do not possess the cash (or other financial assets) that would permit them to buy housing outright. In the early twentieth century, it was difficult or costly to obtain a mortgage for most white households (let alone blacks) and, as a result, rates of homeownership fell short of a majority for both races. In the 1930s, significant changes took place in federal housing policy that greatly enhanced access to mortgage finance, especially among middle-class whites seeking to move from central cities to suburban areas. Indirectly, these changes led to increases in black homeownership in central cities—a process known as "filtering"—while rising incomes and other factors (veteran status) enabled some blacks to qualify for mortgage finance. Still, the majority of prospective black homeowners faced great difficulties in acquiring a mortgage, either because of a lack of income, irregular employment, or outright discrimination by mortgage lenders. Following the passage of a federal "fair housing" law in 1968 and subsequent related legislation, access to mortgage finance by black households improved. Banks and other financial institutions are now required to set aside a certain portion of their funds for community reinvestment, which increased availability of mortgage finance to blacks and other minorities. Despite these changes, some black households still face difficulties in getting a mortgage. In one well-known study (Munnell, et. al. 1996) researchers used data on approximately 3,000 mortgage applications in Boston in 1990 to examine the effects of race on mortgage approvals. Using statistical techniques to control for an unusually long list of possible factors (for example, household income, credit history) that might have affected this probability, the results showed that the probability that a black household would be denied a mortgage was 82 percent higher than an otherwise equivalent white household.[16]

Recent decades have also seen substantial growth in so-called "sub-prime lenders"—financial institutions that offer loans to households that may not qualify for conventional mortgage finance. Unfortunately, such loans come at a price—higher fees and interest rates; while most sub-prime lenders operate within the boundaries of the law, on occasion the fees and interest rates charged lead to accusations of "predatory" lending. Black households are much more likely to use sub-prime lenders than white households and, as a result, may have greater difficulties making mortgage payments and thus face a higher risk of foreclosure (Ross and Yinger 2002, p. 24). Despite such problems, there is little doubt that improved access to mortgage finance, particularly since 1970, has enabled many black households to become homeowners who, in earlier decades, would have been denied the opportunity.

CONCLUSION

Racial differences in wealth have narrowed over the long sweep of American history. Despite this convergence, the racial wealth gap in the contemporary United States is very large, much larger than the racial gap in income or educational attainment. Racial convergence over the long term has been especially significant in the case of home ownership but, even so, the home ownership gap is still large in absolute terms, as is the gap in the value of homes that are owned.

Ultimately, racial differences in wealth derive from racial differences in inheritances and inter-vivos transfers, in incomes, in rates of saving, and in the allocation of wealth across different types of assets. Policies that alleviate racial differences in schooling and other types of human capital offer important scope for narrowing the racial wealth gap, because higher levels of human capital are associated with higher incomes for both blacks and whites. Continued and vigorous enforcement of fair-housing legislation may help sustain the long-run gains in black homeownership. In addition, policies that provide greater information about and easier access to the full range of financial assets now available in the United States might encourage some black households to shift their wealth holdings in ways that might yield a higher overall rate of return, and thus narrow the wealth gap with white households.

REFERENCES

Altonji, Joseph G. and Rebecca M. Blank. "Race and Gender in Labor Markets," in Orley Ashenfelter and David Card (editors) *Handbook of Labor Economics*, Volume 3. Amsterdam: North-Holland, 1999.

Becker, Gary. *The Economics of Discrimination*. Chicago: University of Chicago Press, 1957.

Blau, Francine D. and John W. Graham, "Black-White Differences in Wealth and Asset Composition," *Quarterly Journal of Economics* 105 (May 1990): 321–339.

Collins, William J. and Robert A. Margo, "Race and Homeownership: A Century's View," *Explorations in Economic History* 38 (January 2001): 68–92.

———, "Race and the Value of Owner-Occupied Housing, 1940–1990," *Regional Science and Urban Economics* 33 (May 2003a): 255–286.

———, "Historical Perspectives on Racial Differences in Schooling in the United States," in E. Hanushek and F. Welch, eds. Handbook of the Economics of Education. Amsterdam: North-Holland, 2005, forthcoming.

———, "Race, Family Structure, and Homeownership in Twentieth Century America," in Edward Wolff, editor. *What Has Happened to the Quality of Life in America and Other Industrialized Nations?* New York: Edward Elgar, 2004a.

———, "The Economic Aftermath of the 1960s Riots: Evidence from Property Values," National Bureau of Economic Research Working Paper No. 10493, Cambridge MA, May, 2004.

David M. Cutler, Edward L. Glaeser, and Jacob L. Vigdor, The Rise and Decline of the American Ghetto, *Journal of Political Economy* 107 (1999): 455–506.

Higgs, Robert, "Accumulation of Property by Southern Blacks Before World War One," *American Economic Review* 72 (September 1982): 725–737.

Higgs, Robert and Robert A. Margo, "Black Americans: Income and Standard of Living from the Days of Slavery to the Present," in Julian L. Simon, editor. *The State of Humanity*, pp. 178–184. Blackwell Publishers: Cambridge, MA, 1995.

Munnell, Alicia H., Lynn E. Browne, James McEneney, and Geoffrey M.B. Tootell, "Mortgage Lending in Boston: Interpreting HMDA Data," *American Economic Review* 86 (March): 25–53.

Pope, Clayne, "Inequality in the Nineteenth Century," in Stanley L. Engerman and Robert E. Gallman, editors. *The Cambridge Economic History of the United States, Volume II: The Long Nineteenth Century*, pp. 109–142. New York: Cambridge University Press, 2000.

Ross, Stephen L. and John Yinger, *The Color of Credit: Mortgage Discrimination, Research Methodology, and Fair-Lending Enforcement*. M.I.T. Press, Cambridge MA, 2002.

Ruggles, Steven, Matthew Sobek, et al. *Integrated Public Use Microdata Series. Historical Census Projects*, University of Minnesota, Minneapolis, 2003.

Schuman, H., C. Steeh, L. Bobo, and M. Krysan, *Racial Attitudes in America: Trends and Interpretations*, Harvard University Press, Cambridge MA, 1997.

Wolff, Edward N., "Recent Trends in the Size Distribution of Household Wealth," *Journal of Economic Perspectives*

NOTES

1. At the level of individuals or households and possibly even at the level of a nation as a whole, it may be important to distinguish between gross and net wealth.

Gross wealth is the monetary value of physical resources. An individual's ownership of wealth may be partial; for example, in the case of owner-occupied housing, there may be a mortgage or other lien on the property. For this reason, net wealth is defined as gross wealth less liabilities (such as mortgages).

2. This is also true for public wealth; however, the presumption is that the benefits of such wealth are shared more or less equally among a society's members. This assumption, of course, may not be true; in the case of African-Americans, equal access to public wealth in the form of public school buildings, for example, was systematically denied during the period of *de jure* segregation in public education.

3. The seminal theoretical work in this area is Becker (1957). In the decades since Becker's treatise, a variety of other theoretical approaches have been elaborated. See Altonji and Blank (1999) on labor market discrimination.

4. In general, the return on wealth may take two forms: interest or a "dividend" on the principal (as, for example, when a bank pays interest on a savings account) and "capital gains" (changes in the value of the asset in which savings is allocated—for example, owner-occupied housing—from one year to the next). Interest or dividends are either zero or positive, but capital gains can be negative—an asset can decline in price from one year to the next.

5. An *inter-vivos* transfer occurs when one person transfers wealth to another while both are living; for example, a parent may give a child a down-payment for a house.

6. Computed from figures reported in Pope (2000, p. 117).

7. Computed from Table 1 of Higgs (1982, p. 729). Because it is difficult to devise a completely consistent definition of a "household" from the censuses for the late nineteenth century, the state auditor data have been usually expressed on a per capita rather than per household basis. The black-white ratios most likely would look slightly higher on a per household basis but it is unlikely that the trend would be affected.

8. Examples are the Survey of Consumer Finances, the National Longitudinal Surveys, and the Panel Study of Income Dynamics. The Survey of Consumer Finances is conducted on a periodic basis by the Federal Reserve; it is a random sample of households, and a large number of questions are asked about assets, debt, and other aspects of consumer finances. The National Longitudinal Survey and Panel Study of Income Dynamics are specialized surveys of households that are followed over time.

9. The lower level of business assets is a consequence of a lower rate of self-employment among black households; a portion of the self-employed are business owners, and a portion of these are quite successful, generating considerable wealth in the form of business assets.

10. The statistical technique used by Blau and Graham was multiple regression analysis, a technique widely used in the social sciences to assess the quantitative impact of one or more variables (for example, income, education) on an outcome (wealth). In the data analyzed by Blau and Graham, a higher level of income was positively associated with a higher amount of wealth among both black and white households and, on average, black households had lower incomes than white households. However, the statistical effect of income on wealth was not large enough to account for the racial difference in average wealth, given the racial difference in income. A similar result applies in the case of racial differences in education.

11. Changes in the "quality" of goods is one such factor; the characteristics of owner-occupied housing today are much different from housing a century ago.

12. It is likely that this figure is understated because the data from the Survey of Consumer Finances refer to net worth, which can be negative (because of liabilities), while that from the 1870 census refers to gross wealth, which cannot be less than zero (net worth = gross wealth − liabilities).

13. The black/white ratio of per capita incomes has been estimated at 0.24 ca. 1870; see Higgs and Margo (1995, p. 179). In 2001, the ratio, as reported by the Bureau of the Census, was 0.62 (computed from Tables P-1a, P-1b, www.census.gov/hhes/income/histinc). If Hispanics are excluded from the computation of the white average, the ratio in 2001 is 0.57.

14. No sample exists for 1890 because the original census returns were destroyed in a fire. The earliest sample, therefore, containing information on home ownership is 1900. No sample currently exists for 1930 which was subject to confidentiality restrictions until very recently, but one is expected eventually.

15. Collins and Margo (2003a) also show that this deterioration in the relative value of black-owned housing was especially severe in the nation's most segregated cities.

16. For a detailed discussion of Munnell, et. al. (1996), see Ross and Yinger (2002, chs. 4,5).

Chapter Three

"Location, Location, Location": Residential Segregation And Wealth Disparity

M. Elizabeth Kirkland and Sheila R. Peters

INTRODUCTION

Home ownership is a form of wealth. For many Americans, most of their wealth is in fact in their homes—homes are most people's single largest asset. Part of the modern American ideal of home ownership—beyond the real and symbolic values of stability, sanctuary, and sustenance—is the ability to maintain a landed asset over a period of time and to generate and accumulate savings from that asset. The tangible, investment aspect of home ownership enables families to propel their gains into education, business, financial assets, retirement, and intergenerational bequests. And yet, white Americans own homes at a rate 57% higher than African Americans (U.S. Census Bureau, Annual Statistics, 2005).

Beyond home ownership, *where* one lives—owning as well as renting one's space—is a form of wealth. To the extent that space and the housing stock are racialized, wealth is racialized. To the extent that access to housing and ability to accumulate equity in our homes is race-dependent, we have wealth disparities based on race. As the scholar john a. powell says with regard to housing, "Geography does the work of Jim Crow laws" (Background reading, *Race— The Power of an Illusion*, 2003). Racial residential segregation—in which racial and ethnic groups live separately from one another, in different areas of their city—generates, perpetuates, and solidifies this particular form of wealth disparity. Particularly, we examine how the racial wealth disparity via residential segregation has been perpetrated. We discuss how deftly and dramatically portions of the United States government, industry, and white Americans carved a residential color line and racialized space in the twentieth century, and how this perpetration continues in the twenty-first.

Nature itself has offered a panoramic view of the wealth disparities associated with residential location and access to homeownership. With the horrific unfolding of the Hurricane Katrina tragedy in the Gulf Coast, governmental response particularly to the poor and people of color was significantly delayed. Today, many of these persons remain displaced across the United States. It is these groups—the nonwhite and the poor—who were unlikely to own their housing, likely to live in areas most affected by the hurricane and its aftermath, and even more likely to struggle through the prolonged displacement. Those who were renting their space long for home—the life experiences and memories. How likely are renters to relocate to their pre-Katrina homes?

THE URBAN MIX OF THE 1800S, AFTER THE CIVIL WAR

We are a nation segregated residentially by race. Race is the primary determinant of where Americans live, and we tend to live apart (Glaeser and Vigdor, 2001). Yet, little more than a century ago, our urban areas were integrated mélanges of black and white neighbors. Before the twentieth century's problem of the color line, in the latter part of the nineteenth century, racial residential *integration* was the norm for blacks and whites, in northern as well as southern cities (Massey and Denton, 1993). It is certainly true that urban blacks suffered numerous hardships and disadvantages in the decades following the Civil War, but they were not residentially segregated from whites. It is broadly acknowledged that blacks and whites in post-Civil War America shared urban neighborhoods, and thus as well shared a common language and culture, interacting socially and personally on a regular basis. (For a thorough review of the detailed literature on residential segregation in this period, see Massey and Denton, 1993.) In the latter 1800s, in most American cities of the South and the North, black residents and white residents shared a residential pattern inconceivable by today's segregated standards. Certain areas of cities could be identified as places where many African Americans lived, but these areas were not predominantly African-American, and most African Americans did not live in them. (In addition to Massey and Denton, see also, for example, Katzman (1973) with regard to Detroit, Michigan, Gotham (2002) with regard to Kansas City, Missouri, and Lovett (1999) with regard to Nashville, Tennessee.)

How did such racially interspersed neighborhoods in cities across the United States become the segregated areas of today? What events transpired to divide black and white residents? What forces transformed the residential mix and carved the color line across our cities? This chapter provides, first, an overview of the twentieth century transformation from residential integration to segregation, particularly from around 1900 until the Civil Rights Era, and, secondly, an examination of the post-Civil Rights forces—the contemporary system of racial residential segregation—that continues to shore up and carve anew the color line.

THE TURN OF THE CENTURY AND
A VIOLENT TURN TOWARD SEGREGATION

It was in 1903 that W. E. B. DuBois identified the color line as the problem of the twentieth century. Indeed, the post-Civil War prevalence of urban integration—blacks and whites residing among one another in a scattered fashion throughout American cities and in a more concentrated pattern in enclaves—began dissipating just before the 1900s. Historians note that the twentieth century ushered in the complimentary and hugely transformative trends of industrialization and blacks' rural-to-urban, as well as southern-to-northern, migration. Douglas Massey and Nancy Denton, in *American Apartheid: Segregation and the Making of the Underclass*, recount in detail how these technological and demographic trends are credited with elevating tensions in race relations and with heralding the beginning of a steady rise—unrelenting, up through the 1960s—in residential segregation between blacks and whites.

In the North, industrialization transformed large areas of cities into burgeoning manufacturing districts filled with large and small factories and plants, and dense housing for the requisite work force. Streets once lined with homes and small shops became blocks of teeming tenements and row houses. Meanwhile, blacks from the South had begun to migrate north by the tens of thousands in the final decade of the 1800s, and they filled the new demand for labor and changed the face of the urban streetscape of northern cities. Nearly 200,000 southern blacks moved north between 1900 and 1910, and the outbreak of World War I further fueled the dual trends of black migration to the North—over a half a million between 1910 and 1920—and industrial development (Polikoff, 2006).

Heightened racial tensions arose from the confluence of industrialization, the consequent housing density, and the large proportional increase in black population experienced by whites in northern cities. The typical migration pattern involved African Americans moving initially into compressed areas of industrial sections of cities and then moving or attempting to move out of the decaying, overcrowded areas into adjacent or other parts of the city (Polikoff, 2006). From 1900 through the 1920s, as this migration sequence unfolded constantly against a backdrop of exploding industrialization, northern cities saw repeated and often large-scale incidents of white-on-black racial violence (Massey and Denton, 1993). In "thousands of small acts of terrorism" (Meyer, 2000), whites waged violent battles against black residential integration, household by household, and block by block. African-American homes were invaded, burned, or bombed; individual blacks were beaten, shot, or lynched; white gangs asserted a threatening presence in city streets; and race riots instigated by whites periodically broke out in northern cities. The ongoing threat of violence, in turn, propelled even more segregation, as whites became increasingly intolerant of any African-American presence in their neighborhoods and as blacks increasingly sought comfort and security in neighborhoods with other blacks (Massey and Denton, 1993).

Southern cities, meanwhile, certainly experienced racial violence in the early 1900s—primarily, the thousands of lynchings by white Americans—but were not afflicted by large-scale race riots, and residential segregation increased at a slower rate. There was less intense industrialization and greater reliance on the Jim Crow system of racial subordination; ironically, the very system which elevated whites' status by subordinating blacks allowed for more integrated residential patterns. Charles S. Johnson (1943), reflecting on the more integrated residential patterns in southern cities, noted that African Americans' "place [was] so well defined in social space that their location in ecological space [did] not loom as a great issue. In the North, however, where their social status [was] more anomalous and where they [had] no customary place in the community," their place of residence was more fraught with meaning and potential and thus tended to be more segregated.

Race relations and residential patterns after the turn of the century were thus defined and transformed by societal and economic shifts. Whites' violent creation and reinforcement of a residential color line met with very little deterrence from police and the law; they acted with "virtual impunity" (Polikoff, 2006). The early decades of the 1900s thus ushered in ever-increasing black-white residential segregation and an ever-hardening color line, fueled particularly by racial prejudice expressed through violence.

INSTITUTIONAL AND GOVERNMENTAL METHODS OF CARVING THE RESIDENTIAL COLOR LINE

Industrialization, migration, and the unremitting, undeterred white violence may have wrought the initial trend toward black-white residential segregation, but for most of the twentieth century, the avenues for residential segregation have been institutional and governmental, on a massive scale. Through a variety of practices—from neighborhood associations and real estate industry policies through legislation and federal government property appraisal programs—the color line has been carved into the urban landscape. On these multiple fronts, while outright racial violence has been largely subverted, racial fears and prejudices have been expressed, and the color line of residential segregation has been forged and maintained. These forces exert a "structural violence" (Farmer, 2003) through institutional forms of oppression.

For several years in the early 1900s, whites in many southern cities began legislating residential segregation through city ordinces. Typically, such laws actually dictated where blacks and whites could and could not live, and were buttressed by the expressed purposes of preserving public welfare and even improving race relations. Their effect was, of course, to create separate black and white residential areas. Although segregation ordinances were first declared unconstitutional by the U.S. Supreme Court in 1915, cities continued for several years to draw lines dividing black from white residents, in order to attempt to force residential segregation through legislation (Johnson, 1943).

Neighborhood associations, formed typically by middle-class urban whites, were another common method for maintaining the black-white color line in residential segregation. Throughout city after city, these organizations worked toward their primary goal of preventing the movement of African Americans into white neighborhoods, through a variety of efforts. They lobbied city governments for the passage and enforcement of discriminatory ordinances, for the closing of streets where blacks resided, and for the closing of hotels and rooming houses frequented by blacks (Massey and Denton, 1993). Through fundraising and donations, they purchased property from black homeowners in their neighborhoods, bought property from owners who were renting to blacks, bought vacant homes, and paid money to black renters who agreed to move away, all in the effort to keep their neighborhoods white (Gotham, 2002). Neighborhood associations also brought lawsuits against real estate agents who sold homes to blacks, organized demonstrations against blacks moving in, and boycotted white businesses and real estate agents patronized by blacks (Massey and Denton, 1993).

Real estate boards were another organizational structure for the maintenance of the black-white color line. The National Association of Real Estate Brokers proclaimed in its code of ethics that "a Realtor should never be instrumental in introducing into a neighborhood . . . members of any race or nationality . . . whose presence will clearly be detrimental to property values in that neighborhood" (Gotham, 2002, p. 34–35). Published real estate textbooks and guidelines explicitly and forcefully advocated racial segregation, with the stated goal of keeping white neighborhoods white. Local real estate boards across the country followed suit. Homogeneity—specifically, the exclusion of nonwhite residents—was the ideal.

These local real estate boards played the critical role of creating racially re-strictive covenants for use by white homeowners and white neighborhood as-sociations. Race restrictive covenants were collective, contractual arrange-ments between property owners and their neighborhood associations, through which property owners agreed not to permit blacks (and other ethnic groups) to purchase, rent, or otherwise occupy their property. Such covenants were in widespread use throughout the country from 1910 until they were declared unconstitutional in 1948, and even continued to be recorded and applied for up to two decades beyond the time they were outlawed by the U.S. Supreme Court (Massey and Denton, 1993).

Four decades of legally enforceable race discrimination in housing, in the form of restrictive covenants, on top of the effects of racial legislation and in addition to the concerted efforts of neighborhood associations and real estate boards, carved the color line deeply across American cities and towns. Through, and in addition to, the tangible geographic divisions, the actions and initiatives of local private institutions wrought a less visible but equally pow-erful aspect of segregation: a racial ideology. This ideology portrayed blacks as harmful to neighborhood stability, desirability, and property values (Gotham, 2002).

This color line, it is important to note, represented not only a physical, ge-ographical division of race, but a racialization of financial worth as well. Just as the real estate industry admonished realtors to keep neighborhoods white in order to maintain property values, part and parcel of the racial ideology was the ascribing of monetary worth to homes based on their location on streets and in areas without nonwhite residents. Gotham (2002) has evaluated in great detail the role of industry in promulgating racial residential segrega-tion and uneven development, and points up in particular the profit motive that linked racial ideology to property value: the preservation of segregated housing was "not incidental to real estate profit-making but intrinsic to it." Community leaders, through real estate organizations and neighborhood as-sociations, assigned and marketed positive attributes—such as security, hard work, upward mobility, moral character—and, most significantly, outright su-perior financial value to homes in all-white neighborhoods.

> The rise of the real estate industry was intimately bound up with the emergence of new meanings of White racial solidarity and homeowner identity that were forged through the promotion and protection of the status value of "home" and "neighborhood" . . . Racial restrictive covenants, like other segregative land-use tools, encoded possession and racial difference in urban space, and helped le-gitimate and popularize the notion that racially diverse neighborhoods were in-ferior and less valuable than all-White homogenous neighborhoods, a belief that still continues . . . [E]arly-twentieth-century meanings that people assigned to

home, neighborhood, and community were intimately connected to constructions of race and racial identity that together racialized space in the emerging segregated metropolis (Gotham, 2002, p. 47).

Not long after private institutions began carving the color line across American municipalities, the United States government also joined in the sponsorship of residential segregation. Beginning in the 1930s, the United States government radically changed the way in which Americans could own their own homes. Prior to that time, mortgage financing as we know it today did not exist; a homebuyer would have to pay at least half of the cost of the home, in cash, up front, and pay the remainder soon thereafter (Jackson, 1985). In 1933, at a time of economic crisis for homeowners and the housing industry, the federal government sought to make home ownership an attainable goal for Americans through accessible (low down-payment, low interest), long-term mortgage financing arrangements. This completely opened up the home owning possibility for average Americans—although, as it came to be implemented, only for average *white* Americans—for the first time.

To implement its program, the government devised an evaluation system by which to rank urban neighborhoods. The creation of the Home Owners' Loan Corporation (HOLC) brought about a nationwide property appraisal system, in which every block of every city in America was assessed for creditworthiness and assigned a rating of neighborhood quality (Jackson, 1985). Racially homogenous, new, all-white neighborhoods ranked highest, and the second rating went to outlying, working-class, white neighborhoods. The third tier of neighborhood quality rating encompassed racially mixed neighborhoods, or neighborhoods of lower economic status that were white but were located near black areas; predominantly black neighborhoods, regardless of the income of the residents or condition of the housing, were rated lowest. On HOLC maps, lines of different colors were drawn around these different categories of neighborhood, with the lowest tier—black neighborhoods—getting "redlined."

The HOLC itself was not a major provider of mortgage funds over the long term, but in its first two years the HOLC provided loans to one-tenth of all owner-occupied, non-farm residences in the country (Jackson, 1985). What's more, the HOLC itself is not known for discriminating against minority homeowners and predominantly black neighborhoods; Jackson cites "strong evidence . . . that the HOLC did in fact issue mortgage assistance impartially and make the majority of its obligations in [third- and fourth-ranked] neighborhoods." The HOLC's legacy lies in the rating system it spawned, which took on a life of its own and became the model for private banks as well as for future government agencies. Private banks adopted the federal government's residential categorizations and redlining approach, in which homeowners in newer, all-white neighborhoods were virtually guaranteed mortgage financing, and properties in second-ranked neighborhoods, also white, were generally deemed eligible. Homes in the third and fourth categories—homes in black areas, in areas with some black residents, or in areas deemed to be undesirably near to areas with black residents—were considered unworthy of mortgage lending, and therefore ineligible for mortgage loans.

Even more significantly, ensuing government loan programs—under the Federal Housing Administration (FHA), created in 1937, and the Veterans Administration (VA), created in 1944—followed the HOLC model of categorizing neighborhood quality on the basis of whiteness. These two loan programs—the FHA primarily, and the VA which followed on the heels of the FHA—are said to have "revolutionized the home finance industry" (Jackson, 1985) by enabling home ownership, making it cheaper to buy than to rent (at least when comparing a suburban purchase to an urban rental), and taking the white middle-class out of the inner city. An FHA loan was predicated on an acceptable appraisal of the neighborhood where the property was located (in addition to the acceptability of the property itself and of the homebuyer). Jackson details the euphemistic criteria used to measure neighborhood quality: the two most heavily weighted categories were "economic stability" and "protection from adverse influences," and both were applied so as to avoid heterogeneous environments and "inharmonious racial or nationality groups" (Jackson, 1985, quoting the 1939 FHA *Underwriting Manual*). The FHA is said to have exhibited an "obsessive concern" (Massey and Denton, 1993) with separating race and social class, going so far as recommending the use of restrictive covenants and compiling maps and reports of the present and predicted future residential patterns of black households (Jackson, 1985). In Jackson's words, "previously, prejudices were personalized and individualized; FHA exhorted segregation and enshrined it as public policy."

Built upon the ranking system set by the HOLC, the redlining practices of the federal government through the '40s and '50s, in tandem with the racially discriminatory credit practices of private banks, carved the color line across the nation in grand fashion. From the refashioning of the provision of mortgages in 1933 until the Civil Rights legislation of the 1960s, *home ownership was tied to financing and financing was tied to race.* According to one estimate, over $120 billion in new housing loans alone was underwritten by the federal government between 1934 and 1962, and less than 2% of that went to nonwhites. (Background reading, *Race—The Power of an Illusion*, 2003). During this period, virtually the entire residential market—both government and private sectors—became undergirded and largely segregated by the officially sanctioned and ubiquitously replicated standards of racial discrimination.

By denying home lending opportunities to integrated neighborhoods and predominantly black neighborhoods, while at the same time providing such opportunities to whites (only if they resided in white neighborhoods), the United States government officially adopted standards of racial discrimination in housing. This racialization of property values, first promulgated through real estate industry efforts and neighborhood associations, was now packaged into government policy through a rating system that made race the primary determinant of investment-worthiness. According to Massey and Denton, "it bureaucratized [the racial discriminatory standards of property valuation] and applied them on an exceptional scale. It lent the power, prestige, and support of the federal government to the systematic practice of racial discrimination in housing" (Massey and Denton, 1993). Redlining—the policy of providing generous packages of financial assistance to only white homeowners, and *only* if the home is not located near to nonwhites—became the law of the land, and remained so for decades.

Thus the United States saturated the nationwide housing market, through governmental agencies and mimicked by the private lending industry, with massive financial assistance to white, middle-class homeowners. These white beneficiaries were usually also suburbanites. Indeed, the government's foray into homeownership support contributed mightily to the growth of suburbia and decay of inner-city neighborhoods. The guidelines and practices of the FHA favored the construction of single-family homes and discouraged multi-family dwellings, made it easier to purchase a new home than to modernize an old one, and gave a low neighborhood rating to more densely built and older areas (Jackson, 1985).

In a separate, equally impactive string of initiatives—arising also out of the strictures of the Great Depression but later implemented to redress inequalities—the United States government provided a different type of housing assistance to the poor and those otherwise unable to partake in the largesse of homeownership opportunities. In 1937, the United States Housing Act (USHA) launched the public housing program for the country, which, over the ensuing decades, has actually reinforced and compounded the imbalances wrought by homeownership assistance: namely, racial segregation and the urban-suburban divide.

Jackson (1985) enumerates three key components of the public housing legislation that reinforced and furthered existing social inequities. For one thing, federally subsidized housing was predicated on locally, voluntarily generated requests, and a second feature was the fact that the law required that a community create a municipal housing agency in order to qualify for public housing. "Because municipalities had discretion on where and when to build public housing, the projects invariably reinforced racial segregation. A suburb that did not wish to tarnish its exclusive image by having public housing within its precincts could simply refuse to create a housing agency . . . .[Further,] housing authorities were typically made up of prominent citizens who were more anxious to clear slums and to protect real-estate values than they were to re-house the poor" (Jackson, 1985). In effect, public housing assistance under the USHA (and subsequent legislation, primarily the Housing Act of 1949) di-vided the country into communities that did and did not seek public housing. A third aspect was a requirement that for every unit of public housing, one di-lapidated unit must be razed; it was axiomatic, then, that areas without signif-icant numbers of substandard housing would not acquire public housing. Po-likoff (2006) highlights the additional element of the "neighborhood composition rule," according to which the racial occupancy of a public hous-ing development was required to reflect the racial makeup of the area. Thus, Jackson concludes, "public housing was confined to existing slums. It further concentrated the poor in the central cities and reinforced the image of subur-bia as a place of refuge from the social pathologies of the disadvantaged."

Indeed, the "filtering" process, referred to by Margo and Collins in Chap-ter II, was a way in which some African Americans in the '40s and '50s were able to get housing: as whites, pursuing the home loans that were available to them, evacuated the inner city, urban housing stock could sometimes be pur-chased by blacks, to whom such home loans were not available. To cast this as a positive development, though—to highlight this filtering process simply as an increase in black homeownership—is a distortion, much as if one were to brew a pot of coffee and describe as beneficial the grounds that were left behind. Black homeowners in the inner city acquired the dregs that were deemed unsuitable for investment, from those who were given access to something far more valuable. Much of the residential pockets of America's inner cities rapidly became the black ghetto.

The black ghetto today lies at the extreme of the wealth disparity that de-rives from residential segregation. Polikoff (2006) illuminates the dual iconography (and reality) of black Americans: the black middle and upper class, on the one hand, with a trajectory of progress and promise, and the poor and working class, on the other. He argues for dismantling the ghetto in part because, he asserts, the stigmatizing effect of the ghetto feeds and sustains racial inequality for all African Americans, in all arenas, including education and employment, but particularly in the realm of the dual housing market and residential segregation—which encompasses wealth disparity, homeowner-ship disparity, and home-value disparity. His concern is that the dual housing market and residential segregation will remain entrenched so long as the black ghetto, which he considers "the modern successor to black slavery and Jim Crow," is allowed to persist. Polikoff even sounds an alarm that it is pos-sible that black urban poverty, in its damaging effect on race relations and its sustenance of white prejudice, could foretell a decline in fortune and promise of the ascendant black middle class, a regression from the progress so recently attained, a turn for the worse in the form of greater disparity of wealth and even higher levels of segregation. This is part of the vicious cycle described by many sociologists and historians over the years, in which white prejudice and discrimination, inadequately deterred, force substandard circumstances onto black Americans, with which white Americans in turn buttress their ongoing prejudice and discrimination.

In sum, institutional and governmental forces first carved and then reinforced the residential color line across American metropolitan areas. In accordance with the critical race theory approach espoused by Tony Brown in Chapter V, the examination and comprehension of this massive historical and systematic effort is essential to our understanding of race relations at the dawning of the Civil Rights Era as well as of the racial residential segregation in which we live today.

THE CONTEMPORARY SYSTEM OF
RACIAL RESIDENTIAL SEGREGATION

Although the Civil Rights Act of 1866 enunciated quite clearly that "all citizens shall have the same right as is enjoyed by white citizens to purchase real property," the United States government and the real estate and lending industries proceeded to systematically deny that right. One century on, in one of the successes of the Civil Rights Movement, the Fair Housing Act of 1968—seen as groundbreaking, transformative legislation—reasserted that racial discrimination in the housing market is illegal. Real estate agents, landlords, buyers and sellers of homes, as well as those who finance and insure these transactions, are forbidden by law to discriminate on the basis of race. After about 70 years of aggressively enforcing, financing, and ascribing value to racial residential segregation, white America outlawed the entire policy and practice.

Nevertheless, racial discrimination continues to pervade the mortgage lending industry and the housing market, maintaining and carving anew the color line of residential segregation. In an ongoing epilogue to the Civil Rights legislation that purported to guarantee fair housing, investigations and analyses show that nonwhite Americans are at a significant disadvantage, by virtue of their race, when trying to find an apartment, looking for a new house, or applying for a mortgage to make a home purchase possible. The contemporary system of racial residential segregation can be discerned through examinations of the home financing and housing search processes.

As for mortgage financing, white Americans enjoy a significant advantage when seeking a home loan, and this fact is born out in numerous analyses of mortgage funding decisions. The seminal research study of mortgage lending discrimination, known as the Boston Fed Study, revealed that black and Hispanic applicants were 80% more likely to be turned down for mortgages than white applicants with the same personal and property characteristics (Munnell, et al., 1996).

Data released through the Home Mortgage Disclosure Act (HMDA) has, before and since the Boston Fed Study, revealed severe racial disparities in mortgage approval rates—for conventional home purchase loans in 2000, for example, blacks were twice as likely as whites to be rejected—but the HMDA data does not account for certain presumably important variables in the loan decision, such as the applicant's wealth and credit history. It is on that basis that detractors have argued that the HMDA data are misleading and that the racial disparities they show in loan approval are a consequence not of the applicant's race but of the applicant's lack of creditworthiness, unrevealed by the limited data. The Boston Fed Study debunks that argument. It accounted for all variables in a mortgage application that could possibly be relevant to creditworthiness, including credit history and wealth, and found that rejection rates for blacks and Hispanics were, indeed, nearly twice as high as for otherwise identical white applicants.

The Boston Fed Study provides an enlightening perspective on the operation of the mortgage lending industry, with regard to how mortgage decisions are actually made. The analysis of mortgage applications in the Boston Fed Study revealed that an applicant's race was a stronger predictor of loan denial than almost all economic characteristics (Munnell, et al., 1996). Particularly, an applicant's income and net wealth were less predictive of loan denial than race. An applicant's mortgage history or credit history, as well as the property's appraised value or its use as a multi-family dwelling, were also less predictive of loan denial than race. Only bankruptcy or a failure to obtain mortgage insurance outweighed race as predictors of home loan denials. To put it another way, mortgage applicants' nonwhiteness was more likely to contribute to loan application rejections than weaknesses in income, wealth, credit history (short of bankruptcy), and debt.

Racial discrimination in mortgage approval limits the choices of minority homeseekers and eliminates or narrows the locations in which they might otherwise choose to live. But the racial disparity in mortgage lending constitutes only a snapshot view of one aspect—the "grant" or "deny" stamp on the mortgage application—of the housing search. In fact, by the time minority applicants reach the point of mortgage rejection, many others have already been eliminated from the process through earlier means of discouragement. Other studies of the lending industry point to racial discrimination that precludes nonwhite homeseekers from even reaching the point of applying for a mortgage. The most common way of discovering whether minority persons receive fair and equal treatment in the housing market is through paired audit studies, in which white and nonwhite testers pose as homeseekers with the same financial and personal characteristics—that is, they are virtually equal, for purposes of getting a home, except as to race. Discriminatory techniques uncovered by audits of the lending industry include: coaching whites, but not blacks, on particular ways to improve their creditworthiness so that they can meet underwriting standards; providing less information to potential black applicants than to whites; urging potential black applicants, but not their otherwise equal white counterparts, to go to a different lender; emphasizing to black customers, but not to whites, that mortgage application procedures are onerous and complicated; communicating more options to white customers than to blacks (Yinger, 1996).

Similar to the process of obtaining a home mortgage, studies reveal that the process of searching for a house or an apartment is likewise fraught with racially discriminatory constraints. The nonwhite homeseeker faces racial discrimination from the moment, quite literally, that he or she begins to look for a house or apartment. Thousands of paired tests in cities across America in the years following civil rights legislation have uncovered specific, documented, measurable discrimination (Turner, et al., 2002; Yinger, 1995). As in the approach for uncovering racial discrimination by bankers and lenders, in a paired test of real estate and rental agents, two individuals—one minority and the other white—are assigned similar family and economic characteristics and pose as otherwise identical homeseekers, inquiring after the same advertised housing unit, with comparable housing needs and resources. As in the mortgage approval arena, whites are favored over otherwise equally situated nonwhites. Whites are more likely than blacks and Hispanics to be told that the advertised house or apartment is available, whites are more likely to be shown the house or apartment, and whites are more likely to be told about and shown additional homes (Turner, et al., 2002). Blacks, on the other hand, are more likely than whites to be shown additional homes that are less expensive than the advertised home.

All of these discriminatory acts affect the outcome of the housing search and where people end up living, but perhaps none so much as the particular technique known as racial steering, a racially discriminatory real estate practice—a "particularly elusive type of discrimination" (Yinger, 1995)—that is actually thriving. Under the Fair Housing Act of 1968 and subsequent amendments, real estate agents may not direct people to a particular community or neighborhood because of their race, discourage people from occupying any home because of the race of the persons in the surrounding neighborhood, fail to inform people of desirable features of a home or neighborhood in order to discourage their interest, or communicate to potential homebuyers that they would not be comfortable or compatible with neighborhood residents. And yet, housing discrimination studies reveal that real estate agents are less likely to recommend and show houses in predominantly white areas to blacks; black homeseekers are more likely to be guided to less affluent, less white neighborhoods. In fact, according to the periodic, nationwide assessment by the Department of Housing and Urban Development (HUD), racial steering is on the rise; the HUD housing discrimination study conducted in 1999 uncovered a significant increase in the incidence of racial steering from HUD's previous study in 1988 (Turner, et al., 2002).

The marked increase in racial steering is particularly disturbing when considered against the backdrop of legislation. The Fair Housing Act of 1968 had lacked strong enforcement provisions, but subsequent legislation passed by Congress in 1988 strengthened the government's hand against housing market discrimination with increased penalties for discriminatory acts, expanded potential for involvement of the United States Justice Department, and the empowerment of HUD to investigate and file cases (Polikoff, 2006). Disappointingly, however, in the aftermath of these heightened enforcement capabilities, blacks and whites in particular have been found to be even more likely to be recommended and shown homes in different neighborhoods. The gross incidence of steering based on neighborhood racial composition rose significantly in the decade following the 1988 legislation, as did a particular type of steering known as "editorializing," in which real estate agents provide gratuitous commentary that conveys more information to white homeseekers and encourages them to choose neighborhoods with more white inhabitants (Turner, et al., 2002).

The National Fair Housing Alliance grapples with this seeming inability of our nation's laws to rein in the rampant discrimination in the housing market. The Alliance, which collects information on housing discrimination from local, state, and federal government agencies and conducts its own testing as well, estimates that more than 3.7 million violations of the Fair Housing Act occur annually, with more than 99% of them going unreported (National Fair Housing Alliance, 2006). One hundred years ago, white Americans enjoyed virtual impunity as they violently forged a residential color line; the contemporary system of racial residential segregation, it would seem, operates with similar impunity.

THE COLOR LINE REMAINS

The color line—that twentieth-century problem—is still with us. Margo and Collins in Chapter II provide data that reveal the disparity in black-white homeownership, as well as the racial disparity in home value, throughout the twentieth century and up through the 1990s. Additionally, more recent statistics illustrate the ongoing disparity. United States Census figures from 2005 document a white homeownership rate of 75.8% and a black homeownership rate of 48.2% (U.S. Census Bureau, Annual Statistics, 2005). As for the disparity in home value between whites and African Americans, there is strong evidence that residential segregation contributes to the gap. One study found that houses in neighborhoods that are more than 10% black have 16% less value than equivalent houses in all-white neighborhoods (Shapiro, 2004). Furthermore, a 2001 study by the Brookings Institute found a direct correlation between home value and residential segregation: the higher the level of residential segregation, the greater the disparity in black-white home value (Shapiro, 2004).

Certainly the monetary and investment value of homes are contemplated as wealth, and those amounts differ between black and white households: homes owned by African Americans, or located in areas that are not overwhelmingly white, hold and accumulate less value. But such homes also constitute and generate less wealth in other, less tangible forms as well. The location of one's home is related to the quality of education, availability of employment, accessibility of cultural and commercial amenities, the provision of municipal services, and even the relative protection of the surrounding environment (Gotham, 2002). The familiar mantra of real estate — "location, location, location!" — is a behest to buy where one's property value will rise, or at least hold its own in tough times; how much is it a call to mind the color line and to be wary of racial differences in neighborhoods? This simple advice represents, without mentioning race, the common wisdom that the best home equity opportunities are found in the best locations, and twentieth century history reveals that the best locations are white.

On a parallel but not unrelated plane, fifty years on from *Brown vs. Board of Education*, the United States continues to grapple with issues of school segregation and, particularly, the question — once thought to have been answered by *Brown* — of the educational benefits of diversity. In a *New York Times* piece concerning the United States Supreme Court's consideration of racial balancing efforts by public schools, a researcher of school desegregation is reported to have found little connection between racial integration in schools and student achievement (Rosen, 2006). This scholar advocates an end to race-conscious school assignment schemes, arguing: "We have racially imbalanced neighborhoods and cities based on where people choose to live. What's wrong with racially imbalanced schools?"

This "choose to live" argument points up two critical aspects of the wealth disparity that arises out of racial residential segregation. One is the fallacious assertion that people have the choice, free of racial discrimination, to live where they do. With high rates of racially discriminatory treatment throughout the home search process, one's choice of location is restricted by one's race, if one is not white. With high rates of racially discriminatory mortgage approval, where lenders are found to give greater consideration to the applicant's race or ethnicity than to such factors as income, employment, assets, or debt, one's ability to choose one's housing and location—indeed, to become a homeowner at all—is constrained if one is African American. The other noteworthy aspect of the "choose to live" argument is the concept that segregated schools bear some connection to segregated housing. Indeed, the racial segregation and inequality in our nation's public schools (a subject for another chapter!) is of course integrally bound up with our contemporary system of residential segregation. Racial residential segregation has long been understood as the linchpin for other forms of racial segregation, as the "basic structure" (Johnson, 1943) or fundamental "institutional apparatus" (Massey and Denton, 1993) that supports and binds together other forms of racial discrimination and subordination. However, while it is quite correct to link racially imbalanced schools to residential segregation, it is utterly incorrect to label it a choice and to assert there's nothing wrong with it.

Despite the common assumption that racial residential segregation—and the attendant wealth disparity—has always been with us, it is a modern, twentieth century, institutionally generated phenomenon. White racial prejudice, private profit-oriented initiatives, and large-scale governmental policies combined to produce the racial residential segregation of the twentieth century. Residential segregation between blacks and whites steadily increased for the first seven decades of the twentieth century. Moreover, countervailing trends—including the Civil Rights movement, the Fair Housing Act of 1968 and its enforcement provisions of 1988, the Home Mortgage Disclosure Act of 1975 and its ensuing amendments, the Community Reinvestment Act of 1977, Housing and Urban Development's Hope VI program of the 1990s, the emergence of a large black middle class population, and the seemingly improved racial attitudes of whites—have done astonishingly little to erase the residential color line. Since 1970, levels of black-white segregation have begun to decrease, but the decrease is minimal, and current segregation levels, by any measure, are extremely high, far greater than the integrated residential patterns of a hundred years ago. Meanwhile, a contemporary system of racial residential segregation continues to divide residents by race and to make whiteness a property value. Thus, American metropolitan areas at the dawn of the twenty-first century are left with deeply carved and seemingly intractable racial residential segregation.

The truth was brought to light in the aftermath of Hurricane Katrina. Perhaps one of the greatest outcomes of this natural disaster is that the ongoing structural human disasters of residential segregation, poverty, and environmental racism were made bare to the world. Where one lives determines how our emergency response system functions. The more affluent communities are faring better in the ongoing recovery effort. When government has been asked to provide emergency housing and assistance to those in greatest need, bureaucracies have stymied the process. With the rich cultural heritage of the Bayou culture, will New Orleans recapture its original heritage or will individuals with resources transform the home of the French Quarter into a racially segregated space shaped by income? Moreover, with the displacement of hundreds of thousands, who will be able to realize a dream of returning and reclaiming their homes? Our ultimate response to Hurricane Katrina may give stark attention to the structural barriers for the poor and the African American to gain access to the rebuilding of New Orleans and the Gulf Coast region.

The color line was awkwardly revealed in the aftermath of Hurricane Katrina. For some of the most disenfranchised residents of New Orleans, there are those who wonder if their communities were targeted in the early stages of recovery. Some wonder if specific areas were sacrificed to allow other cherished areas to be spared. How much is the residential segregation of New Orleans reflective of American cities? Are other racially segregated communities at greater risk for limited economic growth and environmental hazards? In the Ninth Ward, if more residents had been homeowners, would the treatment of their neighborhoods in the aftermath have been different?

The racialization of wealth limits opportunity and access to wealth-generating activities. The poor—disproportionately of color—are likely to live in spaces that are potentially unstable in long term planning. Therefore, scholars and activists need to concentrate on not only raising the awareness of institutional barriers to homeownership and wealth, but on effective practices to reduce these wealth disparities. Governmental programs and policies are insufficient at best. The return to once abandoned central cities may have dilatory result on the disenfranchised who are most likely to be displaced as a result of gentrification. If America is to truly be one of the most powerful leaders of the free world, America must find pathways to freedom for all. Wealth including home ownership should be an accessible right, rather than a fading dream. Home ownership builds more than wealth potential. Homes are the foundations of communities, and if American communities are to be transformed into culturally diverse spaces that honor and respect the human spirit, human capital must be elevated over bricks and mortar.

REFERENCES

DuBois, W. E. B. (1903). *The Souls of Black Folk: Essays and Sketches.* New York: Fawcett.

Farmer, P. (2003). *Pathologies of Power: Health, Human Rights, and the New War on the Poor.* Berkeley and Los Angeles, California: University of California Press.

Glaeser, E. and Vigdor, J. (2001). Racial Segregation in the 2000 Census: Promising News. Washington, D.C.: Brookings Institution.

Gotham, K. F. (2002). *Race, Real Estate, and Uneven Development: The Kansas City Experience, 1900–2000.* Albany, NY: State University of New York Press.

Jackson, K. T. (1985). *Crabgrass Frontier: The Suburbanization of the United States.* New York, NY: Oxford University Press.

Johnson, C. S. (1943). *Patterns of Negro Segregation.* New York, NY: Harper and Brothers.

Katzman, D. M. (1973). *Before the Ghetto: Black Detroit in the Nineteenth Century.* Urbana: University of Illinois Press.

Lovett, B. L. (1999). *The African-American History of Nashville, Tennessee, 1780–1930.* Fayetteville: University of Arkansas Press.

Massey, D. S. and Denton, N. A. (1993). *American Apartheid: Segregation and the Making of the Underclass.* Cambridge, MA: Harvard University Press.

Meyer, S. G. (2000). *As Long as They Don't Move Next Door.* Lanham, MD: Rowman and Littlefield.

Munnell, A. H., Tootell, G. M. B., Browne, L. E., and McEneaney, J. (1996). Mortgage Lending in Boston: Interpreting HMDA Data. *The American Economic Review*, 86, 25–53.

National Fair Housing Alliance (2006). Unequal Opportunity—Perpetuating Housing Segregation in America. Found on line at http://www.nationalfairhousing.org/resources/news/Archive/resource_20628126054870386567.pdf.

Polikoff, A. (2006). *Waiting for Gautreaux: A Story of Segregation, Housing, and the Black Ghetto.* Evanston, IL: Northwestern University Press.

Background readings, *Race—The Power of an Illusion.* A PBS production. California Newsreel, 2003. Found on line at http://www.pbs.org/race/000_General/000_00–Home.htm.

Rosen, J. (2006). Perhaps Not All Affirmative Action is Created Equal. *New York Times*, June 11, 2006.

Shapiro, T. M. (2004). *The Hidden Cost of Being African American: How Wealth Perpetuates Inequality.* New York, NY: Oxford University Press.

Turner, M. A., Ross, S. L., Galster, G. C., and Yinger, J. (2002). Discrimination in Metropolitan Housing Markets: National Results from Phase I HDS 2000. The Urban Institute. Submitted to U.S. Department of Housing and Urban Development.

U.S. Census Bureau, Annual Statistics, 2005, Homeownership Rates by Race and Ethnicity of Householder, Table 20. Found on line at http://www.census.gov/hhes/www/housing/hvs/annual05/ann05t20.html.

Yinger, J. (1996). Discrimination in Mortgage Lending: A Literature Review. In *Mortgage lending, racial discrimination, and federal policy*, edited by J. Goerring and R. Wienk, 365–397. Washington, DC: Urban Institute Press.

———. (1995). *Closed Doors, Opportunities Lost: The Continuing Costs of Housing Discrimination.* New York, NY: Russell Sage Foundation.

Chapter Four

Corporatism and Inequality:
The Race to the Bottom (Line)

Bruce Barry and Jason Stansbury

As a subject area in higher education, "management" can be construed broadly as the study of virtually all aspects of commerce, given that universities often label their units devoted to the study of business as schools, colleges or departments of management. More narrowly, however, management as an intellectual enterprise encompasses behavioral- and social-science subjects within business academia that address individual, organizational, and strategic behavior. Although no one model prevails, it is common for university business schools to encompass subareas or departments for such subjects as accounting, finance, marketing, operations, information systems—and management. In this narrower, departmental vein, the academic field we call management is an interdisciplinary venture underpinned by multiple social and behavioral sciences—most prominently social psychology, sociology, and economics, but also anthropology, political science, and law, among others. Among academic researchers and teachers in management, some have earned doctorates within a business school behavioral science specialty, such as organizational behavior, human resources, or strategic management, while others have terminal degrees in these outside yet underlying disciplines.

It is intellectually risky to paint the contours of a broad academic field with a single brush stroke, but we can say in rough terms that the aims of management research are to understand and influence the science and practice of organizational arrangements and processes. Mainstream scholarly research in management tends to be empirical within a normal, positivist tradition of social science theory development. Exemplary research published in prestigious scholarly journals is aimed typically (but not always) at both the development of sound middle-range theory and the influence of contemporary management practice. Even the most academically abstruse of management journal articles, whether empirical or purely conceptual, often includes a section on the "management implications" of the research.

In this chapter, we search for an understanding of how the scholarly field of management tackles, copes with, or perhaps just conveniently avoids the subjects of race and wealth inequality in contemporary America. Doing so means confronting an inescapable paradox between the imposing and expanding power of corporate capitalism on the one hand, and the depressing and stubborn reality of poverty and economic inequality in American society on the other. The questions are, "how do those intersect?" and "how does the field of management come to grips with that intersection?" The chapter is structured into three major parts: First, we present a brief overview of poverty and corporatism, followed by a discussion of existing management scholarship on the intersection of poverty, race, and inequality; Second, we discuss underlying conceptual frameworks that create tensions in management scholarship between economic and social imperatives; Last, we conclude with a few speculative words about future directions for more and better management research attention to these issues.

MANAGEMENT SCHOLARSHIP ON
POVERTY, INEQUALITY, AND RACE

An examination of management scholarship on race and wealth yields a surprising finding: to the extent that there is any management literature on race and wealth, that literature deals either with poverty alone (without regard to race), or with race as it impacts the careers of minority managers (most of whom earn middle-class incomes or more). We are not aware of published management scholarship that examines management's descriptive or normative influence over the systematically higher poverty and lower access to resources that (in the U.S.) afflict many African American, Latino, and Native American communities. In light of management scholarship's separation of race and poverty, we divide our own introduction to the management literature on race and wealth into two subtopics. The first topic looks at the literature on management and the alleviation of poverty, and the second topic looks at the literature on race and career outcomes for managers.

Poverty and Corporatism

Extending our inquiry past the front door of the firm, to poverty and inequality in the community, calls for a reminder of the grim scope and persistence of the problem. It is easy to become almost numb to the parameters of these issues, so they bear repeating. The poverty rate in the United States is stubbornly high: the poverty rate of 12.5% in 2003 was up from 12.1% in 2002, after having declined from roughly 15% in 1993 (DeNavas-Walt, Proctor & Mills, 2004). American *child* poverty is especially troubling when compared with other countries; Italy and the United Kingdom are the only western industrialized nations whose child poverty rates approach the 2000 American level of 22%, at 16.6% and 15.4% in 1999, respectively (Luxembourg Income Study, 2004). Wealth disparities across races are also large across most ages of adulthood, even when you take education into account (Sholz & Levine, 2002).

Dispiriting numbers such as these grow even more so when one's perspective shifts from the U.S. to global poverty. Income poverty worldwide is sometimes measured in terms of the number of people who live on less than a dollar or two a day, and statistics show that in 2001 over 2.7 billion people lived on that little (World Bank, 2005). Also remarkable is a comparison between 1990 and 2000—a period of unprecedented economic growth in many parts of the world—showing that (with the exception of East Asia) the millennium began with as many or more people living on less than two dollars a day than did in 1990 (Chen & Ravallion, 2004). Figures like these tell a compelling story, but they mask the sober reality that poverty is about hunger and unemployment and lack of shelter, about illness without access to health care and illiteracy without access to education, not only now but also into the future. It is a form of "powerlessness, lack of representation, and [lack of] freedom" (World Bank, 2004).

The issue before us here is the connection between this grim reality and the academic field of management. We have come to notice what is, in the kindest possible terms, a markedly calloused detachment on the part of our field toward this enduring social pathology. It is a detachment that we argue has evolved and expanded since the war on poverty began. We develop this (admittedly cynical) thesis from three angles. First, what does the field of management have to say, both to itself and to practitioners? Second, what kind of underlying conceptual evolution have we seen among social theorists and ethicists about this issue? Finally, what can we say about the approach taken by current management practice toward this issue?

One idea threaded through all three questions is *corporatism*, which refers to the extent of influence that private organizations have over government and policy. After World War II, benevolent forms of corporatism in Europe supplemented representative democracy; for example, tripartite councils brought business, government, and labor to the table together in Western European nations, and later in the former Eastern Bloc, Southeast Asia, and Latin America (Fashoyin, 2004). The interesting thing about the word "corporatism" is that it has come to refer in many circles to a kind of sinister influence of corporations over public policy, and to an antidemocratic belief that government and society should be led in a big way by corporations (Klein, 2000). Our point is this: It can be said that corporations are more powerful in America than they have been before, but on issues of poverty and inequality corporations are not powerless but essentially valueless. They do not lack power, but choose or perhaps are forced to exercise almost no power in these areas.

Management on Poverty and Inequality

So, what does the field of management have to say about this intersection between management, poverty, inequality, and race? On the scholarly side, the answer is "not much at all." To explore this, we took advantage of a search engine maintained by the Academy of Management, an international scholarly professional association devoted to research in the theory and to a lesser extent the practice of management, organizational behavior, and strategic management. The Academy of Management has been publishing journals and holding academic conferences for forty years. With the word *poverty* entered as a search term, over forty years of journals and conferences produced seven hits in all, of which four are irrelevant because the authors just happened to use the word "poverty" as a noun in another context. The search yielded one journal article from the late 1960s, and a conference paper from 1988 (Steidlmeier, 1988). In forty years of what many would consider to be the premier journals in the management field, there is only a 1968 study of leadership and organizational issues in so-called Neighborhood War-On-Poverty Centers (Delbecq & Kaplan, 1968). In the same search engine, the word "inequality" elicited three hits over forty years, one of which is irrelevant because it used the word "inequality" in a different context. There is one theory paper (Fondas, 1993) and one conference paper on salary and equality between male and female employees (Auster, 1989). Praveen and Cullen (2002) have an interesting conference paper reporting on a multination study exploring whether managers are more likely to justify unethical behavior if they are in countries with high social and economic inequality. The answer, by the way, was yes.

Our thought after this search-engine parlor game was "well, management theory is really not about the study of social problems, except as they arrive within the purview and mission of the firm," but we also thought "then again, the firm is the cornerstone of market capitalism." The social and economic structure of communities and societies is plainly and at least in part an outgrowth of firm behavior, and increasingly of corporate political influence.

Interestingly, the theoretical inattention of management scholars toward these issues has not stopped them from trying to tell business leaders how to think and what to do about these problems. An engaging way to assess that kind of didactic role is to look at the most venerable of management journals intended for high-level executive audiences—the *Harvard Business Review* (HBR). A walking tour through 40 years of HBR's coverage of poverty starts with a 1964 piece called "Poverty and Profits." This is not a single article but a collection of short essays, which the editors introduced with this remark:

> How do you encourage initiative on the part of those who have been brought up in destitute, broken homes, where there is no parent who goes to work every morning? . . . Not by a dole. Even technical training fails the purpose of making the unemployed more employable, when the unemployed in question has built a way of life around getting the most out of various kinds of relief (as demonstrated among hard core unemployed Negroes in the South). (Hostetler, Kelso, Adler, Long, & Oates, 1964: p.6)

The other contributors to this multi-essay forum were more analytical and by extension less troubling. Norton Long, a sociologist, wrote that "what the poor need is employment, and in a capitalist system employment depends on someone being able to make a profit from their employment . . . To pretend otherwise is . . . both self-defeating and intellectually dishonest" (Hostetler et al, 1964: p.16). Long wrote "the most powerful force in our society as currently organized, with the possible exception of war, is in fact the search for profit" (Hostetler et al, 1964: p.18). So, anything that is done about poverty presumably must come in that context. Corporate lawyer Louis Kelso, another contributor, wrote:

> [T]he solution to our problem . . .lies in recognizing that some of our wealth is produced by labor, and much—an increasing portion—is produced . . . by capital instruments . . . As more of our wealth is produced by capital, more of our families *must* participate in production as owners of capital. . . The goal of labor should not be toil for all but *participation in production for all* (Hostetler et al, 1964: p. 14–16; emphasis in original)

Kelso proposed a system of loaning poor people money to buy stocks they can't afford. Essentially, the idea was to get people credit so they can become owners. Overall, the logic of the status quo seems unassailable to these authors, who therefore focus on devising a means of access to the system for those who have none.

Skip ahead a few years to 1968, and we find a piece in HBR by Leland Hazard, an executive turned business school professor, who argued that existing anti-poverty programs were economically self-defeating due to their inflationary effects, and that capitalizing on the administrative and allocative skills of business could make effective progress in eliminating "real poverty,"

though not relative poverty (Hazard, 1968). Hazard proposed that government form a high-level business council on poverty and welfare that would
bring executives together and apply their skills to public sector efforts on social welfare. He makes this interesting point:

> Industrialists eschew involvement in high-level social welfare planning [be-
> cause] the programs may often be controversial. . . Executives really want to do
> the safe thing—be on hospital boards, most college and university boards, the
> Boy Scouts, the Girl Scouts, either of the Y's and . . . the Salvation Army . . .
> but he had best not pioneer in mental health, penal reform, or the benign use of
> drugs—or write poetry (Hazard, 1968: p. 6)

Hazard closes the article by saying "If industry does not develop the will to
help the poor, if it does not use for the poor the skills which it possesses, then
it must remain silent while government fumbles. Put up, or shut up" (Hazard,
1968: p. 169–170).

Fast forward to 1991, and we find two prominent sociologists, Mary Joe
Bane and David Ellwood, offering a polemic to HBR readers about poverty
with a very different kind of message. Instead of thinking about the poor as
residing outside the corporation's doors, they proposed thinking of poverty as
something that exists within a corporation because the poor are its workforce:

> Poverty is a business issue, then, because most poor people are part of the cur-
> rent or future U.S. work force. And this poses a problem for managers. In a more
> competitive and fast-changing economy, the performance of companies increas-
> ingly depends on the capabilities of their employees. . . . And yet, for 8 million
> American workers—roughly 7% of the entire U.S. labor force—the experience
> of work isn't empowerment but quite literally impoverishment (Bane & Ell-
> wood, 1991: p. 58)

Bane and Ellwood look at 1988 data and find that roughly half of the adult
poor work. This catalyzes a polemic of sorts urging new public policies
around child care, health care, support payments, child support, and so forth.
Notwithstanding its appearance in the staid HBR, it comes off more as a con-
sciousness-raising, public advocacy sort of piece than a call for direct action
by business leaders in the reduction of poverty.

Move ahead another decade to 2002 and the emphasis shifts dramatically.
Prahalad and Hammond argue in HBR not for workforce or community development, but for businesses to fulfill their potential to make profits off of
poor people (Prahalad & Hammond, 2002). Arguing that prosperity comes to
the world's poorest regions through the involvement of multinational corporations, Prahalad and Hammond challenge two common assumptions: first,

that the poor have no money (when in fact their incomes may be low but their aggregate buying power is quite large), and second, that poor people are too concerned with meeting basic needs to spend on nonessential goods (when in fact the poor often do buy luxury items). We see, again, the recurring argument that business efficiency holds the key to alleviating poverty, but this time through sound business strategy rather than philanthropy or strategic human resource management (Prahalad & Hammond, 2002).

An HBR article by Michael Porter (2002), a widely-known writer on corporate strategy, discussed the competitive advantage of corporate philanthropy. Porter argued that social and economic value could be simultaneously created by treading a middle ground between both philanthropy and business. The argument is perhaps best encapsulated in the statement:

"There is no inherent contradiction between improving competitive context [i.e. external factors that impact a company's competitiveness] and making a sincere commitment to bettering society. Indeed, as we've seen, the more closely a company's philanthropy is linked to its competitive context, the greater the company's contribution to society will be. . ." (Porter, 2002: p. 59).

This can be construed as letting business off the hook, arguing that if firm leaders do what comes naturally—pursue strategic self-interest—social value will follow.

In summary, it can be said that over four decades there has been an escalation of calls for business to be engaged in these problems, for different reasons at different times. Early on, there is Hazard's call for businesses to share their leadership (Hazard, 1968), followed later by Bane and Ellwood's appeal to workforce interests (Bane & Ellwood, 1991), and most recently a shift in emphasis to the market potential of philanthropy (Porter, 2002). Yet viewed through a different lens, we end up in the same theoretical and ideological place after forty years that we were at the start of this little walking tour: knee deep in a rational, neoclassical economic model of self-interest that undergirds market capitalism. There is little to suggest that the field of management is speaking to its professional practitioners about any evolution away from that fundamental neoclassical assumption.

Management and Race

The form and focus of the management literature on race further illustrates the neoclassical paradigm mentioned above. A number of empirical studies have investigated the impact of race on such outcomes as job satisfaction, salary, promotions, and social networking, which are important insofar as organizations are generally thought to prosper when they retain and motivate talented employees (Wright & McMahan, 1992). Of course, increased job satisfaction, higher salaries, more frequent promotions, and enhanced social networking are also thought to be overwhelmingly beneficial to minority employees; membership in business organizations is the condition that enables minority employees to benefit from most findings of management scholarship.

Powell and Butterfield (1997), in a study of advancement, examined the promotion rates of employees of color to senior management positions within a cabinet-level department of the U.S. government. They tested both the direct effect of the applicant's race on promotions, and the indirect effect of race as mediated by other factors that vary systematically with race, in this case years of experience and current membership in the promoting organization. Their sample consisted of 300 applications for consideration for one of 39 jobs filled in the department studied between January 1987 and December 1994; African-American, Native American, Asian-American, and Hispanic-American candidates were consolidated into the categories "women of color" and "men of color." The authors used logistic regression to assess the influence of the independent variables on the review panel's decision whether or not to refer an applicant to a hiring official, and the official's decision whether or not to offer a job. Powell and Butterfield found that race itself was not significantly related to referral for promotion, but that applicants who had less experience and were not employed in the hiring department, both of which were generally characteristic of men of color, were less likely to be referred for promotion. None of the variables significantly predicted the selection decision once an applicant was referred. The sample of women of color was too small to be meaningful (Powell and Butterfield, 1997).

Dreher and Cox (2000) examined whether minority managers realize higher salary outcomes by entering the external labor market as well as by taking advantage of internal opportunities for promotion or lateral job change. They hypothesized that even when controlling for candidate qualifications and industry differences in salary, minority managers would realize lesser gains than their Caucasian male counterparts, due to less extensive social networks and the possibility of lower offers from hiring managers who may have a preference for Caucasian employees or may simply perceive that minority managers will accept lower offers. After surveying 758 graduates of nine prestigious Master's of Business Administration programs, they found that white male managers who changed companies within the ten years since completing their MBAs averaged $24,410 more in annual salary than their counterparts who remained with the same firm, but that minority men and both white and minority women who changed companies realized no significant salary advantage over their counterparts (Dreher and Cox, 2000).

Empirical studies in management, like the ones described above, generally treat race as a simple demographic variable. A single survey item is usually considered sufficient for its measurement, which can then be correlated with the outcomes of interest to support or disconfirm a hypothesis (for example) that minority employees are denied promotion because of their race. The studies above reveal, unsurprisingly, that race impacts the career prospects of minority managers, though perhaps more subtly than it once did.

Parallel to empirical management science is a stream of conceptual scholarship that develops and critiques both the concepts examined in empirical work, and the paradigms that underpin them. Management scholarship on race has been predominantly empirical, but Stella Nkomo (1992) examined several theoretical models of race that have informed discussions of privilege in organizations, detailing both their underlying assumptions and their implications for past and present management practice.

Nkomo characterized the ethnicity paradigm, which emerged in the 1920s to supplant then-prevailing biological theories of racial privilege, as insisting that ethnic categories were not long-term essential differences between groups of people, but rather that assimilation to a dominant culture was a natural and perhaps inevitable process. Prejudice was seen as a failure of individual-level cognition, and would disappear as assimilation progressed or as members of different ethnic groups became more familiar with each other (i.e. the contact hypothesis). This paradigm complemented and legitimated programs of assimilation promoted by industrial firms struggling to integrate immigrants into their production systems.

Nkomo also described the "new ethnicity paradigm" that emerged beginning in the 1970s, and differed from the earlier ethnic paradigm by characterizing prejudice as a natural if unfortunate result of biologically-rooted cognitive biases toward one's own group. While racial differences were not seen as essential, the social psychological processes that accentuated them were thought of as natural and immutable. The new paradigm implied that "racial and ethnic stratification are . . . an almost permanent and inevitable part of human society" (Nkomo, 1992: p. 495). Both ethnic paradigms relied on an individual-level model of prejudice or cultural inadequacy, but did not incorporate historically-rooted group-level effects that contribute to the ongoing under-representation of African-Americans at the top levels of American organizations. Rather, either the failure of an ethnic group to assimilate to the dominant culture was construed as its own failure, or the inequality of organizational outcomes experienced by minority groups was explained as an inevitable consequence of cultural pluralism. Nkomo advocated the development of organizational paradigms that comprehend race as a construct with macro-level implications for employees' power and identity within organizations (1992).

Nkomo also reviewed the existing empirical literature and found that the ethnic paradigms had informed a great many studies, which had investigated the experiences of discrimination, job attitudes, assimilation, and leadership suitability of African-American employees. She advocated the measurement of race not as a single-item demographic attribute of individuals, but rather as a phenomenological experience that is determined by the organization as well as by the individual, and identified a set of research questions that such a paradigm would pose, including "Why, despite national policies like affirmative action, does inequality still exist in the workplace? Are assimilation and managing diversity the only two means of removing racial inequality in the workplace? How do organizational processes contribute to the maintenance of racial domination and stratification?" (Nkomo, 1992: p. 506).

Nkomo's call for a phenomenological account of race that incorporates the macro-level implications of historical position has proven to be exceptionally ambitious for management scholarship. The limited literature reviewed above illustrates the current scope of inquiry, which is limited largely to human-resources outcomes within the organization. Although individual career success in organizations is important both for reducing broad-based inequality among racial groups and for reducing racial tension within organizations, Nkomo (1992) notes that theory and practical recommendations that focus on the individual level are unlikely to substantially ameliorate the macro-level social conditions that hinder individual competitiveness. Moreover, social conditions such as differential access to educational, social, and capital resources are centered outside the employment context, and are therefore beyond the current scope of management scholarship.

CONCEPTUAL UNDERPINNINGS
OF MANAGEMENT SCHOLARSHIP

The neoclassical paradigm of economic thinking has long informed management scholarship at all levels. The assertion that agents' rational self-interest promotes the most efficient allocation of resources (Smith, 1991 / 1776), and the assertion that the most efficient allocation is normative (Bentham, 1970 / 1789), have informed the "creative destruction" theory of market competition (Schumpeter, 1942), the shareholder theory of the corporation (Jensen, 2002), and rational choice theories of individual behavior (Blau, 1964). These fundamental assertions provide the starting assumptions for a great deal of management theory, which in turn frames the questions that empirical techniques answer. However, some scholars (especially in the burgeoning subfield of Critical Management Studies) are loosening these assumptions by asking whether rationality is as efficient as it has been supposed to be, and whether the complete sovereignty of capital over the disposal of the firm is as necessary and beneficial as has sometimes been insisted. The loosening of assumptions is theoretically interesting, and challenges to the neoclassical paradigm have important social implications as well: The appropriate scope of management theory and action may begin to extend beyond the stewardship of the firm for the benefit of its owners.

One alternative approach was defined at some length in Amitai Etzioni's 1988 book *The Moral Dimension*. Etzioni offered a forceful critique of neoclassical economics as unrealistically rationalist, overly utilitarian, and excessively individualist. He first challenged two neoclassical assumptions: that people make decisions rationally, and that people's values can be distilled to a single measure of utility. Etzioni argued that people are not rational calculators of their own aggregate interest; rather, they "brush their teeth but do not fasten their seat belts" (Etzioni, 1988: p. xi), and make decisions based on emotion and intuition as much as by rational calculation. More importantly, they make choices based not only on the personal utility that they expect to gain, but also on the fulfillment of moral commitments that may stand in opposition to their own hedonic good (Etzioni, 1988).

Etzioni also challenged the assumption that markets are self-contained, self-sustaining, and can be analyzed within a model of perfect competition. Instead, he asserted that "the economy is a subsystem of a more encompassing society, polity, and culture" (Etzioni, 1988: p. 5), which for its survival regulates the terms and scope of both exchange and competition. Etzioni also argued that economists who defend the sovereignty and primacy of consumer preferences disregard the fact that preferences are socially born, and that those preferences reflect society's values, culture, and power structure. Individual preferences are social creations, so that both hedonic and moral preferences are valid within their proper context. The social creation of these preferences is one form of collective decision-making, which to Etzioni is necessary for societal sustainability (Etzioni, 1988). That last point especially leads to some of his communitarian prescriptions, which strike us as problematic but are outside the scope of this chapter. Still, his criticism of neoclassical economics is cogent.

A second challenge to neoclassical economics, which comes out of the field of business ethics, is stakeholder theory. Stakeholder theorists argue that the firm is a constellation of competitive and collaborative interests, rather than simply the instrument of the shareholders (Phillips, Freeman, and Wicks, 2003). A shareholder approach argues instrumentally that if owners of the firm or regulators give managers the appropriate mix and balance of incentives, optimizing the share price of the firm will coincide with larger societal

welfare. In that sense, the shareholder approach comprehends a kind of enlightened self-interest. To the contrary, however, if the point is the welfare of
employees, customers, and others, as well as shareholders, then why not pursue such societal welfare directly?

A critique of the stakeholder approach is that it is inconsistent with established and stable systems of corporate law and governance. One critic, Alexei
Marcoux, writing for the Libertarian Cato Institute, charged that "stakeholder
theorists seek a reorientation of corporate law toward the interests of stakeholders, and the insulation of managers from the market for corporate control"
(Marcoux, 2000: p.1). Marcoux complained that stakeholder theory will transform the corporate boardroom from a forum in which economically rational
strategies are adopted in pursuit of firm value into an arena for legislative and
bureaucratic political maneuvering. Abandoning fiduciary duty to shareholders in favor of a multifaceted responsibility to workers, consumers, and other
stakeholders would drive managers to distraction, the argument goes, and
thereby threaten the prosperity that shareholder capitalism has created.

Stakeholder theorists would likely argue that the above case is overstated.
Tom Donaldson and Lee Preston, for example, maintain that managers are
morally required to acknowledge the validity of diverse stakeholder positions
and attempt to respond to them, lest they undermine the legitimacy of the
management function (Donaldson & Preston, 1995). Dennis Quinn and Tom
Jones have argued that there are four normative principles that should guide
this way of thinking: avoid harm to others, respect the autonomy of others,
avoid lying, and honor agreements (Quinn & Jones, 1995). They add that
"Acting with regard to these principles is the moral obligation of all humans,
no matter what profession or position" (Quinn & Jones, 1995: p.30). But this
approach still may leave broader social concerns like poverty and inequality
out of management's purview, because ethics as an academic subfield of management tends to drill down into managerial behavior within the firm, leaving external social concerns as a kind of abstraction.

Ed Freeman, in a 1998 essay, sought to develop a broader concept of stakeholder capitalism, envisioning a world where business and ethics are intertwined, and where values and virtues are part of corporate life (Freeman,
1998). To Freeman, a hyper-competitive and shareholder-driven model of
business is obsolete for thinking about the long-term strategic management of
employees, markets, and even shareholders. A revised model that incorporates the well-being of workers, the satisfaction of consumers, and the health
of the earth is already being enacted by some visionary businesspeople, and
as it takes hold not only among businesses but also among public expectations, the law and the theory will follow (Freeman, 1998). It's a lofty argument. Another form of it that has appeared in the business ethics literature is

the notion of Kantian capitalism. Norman Bowie and others argue that Immanuel Kant's categorical imperative could be used as an appropriate basis for business practice. For example, "on Kantian grounds there is a moral requirement that the corporation provide . . . meaningful work" (Bowie, 1998: p. 1083), defined as work that supports the worker in leading a moral and thus an autonomous rational life. According to Bowie, a Kantian theory of capitalism would offer a universal morality for business, institute firms as moral communities, and establish a more cosmopolitan and peaceful world (Bowie, 1998). Again, lofty stuff. A repudiation by Andrew Stark is worth mentioning because of its vitriol: "Even if one believes this assertion to be true, such a claim is so alien to the institutional world inhabited by most managers that it becomes impossible for them to act on it" (Stark, 1993: p. 46). The insight (and encouragement) we draw from this is that some important ethicists are deeply hopeful that the terms of management thinking are changing to incorporate and address concerns about poverty and inequality. Any sanguinity is necessarily tempered, however, by the competitive reality of managers' institutional worlds: any number of great and good ideas are shelved because of higher competitive priorities or their own imagined unaffordability, often before they have a chance to prove themselves in practice.

CONCLUSION

There are signs that firms take social impact more seriously now than in the past. One is found in the kind of discourse around mission and values in which firms themselves engage. For instance, in its public relations materials, the large pharmaceutical firm Pfizer boasts that "through our support of both local and global initiatives, and by the generosity and compassion of our employees, we strive to make every country and community in which we operate a better place to live and work" (Pfizer, 2004). Wal-Mart, quoting the words of its founder Sam Walton, professes an aim to "give the world an opportunity to see what it's like to save and have a better lifestyle, a better life for all" (Wal-Mart, 2005). Modern industrial corporations are accomplished at talking the talk of social value and enlightened capitalism. However, it is a different (and difficult) matter to make measurable commitments to social outcomes, since that entails engaging the prolific layers and conflicting interests of the financial staff and line organization in addition to the marketing department. Few companies have committed to measurable social goals along with their statements of values; the Dutch brewer Heineken B.V. is an example of one that publishes its results as well as its intentions (Heineken, 2004).

Yet if it is easy to be cynical about the false consciousness of social responsibility in corporate America, we note also a proliferation in recent years of nonprofits, industry associations, and NGOs specifically devoted to corporate responsibility. One prominent example in the U.S. is Business for Social Responsibility (BSR), which has studied such issues as the need to pay employees sufficient wages to meet basic needs, or a "living wage." Indeed, there are living wage movements in many municipalities and communities in America. Less encouraging is a tendency for these associations to be dominated by established interests that have the size and influence to forge the agenda. A compromise negotiated on behalf of developing-nation workers by their governments or by labor unions is questionably representative, just as the will and ability of multinationals to speak for all businesses is suspect (Gilbert & Rasche, 2007).

Which leaves us where? Depressed, perhaps, and troubled. Our field—management—jealously guards its studied and calloused detachment we referred to at the outset from the real problems that exist outside the workplace door. Issues like the widespread backdating of stock options that surreptitiously rewarded executives even as corporate performance faltered (Forelle & Bandler, 2006; Lie, 2005) threaten articles of faith like the efficiency of equity markets and the effectiveness of pay for performance. Management scholars are therefore in the sensitive position of both defending and criticizing a system of economic organization whose operating assumptions are in some respects beginning to look obsolete.

The ideology of American business seems to be that prosperity is defined as money, and as economic station, but not as the kind of society in which one would want to live. This tends to be regarded as a settled issue. It's not that business lacks the power to change, it's that it lacks the impetus, which comes back to the idea of corporatism with which we started. Corporations jealously guard and seek to expand their social and political power, but are generally unwilling to use it to catalyze real change. They construct and maintain an ideological fortress that sits on a foundation of neoclassical economics, which arguably is just as redoubtable around the management academy today as it was forty years ago. This ideological fortress, against which social change on economic policy and inequality cannot hope to advance, is why we expect that we will be able to write this chapter 10 or 20 years from now with very few changes.

REFERENCES

Auster, E. R. 1989. Task characteristics as a bridge between macro- and microlevel research on salary inequality between men and women. *Academy of Management Review*, 14: 173–193.

Bane, M. J., & Ellwood, D. T. 1991. Is American business working for the poor? *Harvard Business Review*, 69 (5): 58–64.

Bentham, J. 1970 [1789]. *An Introduction to the Principles of Morals and Legislations.* New York: Oxford University Press.

Bowie, N. E. 1998. A Kantian theory of meaningful work. *Journal of Business Ethics,* 17: 1083–1093.

Blau, P. 1964. *Exchange and Power in Social Life.* New York: Wiley.

Chen, S., & Ravallion, M. 2004. How have the world's poorest fared since the early 1980s? *World Bank Research Observer,* 19(2): 141–169.

Delbecq, A. L., & Kaplan, S. J. 1968. The myth of the indigenous community leader. *Academy of Management Journal,* 11: 11–25.

DeNavas-Walt, C., Proctor, B. D. & Mills, R. J. 2004. Income, Poverty, and Health Insurance Coverage in the United States: 2003. In U. S. Census Bureau, *Current Population Reports: Consumer Income:* 60–226. Washington, DC: U.S. Government Printing Office.

Donaldson, T., & Preston, L. E. 1995. The stakeholder theory of the corporation: Concepts, evidence, and implications. *Academy of Management Review,* 20: 65–91.

Dreher, G. F., & Cox, Jr., T. H. 2000. Labor market mobility and cash compensation: The moderating effects of race and gender. *Academy of Management Journal,* 43: 890–900.

Etzioni, A. 1988. *The Moral Dimension.* New York: Free Press.

Fashoyin, T. 2004. Tripartite cooperation, social dialogue, and national development. *International Labour Review,* 143(4): 341–371.

Fondas, N. 1993. The feminization of American management. *Academy of Management Proceedings:* 358–362.

Forelle, C., & Bandler, J. 2006. The perfect payday. *Wall Street Journal,* March 18: A1.

Freeman, R. E. 1998. Poverty and the politics of capitalism. *Business Ethics Quarterly: The Ruffin Series,* Special Issue No. 1: 31–35.

Gilbert, D. U., & Rasche, A. 2007. Discourse ethics and social accountability: The ethics of SA 8000. *Business Ethics Quarterly,* 17(2): 187–216.

Hazard, L. 1968. Business must put up. *Harvard Business Review,* 46 (1): 2–11.

Heineken B.V., Social Responsibility. http://www.heinekeninternational.com/responsibility/index.jsp. Accessed on 4/2/04.

Hostetler, L. M., Kelso, L. O., Adler, M. J., Long, N. E., Oates, J. F. 1964. Poverty and profits. *Harvard Business Review,* 42 (5): 6–18.

Jensen, M. C. 2002. Value maximization, stakeholder theory, and the corporate objective function. *Business Ethics Quarterly,* 12 (2): 235–256.

Klein, N. 2000. The vision thing. *The Nation,* July 10. http://www.thenation.com/doc/20000710/klein. Accessed on 9/17/06.

Lie, E. 2005. On the timing of CEO stock option awards. *Management Science,* 51(5): 802–812.

Luxembourg Income Study (LIS) Key Figures, http:/www.lisproject.org/keyfigures/childpovrates.htm. Accessed on 4/1/04.

Marcoux, A. 2000. Business ethics gone wrong. *Cato Policy Report,* 22 (3): 1.

Nkomo, S. M. 1992. The emperor has no clothes: Rewriting 'Race in organizations'. *Academy of Management Review,* 7: 487–513.

Parboteeah, K. P., & Cullen, J. B. 2002. Managers' justifications of unethical behaviors: A 28 nation social institutions approach. *Academy of Management Proceedings:* D1–D6.

Pfizer, "Partnerships for a Healthier World." http://www.pfizer.com/subsitues/philan thropy/caring/index.html. Accessed on 3/3/04.

Phillips, R., Freeman, R. E., & Wicks, A. C. 2003. What stakeholder theory is not. *Business Ethics Quarterly*, 13: 479–502.

Porter, M. E., & Kramer, M. R. 2002. The competitive advantage of corporate philanthropy. *Harvard Business Review*, 80 (12): 56–68.

Powell, G. N., & Butterfield, D. A. 1997. Effect of race on promotions to top management in a federal department. *Academy of Management Journal*, 40: 112–128.

Prahalad, C. K., & Hammond, A. 2002. Serving the world's poor, profitably. *Harvard Business Review*, 80 (9): 48–57.

Quinn, D. P. & Jones, T. M. 1995. An agent morality view of business policy. *Academy of Management Review*, 20: 22–42.

Schumpeter, J. A. 1942. *Capitalism, Socialism and Democracy*. New York: Harper.

Sholz, J. K. and Levine, K. 2002. *U.S. Black-White Wealth Inequality: A Survey*. Dept. of Economics and Institute for Research on Poverty, University of Wisconsin-Madison.

Smith, A. 1991 [1776]. *The Wealth of Nations*. Amherst, NY: Prometheus.

Stark, A. 1993. What's the matter with business ethics? *Harvard Business Review*, 71 (3): 38–48.

Steidlmeier, P. 1988. The business community and poverty. *Academy of Management Proceedings*: 329–334.

Wal-Mart, "Wal-Mart at a Glance." http://www.walmartstores.com/wmstore/wm-stores/Mainnews.jsp?pagetype=news&categoryOID=-8764&catID=-8248&template=DisplayAllContents.jsp. Accessed on 2/17/05.

World Bank, 2007. "Poverty Overview" http://web.worldbank.org/WBSITE/EXTERNAL/TOPICS/EXTPOVERTY/0,,contentMDK:20153855~menuPK:373757~page PK:148956~piPK:216618~theSitePK:336992,00.html. Accessed on 5/1/07.

World Bank, 2005. "World Bank Poverty Report." http://devdata.worldbank.org/wdipdfs/table2_5.pdf. Accessed on 9/30/05.

Wright, P. M., & McMahan, G. C. 1992. Theoretical perspectives for strategic human resource management. *Journal of Management*, 18 (2): 295–301.

Chapter Five

A Selective Review of Sociological Perspectives on the Relationship Between Race and Wealth

Tony N. Brown and Daniel B. Cornfield

To propose a sovereign sociological approach to the study of race and wealth is to do injustice to the breadth of theories that are subsumed within and serve to reify the discipline's identity. Sociology is not only built upon theoretical eclecticism, it thrives on it. This is evidenced by the fact that sociological theories appropriate ideas from history, economics, law, psychology, medicine, and anthropology insomuch as these disciplines offer empirically based perspectives that explain social conflict, consensus, and change.

The co-authors of this chapter are two sociologists, trained and with expertise in distinct research areas. Each of us, for example, has a unique program for research, endorses a particular approach to studying race and wealth, and differentially conceives the central values of the discipline. We can write together, nonetheless, because a common theme (i.e., empirically based explanations for social conflict, consensus, and change) underlies our approaches. However we write separate sections because we are knowledgeable about different theoretical traditions and likely hold different criticisms of the extant literature.

Thus two independent sections comprise the chapter. The first examines race and wealth from an economic sociology theory perspective, which tends to juxtapose race to other factors such as human and social capital, whereas the second examines race and wealth from a critical race theory perspective, which tends to characterize racism as omnipresent and enduring. From mainstream to marginal, the theories presented not only represent a random (albeit small) sample of perspectives a sociologist might invoke to investigate the intersection of race and wealth, but also represent groups of sociologists with divergent interests, values, and backgrounds. We do not wish to imply, however, by use of the labels 'mainstream' and 'marginal' a strictly hierarchical

58   Chapter Five

view of different theories/groups of people comprising the sociological tradition, but rather we wish to suggest that there is a historically grounded, ongoing, and dynamic debate between a hegemonic white perspective minimiz-
ing the importance of race and racism, on the one hand, and a disparaged
perspective that demands the inclusion of race and racism as fundamental sociological concepts, on the other hand. The reader should infer, therefore, that
economic sociology theory research and the types of scholars likely to be its
adherents are more widely accepted than the critical race theory approach and
likewise those endorsing it.

Our collaborative effort, divided into two independent sections, proves the
absence of a sovereign sociological paradigm while displaying the thematic
consistency of sociological thought. The perspectives discussed are not meant
to be exhaustive nor mutually exclusive in content, leaving room for discussion, reconciliation, and constructive criticism across perspectives.

DANIEL B. CORNFIELD

Race and Wealth from the Perspective of Economic Sociology

Racial and ethnic disparities in wealth accumulation in the United States have
been studied from the perspective of economic sociology. Economic sociology, according to one authoritative source, is "the application of the frames
of references, variables, and explanatory models of sociology to that complex
of activities concerned with the production, distribution, exchange, and consumption of scarce goods and services" (Smelser and Swedberg 1994:3; also,
see Guillén et al. 2002).

From the perspective of this branch of sociology, disparities in market
outcomes—wealth, earnings, unemployment, etc.—result from asymmetric
social relations and cultural norms that are embedded in markets and market transactions and that may advantage and disadvantage some groups over
others in economic transactions. Asymmetric social relations include societal relations between racial, ethnic, and gender groups and social classes.
Cultural norms refer to generalized beliefs and attitudes about group relations, such as racial attitudes, ethnocentrism, racial and ethnic identity, gender role attitudes, attitudes about labor-management relations, etc., that economic actors enter into economic transactions and that over time become
infused into economic institutions often as informal, taken-for-granted business practices (Guillén et al. 2002; Portes 1995; Smelser and Swedberg
1994; Smelser, Wilson, and Mitchell 2001; Waldinger and Lichter 2003).

Economic action, the actions and consequences of economic actors in markets, is the chief object of analysis in economic sociology. Economic actors

include such market participants as job seekers, workers, labor unions, professional associations, employers, firms, corporations, entrepreneurs, creditors, suppliers, and consumers. In the field of economic sociology, economic action is conceived as transactions between actors in a market that is embedded within societal asymmetric social relations and cultural norms. These social relations and cultural norms are assumed to constrain and shape the preferences of economic actors, the amount of trust and potential for reciprocal relations among economic actors, and inequalities among economic actors in the accessibility of consumer markets and economic resources such as jobs, credit, product innovations, suppliers and government regulations. The embeddedness of social relations and cultural norms in markets often occurs through formal and informal social networks among economic actors, the depth, density, extent, and social prestige of which afford market participants differential access to markets and economic resources (Bean and Stevens 2003:94–113; Portes 1995; Waldinger and Lichter 2003).

Economic sociological research on racial disparities in wealth accumulation has examined racial and ethnic relations in the deployment of three enduring and overlapping income-generating strategies. These strategies are used by individuals and households to accumulate wealth and experience upward social mobility for themselves and their children. The strategies are: (1) individual accumulation of human and social capital; (2) participation in the labor movement, labor unions, and collective bargaining; and (3) entrepreneurialism.

The first, and perhaps the most pervasive of the three income-generating strategies—individual accumulation of human and social capital, is the effort by an individual worker to enhance her or his employability and productivity and to augment her or his access to lucrative jobs and organizational careers in high-wage, corporate, primary labor markets. Human capital consists of resources (such as education and work experience) that enhance individual productivity. Social capital consists of trusting, reciprocal social networks of referrals and prospective employers—"connections"—that afford a worker access to information, employment gatekeepers, and promising organizational careers. Research on this theme has tended to examine the efforts, careers, and attainments of wage and salaried workers, inferring wealth disparities from disparities in their income and employment attainments. Much sociological research has documented and attributed racial and ethnic differentials in individual attainment of human and social capital to one's social class background, neighborhood effects on schooling and access to educational opportunities, overt and covert ethnic and racial discrimination in personnel decision making and human resource management, occupational segregation by sex, race, and ethnicity, individual occupational attainment, economic sector of one's employment, and the size of one's employer (Bean and Stevens 2003; Berg and Kalleberg 2001; Federal Glass Ceiling Commission 1995; Smelser, Wilson, and Mitchell 2001; Wilson and Jaynes 2000).

In his theoretical synthesis of sociological research on race and work organizations, Vallas (2003) argues that more sociological research has been devoted to race inequalities in labor market outcomes than to the unfolding of race and ethnic relations in the workplace. "As a result," Vallas (2003:380) writes, "a wealth of econometric studies have focused on the distribution of opportunity but have produced remarkably little understanding of the social processes that underlie such disparities and that shape the work situations of historically excluded groups." In order to address this deficit in research, Vallas (2003) presents a new research agenda that emphasizes the impact of the following features of social organization inside workplaces on racial and ethnic disparities in career and labor market outcomes: spatial segregation of racial and ethnic groups of workers; informal social networks; racialized status and skill hierarchies and resistance by dominant-group workers; declining managerial concern with equal employment opportunity linked to mounting economic competition; and ineffective individualistic judicial interpretations and remedies that miss collectively produced racial disparities.

The second income-generating strategy, participation in the labor movement, labor unions, and collective bargaining, is a collective strategy by wage and salaried workers to improve their earnings, hours and working conditions. By organizing themselves into a group, unionized workers augment their bargaining power in negotiations with their employer and thereby pursue improvements in their livelihoods. Today, only 12% of the U.S. labor force belongs to labor unions, and no more than 35% of the national labor force has ever been unionized since the late 19th century. Research has shown that the earnings of unionized workers, especially those of unionized ethnic-racial minorities and women workers, have historically exceeded those of their non-union counterparts. Much sociological research has examined the factors that promote and hinder the development of a racially and ethnically inclusive labor movement (Cornfield 1989, 1999; Cornfield and Fletcher 2001; U.S. Bureau of Labor Statistics 2006).

Including ethnic-racial minorities and women in the ranks of labor union leadership has been an important strategy, if a halting process, for recruiting new, underrepresented worker constituencies into the labor movement. Therefore, this strategy also has served as a key vehicle for revitalizing a labor movement whose sagging membership has resulted from employer resistance to unions, globalization and plant shutdowns, and automation of production processes (Cornfield and Fletcher 2001; Cornfield and McCammon 2003). According to Cornfield's (1989) status-conflict theory, movement inclusivity is enhanced during eras of intense labor-management conflict, in which ideologically universalistic labor leaders perceive the strategic importance of non-union ethnic-racial minorities as prospective union members in the revitalization of a declining labor movement (Cornfield 1989, 1999; Cornfield and Fletcher 2001; also, see Brueggemann and Boswell 1998).

The third income-generating strategy is entrepreneurialism, or self-employment. Unlike the other income-generating strategies, this one also is a wealth-producing strategy insofar as the development of one's own business entails the accumulation of business assets. Less than 10% of the U.S. labor force is self-employed (U.S. Bureau of the Census 2006). Much sociological research has documented ethnic-racial and gender differentials in one's chances of becoming self-employed, as opposed to being a wage or salaried employee. The chances of becoming self-employed have been attributed to one's accumulation of human and social capital, ethnic-racial and sex discrimination in credit and consumer markets, immigration and ethnic niches in labor and product markets, and family resources such as children and childcare (Bean and Bell-Rose 1999; Bean and Stevens 2003:127–130; Carr 1996; Light and Karageorgis 1994; Portes and Zhou 1999).

Much sociological research has addressed ethnic and racial variations in the chances of becoming self-employed (Light and Karageorgis 1994). This line of research, in turn, has compared immigrant and native workers' establishment of and employment in ethnic subeconomies. According to Light and Karageorgis (1994:647), an "ethnic economy consists of the ethnic self-employed and employers, and their co-ethnic employees

In their analysis of the 1990 U.S. Census of Population, Portes and Zhou (1999) describe ethnic-racial variations in men's self-employment rates, an indicator of the chances of becoming self-employed. The self-employment rate is the percentage of civilian workers who are self-employed, as opposed to employed for someone else or unemployed. Portes and Zhou show that the self-employment rate for native-born, African American men was 4.9%, that for native-born, white men was 14.4%, and those for foreign-born, male Chinese, Cubans, Dominicans, Jamaicans, Koreans, Mexicans and Vietnamese ranged from 6.8% (Mexican) to 34.2% (Korean).

Portes and Zhou proceed to examine separately and statistically for each of these groups the factors that influence one's chances of becoming self-employed. Their analysis of the 1990 U.S. Census data shows that, for each group, a unique set of factors influence one's likelihood of becoming self-employed. For African Americans, older and more educated workers are the most likely to become self-employed. For whites, age, education, as well as family resources, including having multiple children and few adults in the household, increase one's self-employment chances. For the foreign-born groups, the same set of factors that influence native-born workers' self-employment rates applies. Furthermore, foreign-born workers' chances of being self-employed are also enhanced by their length of residence in the United States, proficiency in English, and residence in metropolitan areas of high ethnic-group concentration.

Portes and Zhou's findings suggest that race and ethnic disparities in wealth derive in part from race and ethnic disparities in human and social capital accumulation. Taking self-employment rate as an indicator of entrepreneurialism, the findings suggest that African American men's relatively low involvement with entrepreneurialism stems in part from their relatively low accumulations of human and social capital. Portes and Zhou are critical of the statistical method they use in this article for its limitations in illuminating community-level resources and multiplier effects of business creation (1999:164). Nonetheless, regarding the development of entrepreneurialism in African American communities, Portes and Zhou (1999:165–166) conclude,

A history of systematic discrimination and enforced disadvantage has left many African American communities unable to undertake these transformations by themselves. The requisite resources are simply not there. Hence, advocating entrepreneurship as one potentially viable path for African American economic mobility should not be confused with conservative calls for bootstrapping and self-reliance. At least for the start, such efforts would require considerable external support. Affirmative action programs that protect and encourage minority entrepreneurs, currently under attack, represent a key step in the right direction. These market reserves should be supplemented by targeted training programs and business credit facilities . . . Research on the topic can thus make a significant contribution by going beyond simple comparisons across groups to examine the transferability of those features that support the remarkable success of certain immigrant communities.

TONY N. BROWN

Race and Wealth: The Contribution of Critical Race Theory

Sociologists have long debated whether social inequality is functional or indicative of conflict, as well as whether economic or political stability can exist without the unequal distribution of scarce resources. So even though there is no established history of studying race and wealth per se, sociologists have much to say on the matter of social inequality, broadly defined. They have, for example, written about social inequality whose etiology is immigration, industrialism, new world slavery, technology, modernization, the law, political and economic change, sexism, migration, war, and so on.

Race and racism are obviously linked to social inequality but have not received systematic or sustained attention in the mainstream literature. Consistent with this, McKee (1993:338–339) and Winant (2000:178–180) argue that the sociological tradition has failed to adequately theorize and empirically investigate why and how race and racism matter today. This is somewhat surprising given the history of the discipline. For instance, Frazier (1947:265–6) noted that the first sociological treatises to be published in the United States were concerned with race relations.

In response to the seeming neglect of race and racism in the discipline, a group of marginalized theorists and researchers produced in the past, and produces today, scholarship illuminating the historical and contemporary importance of race matters (see Ladner 1973; Blackwell and Janowitz 1974; Willie 1979, 1989; Winant 2000:175–6; Young and Deskins 2001). Their work informs and challenges mainstream sociological thinking. Their work questions the value of sociology as a social science when it excludes race and racism as areas of inquiry, and refuses, based on relevant research findings, to engage in efforts to engineer social justice (i.e., public sociology). And thus, through their work, these theorists and researchers guarantee that race and racism will never be completely ignored in the sociological tradition.

In this section of the chapter, I examine the relationship between race and wealth from a critical race theory perspective. Prior to describing sociological research that exemplifies the perspective, I present a simplified synopsis of sociology's history with regard to studying race and racism, and elaborate critical race theory's contribution to the sociological tradition and to research on race and wealth.

Sociology's History of Studying Race and Racism

This section is not a review of sociological studies focusing on race and/or racism. Instead it describes why these topics are generally under-represented in mainstream sociological research. By selectively reading the intellectual history of the discipline backward, I hope to suggest how we arrived at the current state of affairs and foreshadow the utility of critical race theory to contemporary sociological studies.

Sociological studies of race and racism are rarer than one might expect leaving gaps in the literature and critical questions unanswered in reference to social inequality. Although not all sociologists by formal training, scholars (and activists) like Dolores Aldridge, Ida Wells Barnett, James Blackwell, Stokely Carmichael, Patricia Hill Collins, Oliver C. Cox, Harold Cruse, Angela Y. Davis, W. E. B. Dubois, E. Franklin Frazer, bell hooks, Charles Johnson, Joyce Ladner, Stanford Lyman, Manning Marable, Aldon Morris, Cornel

West, Charles V. Willie, and countless and no less notable others (see Black-well and Janowitz 1974; McKee 1993; Winant 2000:175–6; Young and De-skins 2001:446–455) attempted to requisition a place for race and racism within the sociological canon. And to some extent, they were successful. They used a three-pronged approach. First, they challenged mainstream the-oretical perspectives that excluded race and racism from consideration or that minimized its importance. Second, they criticized empirical research that lit-erally excluded people of color and other minority groups. And third, they conducted research that could not be understood by applying only main-stream concepts. Ultimately and through the tripartite approach, they demon-strated, among other things, that race and racism are important omitted vari-ables within what is perceived as the most significant and widely accepted sociological research (Ladner 1973; Blackwell and Janowitz 1974; Willie 1979, 1989; Young and Deskins 2001).

As a consequence, the discipline of sociology was forced to consider the role it played in recreating social inequality because scholars doing "sociology of race" work asked poignant questions that demanded answers. For example, how could classic Marxist theory explain the exclusion of black workers from labor unions or the ready incorporation of new white immigrants in the work-place before willing black workers (for example, see Glazer 1971)? How could the results from the status attainment literature, which is based on white fathers and sons only, be consistent with the finding that skin tone had a sig-nificant impact on upward mobility in the black community (especially among black women) (for example, see Keith and Herring 1991)? How could social psychologists ignore identity politics as a source of conflict (for example, see Carmichael and Hamilton 1967:44–46)? How could social movement scholars fail to predict the U.S. Civil Rights Movement (for example, see McKee 1993; Morris 1984)? Most important and given their contributions to the develop-ment of the discipline, how could sociologists of color be systematically ex-cluded from editorial boards, tenure-track positions at prestigious universities (see Bonilla-Silva and Herring 1999), and leadership positions in the Ameri-can Sociological Association (ASA)?

In summary, the seeming marginality of race and racism in the mainstream sociological literature certainly reveals something about sociology as an enter-prise but it also reveals something about the nature of individuals who typically represent sociology. First, the typical sociologist tends to under-specify the role of race and racism but tends to overemphasize the role of social class. Second, the typical sociologist often conducts empirical work that does not apply to peo-ple of color or include people of color. These two seemingly deleterious ten-dencies, however, were ultimately beneficial because each encouraged a group of sociologists (most often and visibly black sociologists or intellectuals with a penchant for sociological research) to conduct cutting-edge research causing mainstream sociology to remodel itself to more accurately reflect social reality.

Aligned with scholars (and activists) doing sociology of race work, my perspective on the relationship between race and wealth is informed by critical race theory. This theoretical apparatus explains the operation of race and racism as they relate to myriad phenomena including racial and ethnic disparities in wealth.

Critical Race Theory

Delgado and Stefancic (2001a, 2001b) define critical race theory as a paradigm that generates insights into the contemporary racial predicament to transform the relationships among race, racism, and power. As a social movement and science, it was birthed of the union between critical legal studies and radical feminism in the late 1980s; its named forefather is the law professor Derrick Bell. Most research that invokes critical race theory is published in law and legal studies. For example, critical race theory has been applied to topics in jurisprudence such as: analysis of conflict between integration ideals and clients' interests in desegregation litigation, incremental approaches to achieving social equality, pseudo-neutrality in principles of constitutional law, proliferation of discrimination through anti-discrimination law, racially based jury nullification, and race-conscious districting (see Delgado and Stefancic 2001b; Crenshaw, Gotanda, Peller and Thomas 1995). Despite its initial connection to law and legal studies, with increasing frequency scholars in other disciplines are enamored with the theoretical acumen of this revisionist approach (see Brown 2003).

According to Brown (2003:294), there are five fundamental tenets and themes that support the perspective, research methods, and pedagogy of critical race theory: (1) Racism is ordinary, ubiquitous, and reproduced in mundane and extraordinary customs and experiences. (2) The race problem is difficult to comprehend and possibly impossible to remedy because claims of objectivity and meritocracy camouflage the self-interest, power, and privilege of whites. (3) Races are categories that society invents, manipulates, and recreates. (4) Blacks are competently able to communicate and explain the meaning of race and racism because they are oppressed, and therefore, experiential knowledge is legitimate, appropriate, and insightful. (5) Beyond purely academic or scientific outcomes and implications, critical race theory seeks to engineer social justice.

Critical race theory has greatest utility when applied to vectors of social life where the consequence of race and racism is simply ignored or tends to be more complex than is evident upon cursory examination (see Crenshaw, Gotanda, Peller and Thomas 1995). It follows then that critical race theorists are lawyers, economists, psychologists, historians, political scientists, educators, feminists, and sociologists. What unites scholars from this range of academic traditions is a mission to depict how race and racism operate on multiple levels simultaneously to impact lifestyles and life chances. For instance, critical race theorists illustrate how doctrine, discourse, and deliberate action manifest norms, ideologies, and procedures that sustain racial stratification. Critical race scholars believe that race inequality cannot and should not be reduced to social class inequality. They believe that what people perceive as racial progress often comes with a cost. As a consequence, critical race scholars are often portrayed as pessimists, politicians, and/or activists as opposed to academicians (McWhorter 2001:8–9, 40, 219).

Exemplary Research

The book *Black Wealth, White Wealth: A New Perspective on Racial Inequality* presents sociological research on race and wealth, and manifests the tenets and themes embodying critical race theory. In this book, authors Melvin L. Oliver and Thomas M. Shapiro suggest and demonstrate that the extent and embedment of social inequality have been vastly underestimated because wealth disparities and their reproduction have been neglected (Oliver and Shapiro 1997:134, 176). The authors challenge the way that social inequality is theorized and empirically estimated by sociologists, and they show that studying wealth disparities leads to a more complete understanding of the dynamics of past and contemporary racism. The book opened the door for revisionist empirical analyses of phenomena related to race and wealth such as: trends in asset accumulation, home ownership, effects of poor relatives on wealth building efforts, intergenerational wealth by inheritance, and research on differential taxation by race.

Oliver and Shapiro (1997:4–5, 37, 45, 50) employed three theoretical concepts to explain race disparities in wealth: (1) racialization of state policy (i.e., institutional racial discrimination), (2) the economic detour (i.e., low rate of black self-employment), and (3) sedimentation of racial inequality (i.e., cumulative historical disadvantage). Using in-depth interviews and Survey of Income and Program Participation (SIPP) data (1987–1989), the authors investigated net worth (NW) and net financial worth (NFW) showing that race disparities in these outcomes persist after controlling for variation in many variables (Oliver and Shapiro 1997:127–133). They used a popular quantitative analysis called multiple regression (for a thorough description of multiple regression, see Allison 1999), a technique that examines how several, correlated predictor variables are associated with a single outcome variable. A major strength of multiple regression is that it allows analysts to examine how a single predictor variable relates to an outcome variable while adjusting for other predictor variables that might partially or completely explain away the initial relationship. Mathematically, it is based on estimating how much additional information is provided about variation in an outcome variable by considering variation in a predictor variable controlling for other predictor variables. Using an array of such multiple regression models, they found three classes of factors were related to disparities in NW and NFW: (1) human capital and labor market; (2) institutional and policy discrimination (in particular, differential access to home ownership); and finally (3) intergenerational transmission of wealth (Oliver and Shapiro 1997:127–133, 142, 152). Also the authors demonstrated substantial racial variation in the composition of wealth generating assets (Oliver and Shapiro *1997:104–108*).

Black Wealth, White Wealth: A New Perspective on Racial Inequality implicitly invokes critical race theory and exemplifies its tenets and themes in numerous ways. First, the authors demonstrate how racism operates in a mundane and institutionalized manner often without the intent of individuals to further white privilege simultaneous to subverting blacks' attempts to accumulate wealth. In their description of the sedimentation of racial inequality for example, they state: "Practically, every circumstance of bias and discrimination against blacks has produced a circumstance and opportunity of positive gains for whites. When black workers were paid less than white workers, white workers gained a benefit; when black businesses were confined to the segregated black market; white businesses received the benefit of diminished competition; when FHA policies denied loans to blacks, whites were the beneficiaries of the spectacular growth of good housing and housing equity in the suburbs" (Oliver and Shapiro 1997:51). As manifest in this quote, the authors' complicated and historically grounded approach to understanding the nature of wealth disparities exposes the contemporary interests of whites in maintenance of the racial status quo.

Second and by explicitly addressing the material consequence of race, the authors demonstrate that racial categories, despite dubious evidence of their conceptual validity, nonetheless influence the lifestyles and life chances of blacks and whites and racialized others. Third, Oliver and Shapiro question whether individualistic approaches to wealth building in the black community (e.g., encouraging entrepreneurship) (Oliver and Shapiro 1997:190–3) will have any non-negligible impact without the institutionalization of redistributive and wealth accumulation policies that they ultimately outline in the book's concluding chapter. Basically, they argue that blacks do not lack wealth because of poor saving habits or an inability to delay gratification but rather because of a systematic denial of this nation's promise of equality of opportunity. (Despite distinct theoretical approaches but demonstrating consistency in sociological thought, Oliver and Shapiro's conclusion about the inadequacy of self-employment as a method of building black wealth converges with Portes and Zhou's (1999) conclusion reported at the end of Cornfield's section).

Fourth, the authors heavily relied on respondents' narratives about what wealth means in their everyday lives and the barriers that hinder acquisition and accumulation of wealth. Consistent with the critical race theory tenet that blacks are competently able to communicate and explain the meaning of race and racism because they are oppressed, Oliver and Shapiro (1997:52–3) demonstrated that in-depth interviews are absolutely necessary to capture the experiential dimensions of the processes that the quantitative analysis of the SIPP data validated.

Fifth, it is typical in research such as this to conclude by suggesting directions for future research and presenting implications under the guise of advancing social science for the sake of advancing social science (consistent with the norm of value-free science). Indeed, Oliver and Shapiro do follow the norm to some extent but blatantly violate it when they detail several ways, and more important, reasons to engineer social justice in reference to redistributing wealth. For instance, they state: " . . . the evidence we have presented clearly suggests the need for new approaches to the goal of equality. We have many ideas related to this topic and several concrete suggestions for change that can lead to increased wealth for black and poor families . . . After presenting those recommendations we shall broach the sensitive, yet wholly defensible strategy of racial reparations. Then we will reflect on the leadership role that the black community must play in closing the wealth gap" (Oliver and Shapiro 1997:178). Furthermore, they suggest that our nation needs an "avowedly egalitarian antiracist stance that transcends our racist past and brings blacks into the mainstream" (Oliver and Shapiro 1997:194).

A bold conclusion like that one concisely embodies the essence of critical race theory. This type of conclusion, however, is seldom seen in mainstream sociological research. Undaunted by that fact, theorists and researchers representing the sociology of race tradition hope research like Oliver and Shapiro's (1997) *Black Wealth, White Wealth: A New Perspective on Racial Inequality* motivates more sociologists to claim their rightful position as the social scientists who are commonly expected to do research on social inequality (including race-related) and use that research in the pursuit of social justice.

REFERENCES

Allison, Paul D. 1999. *Multiple Regression: A Primer*. Thousand Oaks, CA: Pine Forge Press.

Bean, Frank, and Stephanie Bell-Rose, eds. 1999. *Immigration and Opportunity: Race, Ethnicity, and Employment in the United States*. New York: Russell Sage Foundation.

Bean, Frank, and Gillian Stevens. 2003. *America's Newcomers and the Dynamics of Diversity*. New York: Russell Sage Foundation.

Berg, Ivar, and Arne Kalleberg, eds. 2001. *Sourcebook of Labor Markets: Evolving Structures and Processes*. New York: Kluwer Academic/Plenum.

Blackwell, James E. and Morris Janowitz, eds. 1974. *Black Sociologists: Historical and Contemporary Perspectives*. Chicago, IL: The University of Chicago Press.

Bonilla-Silva, Eduardo and Cedric Herring. 1999. "'We'd Love to Hire Them But' . . : The Underrepresentation of Sociologists of Color and Its Implications." American Sociological Association's *Footnotes* (March):6–7.

Brown, Tony N. 2003. "Critical Race Theory Speaks to the Sociology of Mental Health: Mental Health Problems Linked to Racial Stratification." *Journal of Health and Social Behavior* 44(3):292–301.

Brueggemann, John, and Terry Boswell. 1998. "Realizing Solidarity: Sources of Interracial Unionism During the Great Depression." *Work and Occupations* 25 (November):436–482.

Carmichael, Stokely and Charles V. Hamilton. 1967. *Black Power: The Politics of Liberation in America*. New York, NY: Random House.

Carr, Deborah. 1996. "Two Paths to Self-Employment? Women's and Men's Self-Employment in the United States, 1980." *Work and Occupations* 23 (February):26–53.

Cornfield, Daniel. 1989. *Becoming a Mighty Voice*. New York: Russell Sage Foundation.

——. 1999. "Guest Scholar Poll Review, September 2, 1999, Shifts in Public Approval of Labor Unions in the United States, 1936–1999," The Gallup Organization, http://www.gallup.com/poll/guest_scholar/gs990902.asp.

Cornfield, Daniel, and Bill Fletcher. 2001. "The U.S. Labor Movement: Toward a Sociology of Labor Revitalization." Pp. 61–82 in Arne Kalleberg and Ivar Berg (eds.), *Sourcebook of Labor Markets*. New York: Kluwer Academic/Plenum.

Cornfield, Daniel, and Holly McCammon, eds. 2003. *Labor Revitalization: Global Perspectives and New Initiatives*. Amsterdam: Elsevier.

Crenshaw, Kimberlé, Neil Gotanda, Gary Peller, and Kendall Thomas, Eds. 1995. *Critical Race Theory: The Key Writings that Formed the Movement*. New York, NY: The New Press.

Delgado Richard and Jean Stefancic, eds. 2001a. *Critical Race Theory: The Cutting Edge, Second Edition*. Philadelphia, PA: Temple University Press.

——. 2001b. *Critical Race Theory: An Introduction*. New York, NY: New York University Press.

Federal Glass Ceiling Commission. 1995. *Good for Business: Making Full Use of the Nation's Human Capital*. Washington, D.C.: Government Printing Office.

Frazier, E. Franklin. 1947. "Sociological Theory and Race Relations." *American Sociological Review* 12(3):265–271.

Glazer, Nathan. 1971. "Blacks and Ethnic Groups: The Difference, and the Political Difference It Makes." *Social Problems* 18:444–461.

Guillén, Mauro, Randall Collins, Paula England, and Marshall Meyer. 2002. "The Revival of Economic Sociology." Pp. 1–32 in Mauro Guillén, Randall Collins, Paula England, and Marshall Meyer, eds., *The New Economic Sociology: Developments in an Emerging Field*. New York: Russell Sage Foundation.

Keith, Verna M., and Cedric Herring. 1991. "Skin Tone and Stratification in the Black Community." *American Journal of Sociology* 97(3):760–78.

Ladner, Joyce, ed. 1973. *The Death of White Sociology*. New York, NY: Random House.

Light, Ivan, and Stavros Karageorgis. 1994. "The Ethnic Economy." Pp. 647–671 in Neil Smelser and Richard Swedberg, eds., *The Handbook of Economic Sociology*. Princeton: Princeton University Press and New York: Russell Sage Foundation.

McKee, James B. 1993. *Sociology and the Race Problem: The Failure of a Perspective*. Urbana, IL: University of Illinois Press.

McWhorter, John H. 2001. *Losing the Race: Self-Sabotage in Black America*. New York, NY: Perennial.

Morris, Aldon D. 1984. *The Origins of the Civil Rights Movement*. New York, NY: The Free Press.

Oliver, Melvin L. and Thomas M. Shapiro. 1997. *Black Wealth, White Wealth: A New Perspective on Racial Inequality*. New York, NY: Routledge.

Portes, Alejandro, ed. 1995. *The Economic Sociology of Immigration: Essays on Networks, Ethnicity, and Entrepreneurship*. New York: Russell Sage Foundation.

Portes, Alejandro, and Min Zhou. 1999. "Entrepreneurship and Economic Progress in the 1990s: A Comparative Analysis of Immigrants and African Americans." Pp. 143–171 in Frank Bean and Stephanie Bell-Rose, eds., *Immigration and Opportunity: Race, Ethnicity, and Employment in the United States*. New York: Russell Sage Foundation.

Smelser, Neil, William Wilson, and Faith Mitchell, eds. 2001. *American Becoming: Racial Trends and Their Consequences,* vol. 1. Washington, D.C.: National Academy Press.

Smelser, Neil, and Richard Swedberg. 1994. "The Sociological Perspective on the Economy." Pp. 3–26 in Neil Smelser and Richard Swedberg, eds., *The Handbook of Economic Sociology*. Princeton: Princeton University Press and New York: Russell Sage Foundation.

U.S. Bureau of Labor Statistics. 2006. "Union Members in 2005." News release USDL 06–99, January 20. Downloaded on September 16, 2006 from: http://www.bls.gov/news.release/pdf/union2.pdf.

U.S. Bureau of the Census. 2006. *The 2006 Statistical Abstract*, table 589. Downloaded on September 16, 2006 from: http://www.census.gov/compendia.statab/labor_force_employment_earnings/.

Vallas, Steven. 2003. "Rediscovering the Color Line within Work Organizations: The "Knitting of Racial Groups' Revisited." *Work and Occupations* 30:379–400.

Waldinger, Roger, and Michael Lichter. 2003. *How the Other Half Works: Immigration and the Social Organization of Labor*. Berkeley: University of California Press.

Willie, Charles Vert. 1979. *Caste and Class Controversy*. Bayside, NY: General Hall.

———. 1989. *The Caste and Class Controversy on Race and Poverty: Round Two of the Willie/Wilson Debate*. New York, NY: Rowman & Littlefield Publishers.

Winant, Howard. 2000. "Race and Race Theory." *Annual Review of Sociology* 26:169–185.

Wilson, Franklin, and Gerald Jaynes. 2000. "Migration and the Employment and Wages of Native and Immigrant Workers." *Work and Occupations* 27 (May):135–167.

Young, Jr., Alford A. and Donald R. Deskins Jr. 2001. "Early Traditions of African-American Sociological Thought." *Annual Review of Sociology* 27:445–477.

Chapter Six

Federalism and Equity: Evolution of Federal Educational Policy

Kenneth K. Wong

Public education faces the challenge of income inequality and racial/ethnic disparities in our society. In the early 2000s, one-third of the nation's public school student population is eligible for free and reduced price lunch. In the nation's largest central city school districts, over 60% of the students are eligible for the school lunch program. African American students constitute over one-third of the enrollment in large central cities as compared to 17% nationwide. A similar trend is seen in the growing Latino population. Schools that have a higher concentration of minority and low-income students are less likely to recruit qualified teachers, offer strong curricula, and maintain high academic performance.

The pervasive impact of poverty and racial/ethnic inequality in public schools raises a fundamental tension in our federal system of government. Given our decentralized system of governance, what is the role of government in addressing social redistributive needs? Decentralization is clearly prevalent in public education, where power and decisions are dispersed among 50 states and 15,000 districts. Historically, state and local governments paid limited attention to the educational needs of disadvantaged students, whose parents were often not well organized and whose neighborhoods were less likely to be economically vibrant. States and districts tended to marginalize schooling opportunities for segments of at risk populations.

The tension between decentralization and inequity constitutes a central concern in the discipline of political science. On the one hand, the U.S. Constitution recognizes the rights of the states to handle their own affairs, including public education. On the other hand, there is pressing public responsibility to address the needs of those who are less fortunate. An understanding of how the government manages this tension between local control and social responsibility lies in the distribution of power and functions between layers of government. The way we govern public education, allocate resources, and organize the delivery of services from one level to the other as well as across a diverse country constitute a natural setting for conducting research on intergovernmental relations in educational policy. In this chapter, I will examine the evolution of the federal role in addressing income and racial/ethnic disparities in public schools. Particular attention will be given to evolving theories of intergovernmental relations, including patterns of conflict and cooperation between the federal and the local government in education policy.

EDUCATIONAL POLICY AS A FIELD OF STUDY

From a broader analytical perspective, this study of federal educational policy draws from a subfield in the political science discipline, namely, the politics of education. To be sure, the politics of education as a field of study owes much of its intellectual roots to its parent discipline. Researchers in educational politics are primarily concerned about power, influence, conflict, and the "authoritative allocation of values" (Easton 1965, Peterson 1974). For example, the politics of education scholarship has contributed to our understanding of governmental efforts to promote racial equity (Orfield 1969, Hochschild and Scovronick 2003). Studies show that minority groups can put pressure on the school bureaucracy to allocate resources in a more equitable manner proportional to the needs of the students. Minority groups are also found to have gained representation in both district and school leadership (Jackson and Cibulka 1992). Equally important are studies that showed that minority representation affects personnel policy, which in turn may have contributed to instructional consequences for low-income students (Meier et al 1989). One study, for example, found that increases in the number of Latino teachers tend to reduce dropout rates and increase college attendance for Latino students (Fraga et al 1986). In other words, representational politics tends to reduce discriminatory practices and facilitate equal schooling opportunities.

The focus on political issues notwithstanding, the study of educational policy constitutes a multidisciplinary approach that goes beyond political science. To a large degree, educational policy researchers have vigorously adopted concepts and methods from various disciplines. As policy makers look for coherence in service delivery and formulate more comprehensive solutions to address chronic social problems, policy analysts become increasingly interdisciplinary in conducting their research. Drawing from economic science, researchers apply the concepts of human capital investment, incentives and rational expectation. From sociology, we learn about the nature and functions of bureaucracy, school organization, the process of producing learners, social capital, and the urban underclass (Wilson 1987). We see the importance of contextualizing our findings, as historians do. As mentioned earlier, like political scientists, we pay attention to the governance structure, the political process, interest groups, and the distribution of power.

The multidisciplinary approach will continue to sharpen our understanding of educational policy for reasons that are related to the nature of investigation. Studies of educational policy are more problem-oriented than theory-oriented. Taken as a whole, the field of study can be broadly characterized as applied social science research. While some studies draw on large scale national databases, many researchers continue to gather information directly from the schools, communities, districts, states, and federal agencies that pertain to the particular needs of a specific context. Further, conversations between educational policy analysts and the policy community are frequent and intense and coordinated efforts are made to disseminate research findings to practitioners. Efforts to link research to practitioners are facilitated by the federally-funded research and development centers and technical assistance centers. This latter is in sharp contrast to the culture of investigation in the social science disciplines, where the leading professional journals aim at addressing the theoretic concerns that are central to the particular arena of discipline knowledge. Many discipline-based journals in recent years have become highly technical and filled with mathematical formulae and formal models with limited discussion on policy implications. Educational policy journals are able to maintain their focus on problems that face policy makers and practitioners.

Educational policy researchers are actively engaged in not only problem identification but also seeking alternative ways to address current and emerging challenges that confront policy makers and practitioners. Quite frequently, educational policy involves debates that are deeply embedded in our civic value systems (Gutmann 1987). Contending beliefs include equity issues for classes of disadvantaged citizens, political accountability that respects the tradition of local control, constitutional guarantees of individual liberty, commitment to efficiency in service provision, and maintenance of democratic representation. Governmental institutions, including school boards, are expected to manage competing values and reconcile contending interests in a changing society. In the field of educational policy, researchers have paid attention to the role of government in managing conflicts. Consequently, studies have addressed such important policy issues as urban education reform, school desegregation, assessment of student progress, service integration, race and gender equity issues, and school finance equity (Wong 1999). These are clearly issues that are central to the functioning and improvement of the public education system.

FROM DUAL FEDERALISM TO MARBLE CAKE FEDERALISM

The role of the government in addressing the needs of disadvantaged students occupies a prominent place in the study of educational policy. The governmental responsibility has undergone major changes as American federalism evolved with the passage of time. While the federal government has assumed new responsibilities to promote equal educational opportunity, state and local governments continue to play a dominant role in governing and managing public schools.

Historically, the federal government has taken a permissive role in education that is consistent with what political scientist Morton Grodzins characterized as "layer cake" federalism. Article I, Section 8 of the U.S. Constitution specifies the "enumerated powers" that Congress enjoys and the Tenth Amendment granted state autonomy in virtually all domestic affairs, including education. Sovereignty for the states was not dependent on the federal government but instead came from the state's citizenry. Consistent with this view, in "The Federalist Papers," which were first published during 1787 and 1788, James Madison suggested a line of demarcation between the federal government and the states (Hamilton, Madison, & Jay, 1961). He wrote, "The federal and state governments are in fact but different agents and trustees for the people, constituted with different powers, and designed for different purposes." (No. 46, p.296, 1961). The dual structure was further maintained by local customs, practice, and belief. It came as no surprise that in his description of the American democracy in the mid-nineteenth century, Alexis de Tocqueville (2000) opened his seminal treatise by referring to the local government's "rights of individuality." Observing the state-local relations in the New England townships, de Tocqueville wrote, "Thus it is true that the tax is voted by the legislature, but it is the township that apportions and collects it; the existence of a school is imposed, but the township builds it, pays for it, and directs it." (p.63). Public education was primarily an obligation internal to the state. The division of power within the federal system was so strong that it continued to preserve state control over its internal affairs, including the *de jure* segregation of schools, many decades following the Civil War.

Federal involvement in education sharply increased during the Great Society era of the 1960s and the 1970s. Several events converged to shift the federal role from permissiveness to engagement. During the immediate post World War II period, Congress enacted the G.I. Bill to enable veterans to receive a college education of their choice. The Cold War competition saw the passage of the National Defense Education Act in 1958 shortly after the Soviet Union's satellite, Sputnik, successfully orbited the earth. At the same time, the 1954 landmark Supreme Court ruling on *Brown v. Board of Education* and the Congressional enactment of the 1964 Civil Rights Act sharpened the federal attention to the needs of disadvantaged students. Consequently, the federal government adopted a major antipoverty education program in 1965, Title I of the 1965 Elementary and Secondary Education Act (ESEA).

The ESEA, arguably the most important federal program in public schools in the last four decades, signaled the end of dual federalism and strengthened the notion of "marble cake" federalism where the national and sub-national governments share responsibilities in the domestic arena. Prior to the 1965 law, there was political deadlock on the role of federal government in Congress. The states outside of the south were opposed to allocating federal funds to segregated school systems. Whereas some lawmakers refused to aid parochial schools, others wanted to preserve local autonomy from federal regulations. Political stalemates were reinforced through bargaining behind closed doors among the few powerful committee chairmen (Sundquist, 1968).

The eventual passage of ESEA and other social programs marked the creation of a complex intergovernmental policy system that is unique in American history. To avoid centralization of administrative power at the national level, the Congress increased its intergovernmental transfers to finance state and local activities. During the presidency of Lyndon Johnson, categorical (or single purpose) programs, including Title I, increased from 160 to 380. By the end of the Jimmy Carter administration, there were approximately 500 federally funded categorical programs. Particularly important was the redistributive focus of many of these categorical programs that were designed to promote racial desegregation, protect the educational rights of the handicapped, assist English language learners, and provide supplemental resources to children from at-risk backgrounds. Despite several revisions and extension, ESEA Title I, for example, continues to adhere to its original intent "to provide financial assistance . . . to local educational agencies serving areas with concentrations of children from low-income families to expand and improve their educational programs. . . which contribute particularly to meeting the special educational needs of educationally deprived children." (ESEA of 1965)

The literature on federalism has looked for structural sources in explaining why anti-poverty policy is more likely to come from the national government. The federal government enjoys a broader revenue base in which taxes are primarily raised on the ability-to-pay principle, and it represents a constituency with diverse demands, including views that are not often supported by the majority (Oates, 1972; Peterson, 1995; Wong 1999). In other words, it has both the fiscal capacity and the political justification (often facilitated by organized interest groups) to take a more active redistributive role.

Federal engagement in redistributive policy is depicted in its spending priorities. According to an analysis of federal spending in public schools between 1970 and 2002, Wong found that federal aid to redistributive programs showed persistent growth in real dollar terms (using 2002 dollars). During the

32–year period, these programs increased from 36% to 63% of the total federal spending in elementary and secondary schools. The school lunch program, for example, increased its funding from $299 million in 1970 to $10.3 billion in 2002. Head Start jumped from $326 million to over $6.5 billion during this period. However, federal redistributive support slightly declined from 60% to 58% of the total federal school spending during 1985 and 1990. A similar decline occurred between 2000 and 2002 when special needs funding dropped from 66% to 63% of the total federal budget for public schools.

Further, federal redistributive grants have taken on several institutional characteristics that resemble a policy framework:

- Grants-in-aid arrangement: where the federal government provides the dollars and sets the programmatic framework, but the delivery of services is up to the state and local agencies.
- Categorical or single purpose grants: where well-defined eligible students are the intended beneficiaries; only they would receive the services.
- Supplementary and non-supplanting guidelines: they are designed to guard against any local tendency to shift federal resources away from the disadvantaged.
- Bipartisan support: Special needs programs are often connected to well-entrenched political interests. For example, the child nutrition program (free lunch program) is supported by the agricultural business.
- Incentives for local government to meet anti-poverty objectives: Federal funds are widely distributed to ensure broad political support. The territorial impact of federal grants has contributed partly to the popularity of Title I in Congress over time. For example, in the1990s, the federal grant provided supplemental resources to 64 percent of all the schools in the nation, covering virtually every congressional district. Clearly, big city districts are not the only beneficiaries of compensatory education funds. Indeed, over 20 percent of federal aid goes to districts with fewer than 2,500 students. Districts with enrollments between 2,500 and 25,000 receive almost 45 percent of the funds. Because there are Title I programs in almost every congressional district, partisan conflict has generally been limited during the appropriations process.

EMERGENCE OF PERFORMANCE-BASED FEDERALISM

While redistributive grants-in-aid have gained bipartisan support overtime, this policy arrangement faces its most serious political challenge in the mid 1990s. The 1994 midterm elections produced the first Republican majority in Congress in forty years. The new congressional leadership claimed a public mandate to shrink the federal role in social programs and to shift programmatic authority to state and local governments. The new House Speaker Newt Gingrich tended to undermine long-term institutional practices in decision-making. He depicted the federal government as the major cause of poverty, the federal bureaucracy as the major source of waste of taxpayers' dollars, and the private sector as the solution to social inequality.

Political confrontation between the Congress and the President became highly visible in education policy during 1995. The Republican leadership, for example, proposed to cut significantly major redistributive programs, including Title I and bilingual education. To demonstrate its control over governmental appropriations, the Republican leadership shut down all federal agencies when the budget expired. In the end, however, the retrenchment tactics backfired. Within two years, education policy regained bipartisan support in the Republican-led Congress.

While federal redistributive education policy seemed to have survived its most serious political challenge, its effectiveness was increasingly called into question in a broadened climate of outcome-based accountability. The passage of Improving America's Schools Act in 1994 signaled the beginning of federal efforts to address accountability in its anti-poverty programs. This legislation aimed at reducing program isolation of at-risk students from their peers, created incentives for whole school reform, and required districts and states to use their system-wide standards to assess the performance of at-risk students.

As the U.S. Congress enacted the No Child Left Behind Act of 2001, President George W. Bush broadened federal involvement toward educational accountability for all children. The federal law requires annual testing of students at the elementary grades in core subject areas, mandates the hiring of "highly qualified teachers" in classrooms by 2005–06, and grants state and local agencies substantial authority in taking "corrective actions" to turn around failing schools. Further, the law provides school choice to parents to take their children out of failing schools. Equally significant in terms of federal intervention is the legislative intent in closing the achievement gaps among racial/ethnic subgroups as well as income subgroups. To support these efforts, the federal government increased its allocation by $1.7 billion to a total of almost $11 billion in the Title I program, in addition to over $900 million for early reading initiatives. Whether these performance-based initiatives are effective in reducing the academic gaps remain to be seen.

POLICY IMPLEMENTATION:
CONFLICT AND ACCOMMODATION

While the redistributive goals have relied on federal funding, support from state and local agencies have been mixed. Since the implementation of federally-funded redistributive services, there have been three perspectives to understanding intergovernmental management of these issues.

The first generation of implementation studies was conducted mostly in the late 1960s and the 1970s, which coincided with a period of policy formation. These studies covered a wide range of policy topics—from compensatory education and busing programs to achieve integration to job training and employment programs in economically depressed communities. Given the "new-ness" of federal antipoverty policy, it came as no surprise that many first-generation studies were highly critical of how the federal program operated. For example, a 1969 study conducted by the NAACP Legal Defense Fund found that federal Title I funds were being used for "general school purposes; to initiate system-wide programs; to buy books and supplies for all school children in the system; to pay general overhead and operating expenses; [and] to meet new teacher contracts which call for higher salaries." Similarly, Jerome Murphy's (1971) analysis of the Title I program in Massachusetts found state and local interests competing against the federal antipoverty intent.

In short, as analysts examined the initial development of the intergovernmental administrative structure in implementing anti-poverty programs, they often found confusion, conflict, and failure to meet national social objectives. In other words, federal resources set aside for the at-risk populations often failed to go to the intended beneficiaries. These first generation studies no doubt raised important political and policy issues—whether the federal government can use grants to overcome structural obstacles that are embedded in constitutional tradition of state rights and local control. Consequently, throughout the 1970s, the Congress adopted an exceedingly well-defined set of regulations to make sure that intended beneficiaries receive services.

A second perspective on intergovernmental relations emerges as the federal grants-in-aid system matures. As the federal government increasingly clarifies its anti-poverty intent, state and local agencies seem more ready to meet programmatic standards. Based on a comparative analysis of federal roles in education, health care, and housing and community development, Peterson, Rabe, and Wong (1986) documented various patterns of state and local response to federal expectations. This study observed two major implementation patterns. While intergovernmental cooperation remained strong in activities pertaining to economic growth, conflict often occurred in redistributive programs. The lack of full federal funding to meet mandated standards can be a source of intergovernmental contention. The federal government, for example, promised to provide 40% of the funds for special education, but in reality, its funding level seldom went over 25% of the program cost. Local and state agencies were also reluctant to change their practices in light of the federal focus. Perhaps most interestingly, Peterson, Rabe, and Wong observed that intergovernmental tension became increasingly manageable with the passage of time. Professional exchange and identify across intergovernmental levels were instrumental in resolving program conflict and facilitating communication.

The second perspective tends to address the methodological concerns of first generation studies. First, these studies differentiate socially redistributive objectives from other purposes in federal programs. Having made explicit the differences in national purposes, these studies considered intergovernmental conflict as a function of social redistribution goals. Second, even when they conducted a single case study, researchers often collected information from multiple years of the implementation process. This longitudinal view enabled policy analysts to denote cycles of political compromise and programmatic accommodation within the complex intergovernmental system. Further, researchers used comparative cases that involved multiple schools, districts, or states. Often, these studies specified the broader institutional context within which federal programs operated.

A third perspective has emerged to focus on accountability and innovation since the 1990s. As the public presses for greater academic accountability, research offers two competing approaches to redesign public education. These views aim at reshaping the ways schools are governed and resources are distributed. First, the No Child Left Behind Act of 2001 grants state and local agencies substantial authority in taking corrective actions to turn around failing schools. In this regard, the federal legislation relies heavily on local capacity to play a supportive function. For example, Chicago, following mayoral control of the school system in 1995, has sharpened its focus on low-performing schools and their students. Low performing schools were put on probation, and in a few cases, reconstitution. Failing students are required to attend summer programs and social promotion has been terminated. The combination of sanctions and support seems to have improved the overall conditions to support student learning in the district. Second, low performing, inner-city schools have been the target of experimental vouchers, where parents are allowed to move their children from low performing public schools to better performing public and non-public schools. Following the state-funded voucher experiments in Cleveland and Milwaukee, the Congress has approved a federally-funded voucher program for low performing, low income students in Washington DC in 2004. Whether these programs will raise student performance remain a key research question.

As the federal government launches its ambitious educational plan in the No Child Left Behind Act, it remains to be seen whether local and state agencies are capable of meeting the goal of narrowing the achievement gaps among various subgroups of students. As Lee and Wong (2004) found, states that were active in accountability during the 1990s did not focus their fiscal efforts to narrow the resource gap between high-needs districts and their more affluent peers. In the current context of NCLB, Hochschild (2003) suggests that accountability-based politics have been facilitated by "issue expansion" in education among governors, mayors, and state high courts. As school reform attracts greater attention from policy generalists, the degree to which these political actors contribute to the implementation of the 2001 federal No Child Left Behind Act remains a key issue. In the long term, the critical challenge lies in the commitment of our intergovernmental system to fully address income and racial/ethnic disparity. Toward this end, a functional, federally funded policy system will continue to play an instrumental role in mediating the tension between decentralized governance and social redistribution.

REFERENCES

de Tocqueville, A. (2000). *Democracy in America*. (H. Mansfield & D. Winthrop, Trans., Ed.). Chicago: University of Chicago Press.

David Easton (1965) *A system analysis of political life*. Chicago: University of Chicago Press.

Luis Fraga, Kenneth Meier, and Robert England (1986) "Hispanic Americans and educational policy: Limits to equal access," *Journal of Politics* 48: 850–876.

Amy Gutmann (1987) Democratic Education. Princeton: Princeton University Press.

Hamilton, A., Madison, J., and Jay, J. (1961). *The Federalist Papers*. New York: Mentor.

Barbara Jackson and James Cibulka (1992) "Leadership turnover and business mobilization: the changing political ecology of urban school systems," pp. 71–86 in James Cibulka, Rodney Reed, and Kenneth Wong, eds., *The politics of urban education in the United States*. London: Falmer Press.

Jennifer Hochschild, "Rethinking Accountability Politics," Chapter 5 in Paul E. Peterson and Martin R. West, eds., *No Child Left Behind? The Politics and Practice of School Accountability*. Washington DC: The Brookings Institution Press, 2003.

Jennifer Hochschild and Nathan Scovronick (2003) The American Dream and the Public Schools. Oxford: Oxford University Press.

Jerome Murphy, "Title I of ESEA: The politics of implementing federal education reform," *Harvard Educational Review*, 41 (February, 1971): 36–63.

JaekYung Lee and Kenneth K. Wong (2004) "The impact of accountability on racial and socioeconomic equity: Considering both school resources and achievement outcomes," *American Educational Research Journal*, 41 (4): 797–832.

Kenneth Meier, Joseph Stewart, and Robert England (1989) *Race, Class and Education*. Madison: University of Wisconsin Press.

Gary Orfield (1969) *The reconstruction of southern education: The schools and the 1964 Civil Rights Act*. New York: Wiley.

Paul E. Peterson (1974) *School politics Chicago Style*. Chicago: University of Chicago Press.

Paul E. Peterson, Barry G. Rabe, and Kenneth K. Wong, "The evolution of the compensatory education program," pp.33–60 (Chapter 2) in Denis P. Doyle and Bruce S. Cooper, eds., *Federal Aid to the Disadvantaged: What future for Chapter 1?* Philadelphia: The Falmer Press, 1988.

James Sundquist (1968) *Politics and policy.* Washington DC: Brookings Institution.

Kenneth K. Wong (1999) *Funding public schools: Politics and policy.* Lawrence: University Press of Kansas.

Chapter Seven

History and Education: Mining the Gap: Historically Black Colleges as Centers of Excellence for Engaging Disparities in Race and Wealth

Roland Mitchell and Reavis Mitchell, Jr.

INTRODUCTION—THE WEALTH GAP
BETWEEN BLACK AND WHITE UNIVERSITIES

The thoughts that went into developing this chapter led us to reflect on discussions that take place in many middle-class African American households regarding race and wealth. In these discussions the question is asked, "Where would we be or what would we have if we were white?" Surely there is no direct correlation between racial identity and the accumulation of wealth, but as pointed out by Collins and Margo in chapter II of this text, as well as by numerous other economists and thinkers (Darity, 1998; Mills, 1997; Marable, 2002, 2000; Shabazz, 2004), the political economy of race in America is such that people of color historically have experienced systemic exclusion from the structures in society chiefly responsible for producing wealth. These structures include but are not limited to high-paying jobs, real estate, investments, savings, inheritances, and numerous other sources of economic, cultural, and political capital (West, 1990, 1999; Dyson, 2002; Gilroy, 2002; Marable, 2002, etc.). For the purposes of this chapter, we argue that participation in higher education is one of the key structures for the accumulation of wealth in American society and that unequal provision for the education of blacks in America undergirds disparities in the accumulation of wealth by African Americans.

Comparisons between several aspects of historically black colleges and universities (HBCUs) and predominantly white institutions (PWIs) provide an interesting perspective from which to frame our discussion of the correlation between racial identity, educational opportunity, and economic standing in the United States. For instance, a comparison of faculty salaries at HBCUs and PWIs during the 2003 academic year reveals that the average salary for the professorial level at HBCUs was $53,000 and at PWIs the average was $65,000. For instructors, the average salary was $41,000 at HBCUs compared to $50,000 at all others (Maxwell, 2003). In this case the difference in being employed by a PWI as opposed to a HBCU represents roughly $12,000 at the professorial level and about $9,000 at the instructor level.

Another example of these disparities exists in the salaries of the presidents/chancellors of HBCUs when compared to their peers at PWIs. The October 14, 1999 edition of *Black Issues in Higher Education* illustrated this disparity by comparing the salaries of two presidents in the Mississippi higher education system. The presidents involved were HBCU President Dr. Clinton Bristow of Alcorn State, whose annual salary was reported as $134,000, and Mississippi State University President Dr. Mack Portera, whose annual salary was $300,000. Although both salaries pale in comparison to the most highly paid university president in America at the time—Shirley Ann Jackson of Rensselaer Polytechnic Institute, whose reported salary was $891,400—the $166,000 difference in salaries between Bristow and Portera dramatically illustrates how race has material consequences in wealth accumulation.

The last and arguably greatest disparity between race and wealth in higher education institutions is evident when comparing the endowments of HBCUs and PWIs. According to *Inside Higher Ed* (2005) the combined endowments of the three wealthiest universities in the United States equals roughly $53 billion dollars: Harvard ($25.9 billion), Yale ($15 billion) and Stanford ($12 billion). A combination of the three best endowed HBCUs equals roughly $854 million: Howard ($397 million), Spellman ($258 Million), and Hampton ($199 million). Consequently, the combined $854 million dollar endowment of the three best endowed historically black universities is still over $24 billion less than Harvard's endowment alone. The best endowed HBCU, Howard University, only ranks 136th on the list of best endowed universities in the nation as a whole and if you added up the endowments of the 10 best endowed HBCUs, they would not equal the 37th ranked Williams College's 1.3 billion dollar endowment (Inside Higher Ed, 2005).

Although there are numerous factors such as institutional type, purpose, and mission that influence disparities in wealth between each of these institutions, the obvious fact plainly stated is that HBCUs have fewer resources than PWIs, and this inadequacy highlights the wealth disparity between blacks and whites in the financing of higher education institutions. The *brain drain* that HBCUs have experienced as a result of the plethora of talented African American students, administrators, faculty, and student-athletes that PWIs have gained since the desegregation of higher education, historically has been both proof of and a catalyst for the continuance of a widening in the extent of these disparities in resources and wealth. Before passage of the 1964 Civil Rights Act, which made access to PWIs more readily attainable for African Americans, 85 percent of all blacks who attended college attended HBCUs (Maxwell, 2003). The reversal of this tradition was starkly evident by 2003, when the 18 percent of all African American students attending HBCUs represented the HBCUs' smallest share of the black college student market to date. That reality brings us back to our original question, "Where would blacks be or what would they have if they were white?" Based upon current trends, the answer for the majority of African Americans who participate in higher education appears to be that they would be in much wealthier institutions.

WHAT IS THE CONNECTION BETWEEN HIGHER EDUCATION AND WEALTH?

A central part of our argument highlights the relationship between higher education and the "American Dream"—specifically, the nation's sentimental attachment to a simulacrum of the Protestant work ethic, in which individuals who say their prayers (to a Judeo-Christian god), go to school, work hard, and save their earnings regardless of their race, class, or family name can accumulate wealth in America. One of higher education's greatest achievements was to inextricably align itself with these ideals. In fact, higher education has so successfully established this perception that now there appears to be a "natural" correlation between participation in higher education and full participation in America.

We say this as a means to emphasize that the inception of the American system of higher education focused on producing ethical leaders through a primarily classical curriculum. This approach to schooling was intended to prepare clergymen and to some extent politicians and an aristocratic business/planter class who would in turn civilize a frontier nation (Brubacher and Rudy, 1976). Training for many of the applied disciplines such as medicine, law, and engineering, that are closely associated with higher education and high-paying jobs today, was provided through apprenticeships considered outside the scope of higher education (Thelin, 2005). As America's economy progressed from a rural and agriculturally based system to one with a more industrialized base, higher education evolved from singularly transmitting moral aims and cultural norms in the Colonial period (Vine, 1976) to the chief training and credentialing gateway into a capitalist work force. Therefore, an education became intimately intertwined with reinforcing the ideas and values that support the current economic and political social order (Watkins, 2001).

The evolution of colleges after the Civil War, the establishment of the agricultural and mechanical colleges in the late 19th century, and ultimately the rise and significant contributions of research institutions prior to World War II reflect the historical importance of higher education for the nation. These changes in the purpose of higher education also reflect the ways universities have evolved to fill the needs of America from its inception as colonial territories to its ascension to world leadership status. Today the relationship between higher education and increased earning potential in American society is quite evident. For instance, the U. S. Census Bureau's *Current Population Survey* averaged the income levels for adults ages 25 to 64 who worked during the years 1997–2000. It reported that the average income ranged from $18,900 for high school dropouts to $25,900 for high school graduates; $45,400 for college graduates; and $99,300 for workers with professional degrees (Day and Newberger, 2002). According to these numbers, it appears that participating in higher education is on the average worth between $19,500 and $73,400 in American earnings each year.

Further, the 2000 U. S. Census reported that 24.4 percent of Americans possess a bachelor's degree, with a steady increase projected to have reached 27.2 percent by 2004. These increases demonstrate that more Americans are participating in higher education than ever before. However, the thesis of this chapter suggests that if disparities exist in America where race and wealth are concerned and education is an essential part of increasing one's income, then racial disparities in access and opportunity exist in higher education as well. The fact that the attainment of a bachelor's degree for the African American lags behind the European American by roughly 10 to 14 percent supports our thesis (Day & Newberger, 2002). And historically, once African Americans enter higher education they experience an overabundance of challenges that have often hindered their progress—particularly at predominantly white institutions which, as we previously stated, enroll the majority of African American students. In the following section we will discuss some of the roots of the problems experienced by black students at PWIs and examine the relationship between these challenges and disparities concerning race and wealth.

CHALLENGES TO AFRICAN AMERICAN STUDENTS AT PREDOMINANTLY WHITE INSTITUTIONS

How serious is the challenge of providing adequate service to African American students in PWIs? In recent decades there has been a significant increase in the inclusion of under-represented groups in higher education. The National Center for Educational Statistics cited (1999) that the enrollment of minority students in the United States had steadily increased over the previous 20 years. Minority students, excluding non-resident aliens, comprised 17 percent of all undergraduate students in 1976 and had expanded to 26 percent by the fall of 1995. This demographic trend toward more diverse student populations in American colleges and in the general population has continued with projections that by 2010 ethnic minorities will become the majority population in the United States (Sue, 1991).

Although increased enrollment, increased retention, and even some broadening of the disciplines in which racial minority students have found success does reflect some progress, there is still great need for improvement (Gilbert, 2001; Wheeler, Ayers, Fracasso, Galupo, Rabin, 1999). Miller made the case in 1995 that ". . . in spite of substantial increases in minority enrollment, there is little reason to believe that the attainment gaps . . . in higher education as a whole will be reduced significantly in the next several years" (Miller, 1995, p. 44). In other words, just getting traditionally under-served students on campus will not be enough to produce real higher education equity. This is especially true for African American students for whom graduation rates are still relatively low. In a study conducted by the *Journal of Blacks in Higher Education* (Cross, 1997) from 1986 to 1989, only 37 percent of all black students that enrolled as freshmen graduated within six years. These averages were nearly 22 percent lower than that of white students over this same period.

These numbers represent to many a persistent set of problems that have historically plagued American higher education. Despite some gains in the present, nearly forty years of institutional and governmental approaches to remedy these problems have resulted in only marginal success. Several scholars, social theorists, and educators have advanced theories about the perverseness of these problems (Banks, 1998a, 1988b, 2001; Nettles, 1995; Pascarella and Terenzini, 1991, etc.). The ideology that undergirds many of these theories is founded in liberal thought that has historically resulted in incremental yet significant changes to the system. From this perspective, although the impact of a history of injustice is profoundly detrimental to African American students, the overall foundation upon which the system is built is a just one (Tozer, Violas, and Senese, 2002). Consequently, factors like discrimination based upon race, gender, sexual orientation, or ability, according to these theories, retard the system and cause it to function in a manner outside the parameter for which it was originally designed. And ultimately, if one works from within the system to effect change, the overall sense of fairness and the influence of its foundation in democratic values will afford opportunities for a more just adaptation of the system to prevail.

In contrast, others have advanced a different set of theories to describe the relationship between the shortcomings of the American higher education system and disparities associated with wealth and race. Of these theories, the line of argumentation we will explore is primarily forwarded in the work of educational historians James Anderson and William Watkins. Their writings provide both a useful backdrop for this study and an important counterpoint to the previously mentioned liberal conceptions for coming to terms with and addressing the effects of racism on American higher education.

WHY BLACK COLLEGES AND UNIVERSITIES?

In Anderson's book *The education of blacks in the South, 1860–1935* (1988), a different view of the purpose and development of the American educational system is presented. Anderson suggested that what has historically been thought of as failures or shortcomings in the American educational system are actually the system functioning the way it was intended to function. Anderson believed that the founders of the American educational system never intended that African Americans receive the same quality of education (nor access to wealth and economic stability through education) as European Americans. In effect, Anderson argued that the system was intended to produce an economic underclass of semi-skilled laborers to do the grunt work needed to support the expanding base of industrial capitalism in America's late 19th and early 20th centuries. Further, Anderson believed that the grunt labor force would be established according to a white supremacist racially inspired hierarchy. In the introduction to *The education of blacks in the South*, Anderson wrote:

> The history of American education abounds with themes that represent the inextricable ties between citizenship in a democratic society and popular education. It is crucial for an understanding of the American educational history; however, to recognize that within American democracy there have been classes of oppressed people and that there has been an essential relationship between popular education and the politics of oppression. Both schooling for democratic citizenship and schooling for second-class citizenship have been basic traditions in American education. These opposing traditions were not, as some would explain, the difference between the mainstream of American education and some aberrations of isolated alternatives. Rather, both were fundamental American conceptions of society and progress, occupied the same time and space, and were fostered by the same governments. (p.1)

Through these and other remarks, Anderson challenged the meritocratic ideology inherent to traditional interpretations of the relationship between education and the "American Dream." He conceded that schooling is important for developing a democratic citizenry in a Jeffersonian sense, but regardless of the rhetoric of the founding fathers, Anderson argued that there was never any intent for African Americans to fully participate in their democracy. The role African Americans were to occupy was that of the laborer as opposed to that of the citizen. Consequently, there was a need for a different type of institution, curriculum, and (most importantly to Anderson) ideology supporting the education of newly freed African Americans.

Watkins built on Anderson's arguments regarding America's two track educational system, specifically focusing on higher education and several of the individuals and foundations responsible for crafting the ideologies that have profoundly influenced the development of colleges for African Americans. In *The white architects of black education ideology and power in America, 1865–1954* (2001), Watkins provided detailed information about white philanthropists, politicians, educators, and business leaders who were instrumental in establishing and financing HBCUs. His work is particularly persuasive in that it provides historical and sociological insights into the ways these individuals set the ideological tone for black higher education. This persuasiveness also lies in his discussion of the connection between the mentalities of this philanthropic class and those of the nation as a whole, which Watkins argued led to the overwhelming success and eventual adoption of their vision by the nation. Watkins suggested that this was done through powerful ideological messages about the relevance and utility of higher education for African Americans within American society. Watkins successfully documented the significant and lasting imprint of this powerful class of philanthropists on African American higher education.

In his discussions of individuals such as General Samuel C. Armstrong, General Clinton B. Fisk, and Thomas J. Jones, Watkins meticulously pieced together a description of how the system of higher education for blacks was developed by the white industrial class to best meet their needs for inexpensive labor. The success of these industrial schools in achieving these objectives, as well as their popularity with both black and white Americans, can be attributed to several interlocking factors. Many argued that, after enduring nearly four hundred years of slavery, newly emancipated African Americans longed for full participation in American society. They, like other groups in America, were expected to believe that the training, skills, and insights they would receive from education would provide them greater access into mainstream American society. Proof of this is evident in the demand for higher education, which probably has been the most enthusiastically supported political reform among African Americans, from slavery to the present (Marable, 2000, p. 215). A compounding factor was that not only the South but the entire nation had to find a way to replace and adequately train an extremely productive labor force. Hence, the nation searched for the means to continue to benefit from the labor of African Americans, while peacefully and inexpensively transitioning them into being the driving engine of an industrial capitalist system. All of this had to be done in a relatively short time frame, while maintaining a race-based caste system.

Watkins spoke of these concerns as the "Negro problem," that the country was keenly invested to address, because resolving the "Negro problem" was essential for the nation's future. In addressing this situation, Watkins wrote, "Failure to properly solve the problem and situate the newly freed slave could mean the undoing of the delicate new relationship between the agricultural south and the emergent industrial north. Solving the problem created the possibility for social stability and economic prosperity" (p. 53). Further, there was the need to get those (such as poor whites in the South) to buy into the new labor scheme despite a constant fear of what nearly four million newly freed, ill-prepared, and low-moraled individuals (in the popular opinion of the time) would do without the opportunity for uplift supposedly inherent in education. Therefore, just as education was important for transmitting certain cultural, political, and moral values during America's Colonial period, education was now marshaled for the same purpose during Reconstruction. The crucial difference was that during Reconstruction education's primary function actually took account of African Americans. This recognition of African Americans in the educational system was founded with the specific intent of establishing what the "American Dream" should be for African Americans — a training ground of sorts in which blacks buy into second-class citizenship status, disguised as superior to the treatment they received as slaves.

In contrast to incrementalist views that argue for small and deliberate adjustments to the educational system, the perspective forwarded by Watkins, Anderson, and others with similar beliefs argued for a radical transformationist approach to understanding the establishment and evolution of the American higher education system (Wade, Thompson, and Watkins 1994; Apple, 1979; Bowles and Gintis, 1976; Liston, 1988). From this perspective, the present educational system is not only functioning the way that it was intended, but no manner of adjustment will afford equity to students of color traditionally on the margins of this system of education — and, in reality, the current educational system functions to keep certain groups of students on the margins. Consequently, the whole system would need to be radically transformed to address its inherent injustice. Critics of this system contend that in a capitalist society one of the major roles of schooling is to reproduce the dominant economic, social, and political order. Based upon the location of African Americans in American society after slavery (and, some would argue, today), reproduction of the dominant order has historically functioned to produce the disparities in educational opportunity and wealth, which this chapter concerns.

AFRICAN AMERICANS DISCUSS BLACK EDUCATION

The premises put forth in Anderson's and Watkins' work challenge representations of both the "American Dream" and liberally inspired revisionist interpretations of the place of African Americans within it. Hence, regardless of
how much the system is tweaked, racist ideologies are such a central part of
its foundation that many would question the viability of depending upon a liberal incrementalist agenda for adequately addressing the problem. It also can
be argued that, as a result of such a damning critique, the very act of obtaining education from either predominantly white or black colleges constitutes
an acceptance of a racist system of schooling for purposes that were not established to benefit African Americans. From this perspective, what are the
historic benefits, legacy, and ultimate utility of HBCUs? Why would black
students choose to participate in traditionally black education?

Although singularly not discussed by the white philanthropic class, African
American educators have debated these issues for over a century. There are two
primary schools of African American thought that we found most pertinent for
engaging the question of black participation in black higher education. First, despite the lasting influences of the "White Architects", the design and evolution
of black higher education did not occur in a vacuum absent black educators and
social critics. Arguably, the most notable of these debates occurred between
W.E.B. Dubois and Booker T. Washington in the last part of the 19th century and
concerned appropriate curricula and aims for establishing higher education for
African Americans. The second line of inquiry we will examine concerns the impact of greater African American control of HBCUs in the mid- to late- 20th century as the schools progressed from their infancy to the modern day. In the next
section we will briefly compare the debates between Washington and Dubois
and the evolution of HBCUs as a result of greater African America leadership.
Our intent is to consider the issues raised by Anderson's and Watkins' critiques
concerning whether black participation in higher education has provided a potential remedy or exacerbated disparities in race and wealth in America.

WHY SHOULD AFRICAN AMERICANS
PARTICIPATE IN HIGHER EDUCATION?

Despite the fact that black colleges are largely the direct product of racial segregation, they have been extremely successful in educating black entrepreneurs, scientists, and intellectuals. This has been accomplished in spite of a
history of societal, governmental, and institutional barriers to black achievement. However, a more direct response to the question of why blacks would

choose to participate and ultimately support black colleges and universities is the comparison of Booker T. Washington and his powerful "Tuskegee Machine's" support of industrial education for blacks to W.E.B. Dubois' call for a classical system of education for blacks. The debates provide a good starting point for our inquiry and offer a glimpse into the evolution of black higher education and its relationship to disparities in wealth and race.

Washington's primary platform was built on his willingness to accept the financial support of white philanthropists who advocated an accommodationist agenda (Bontemps, 1972). This philanthropic support hinged on the millions of dollars Washington was receiving in exchange for his promotion of what, at the time, was a liberal educational and radical social agenda. Anderson (1988) described the prevailing philanthropic beliefs of this time:

> [M]issionary philanthropists were not proposing social changes that were revolutionary by national standards, but they were radical within the Southern social order. Equality was carefully defined as political and legal equality. They consented to inequality in the economic structure, generally shied away from questions of racial integration, and were probably convinced that blacks' cultural and religious values were inferior to those of middle-class whites. Their liberalism on civil and political questions was matched by their conservatism on religious and economic matters . . . Slavery, not race kept blacks from acquiring the important moral and social values of thrift, industry, frugality and sobriety all necessary to live a sustained Christian life . . . Therefore missionaries argued that it was vital for education to introduce ex-slaves to the values and rules of modern society. Without education, they concluded, blacks would rapidly degenerate and become a national menace to American society (p. 241).

Washington's most clearly articulated justification for African American acceptance of this system was presented in what arguably became the most influential public discussion of race by an African American during the Reconstruction era. His speech, referred to as the "Atlanta Compromise," provided conciliation to the South and advocated that African Americans remain silent on issues of political and civil rights. Washington envisioned the relationship between blacks and whites as a delicate balance: "In all things purely social we can be as separate as the five fingers, and yet one as the hand in all things essential to mutual progress." The culmination of these ideals in the realm of higher education was Washington's belief in the need for a strong program of industrial education for blacks that established a gospel of work and money intended to help former slaves "pull themselves up by their bootstraps" out of poverty while providing the nation with a strong labor force. Washington's agenda to black America was referred to as a compromise because through this compromise blacks would submit to the social, political, economic, and educational needs of a racially based market system in exchange for the opportunity to add their overall value to that system. The general intent of Washington's compromise was to allow blacks to eventually earn fuller inclusion through their provision of manual labor and temporary acceptance of second-class citizen status.

In contrast, Dubois (1928) criticized Washington's compromise on the grounds that it "deprived [African Americans] of political rights, made a servile caste, and allowed only the most meager chance for developing exceptional men" (p. 51). Dubois would have several changes in thought concerning these issues throughout his lengthy career as an academic and social critic. In his early work, he wrote about and advocated a broader spectrum of ideas for inclusion of African Americans in mainstream American culture. However, despite Dubois' admiration for Washington and his belief in the nobleness of Washington's cause, Dubois did not agree that submission to an unjust racially based economic order was appropriate. Instead Dubois argued that blacks had an extraordinarily rich and distinct culture that should be marshaled to enrich all aspects of American culture. He described this as "not Africanizing America, for America has too much to teach the world and Africa . . . [Nor would he] bleach his Negro soul in a flood of white Americanism, for he knows that Negro blood has a message for the world. He simply wishes to make it possible for a man to be both a Negro and an American" (p.4). In effect, Dubois called for this inclusion of Negro culture into the dominant white culture through a mutual appreciation of both. Civil and political rights, as well as educational opportunity, were essential to Dubois' vision. Where education was concerned, Dubois believed former slaves were in dire need of the best education—whether it be industrial, classical, or liberal—that the nation could provide in order to assist them in adjusting to their new status as free people.

The agreement between Washington and Dubois on the importance of the goal of black education, but disagreement on the appropriate methods for achieving that goal, led Dubois to develop a triple paradox of critique for Washington's position. In it Dubois contended that Washington's program contained at least three inherent lapses:

> 1. [I]t is utterly impossible, under modern competitive methods, for [working men/women] and property owners to defend their rights and exist without the right of suffrage. 2. [An insistence] on thrift and self-respect, but at the same time . . . a silent submission to civic inferiority . . . 3. Advocacy for common-school and industrial training while depreciating institutions for higher learning; but neither the Negro common-schools, nor Tuskegee itself, could remain open a day were it not for teachers trained in Negro colleges, or trained by their graduates (Dubois 1928, p. 52).

Through these comments Dubois is not debating the importance and value of industrial education for blacks. Dubois is actually concerned with the over emphasis he sees in Washington's argument (and in that of many white philanthropists) for industrial education to the detriment of higher education. Dubois considered this emphasis on an industrial educational system in conjunction with an admonition for African American political and civic docility as intertwined with the establishment of a different, but still economically and politically disenfranchised, status for American blacks.

In essence, the political economy of race and wealth in America played a significant role in shaping the positions that both Washington and Dubois supported. The extraordinary success and political clout enjoyed by Washington during his day demonstrated the influence of his ideas, not only on education but on American society in general. Until his death, Washington's philosophy on the education of blacks was more influential than Dubois'. In particular, the Hampton University model developed by Washington's mentor Armstrong and fully realized in Washington's Tuskegee Institute were held up as the archetype for African American education at its best. Washington's model of African American education gained support from the Peabody, Carnegie, Phelps-Stokes, and Rockefeller foundations further demonstrating white support of industrial education for blacks, as opposed to the more progressive model advocated by Dubois.

Despite the overwhelming influence and popularity of Washington's ideas about schooling, there were other successful examples of higher education for blacks that were not built on the industrial education model. The common schools that would eventually form the base for black higher education practiced a different approach to the relationship between education, leadership, and economic stability. This educational concept was a direct challenge to Washington's compromise and the prevailing southern planter preference for black education geared toward reproducing a racially segregated labor force. Describing the initiators of this movement, Anderson (1998) wrote:

> The black teachers, school officials, and secular and religious leaders who formed the vanguard of the post-war common school movement insisted that the ex-slaves must educate themselves, gather experience, and acquire a responsible awareness of the duties incumbent upon them . . . as citizens in the new social order. Their thinking on these questions indicated virtually no illusion about the power of schooling to ameliorate fundamental economic inequalities. Rather it reflected their belief that education could help raise the freed people to an appreciation of their historic responsibility to develop a better society and that any significant reorganization of the southern political economy was indissolubly linked to their education in the principles, duties, and obligations appropriate to a democratic social order (p. 28).

Through these comments, Anderson describes a different role for the education of African Americans articulated by and for the black community than that provided by the white philanthropist, industrialist, and planter class. In this African American conception of black higher education, there is a separation between educational attainment and economic advancement, with an appeal to education as a path for participation in a democratic society as opposed to participation in a capitalist society. This is a significant distinction, since there appears to be a sense of clarity about the importance of black self-determination for education to survive in a racist society, as opposed to occupying a more significant yet still subordinate role in that society. Further, in this black formulation of the role of education, there is a rejection of the commodification of education and an understanding of the pervasiveness of racially based inequality in this conception of the purpose of education. These educators understood, as University of North Carolina economist William Darity (1998) concludes, that the best predictor of future wealth is past wealth; to suggest that participation in higher education for the former slaves and their immediate descendents would automatically change that reality has to date been unsubstantiated. Consequently, these beliefs led to the establishment and maintenance of schools with different purposes, programs of study, and institutional types for African Americans than the previously mentioned industrial models.

Examples of these different institutional models are found in the early histories of historically black colleges such as Fisk, Talladega, Howard, and Atlanta University. Although these black universities were founded and supported by a similar philanthropic base to those that supported Hampton and Tuskegee, their curricula and missions were much more liberal and progressive. The courses of study at these institutions varied greatly from the singular focus on industrial education for African Americans that was prevalent at the time. Instead, these universities adopted the New England classical liberal curriculum that was used by many northern white schools. The courses taught through this curriculum were typically Latin, Greek, mathematics, science, philosophy, and in some cases a modern language (Anderson, 1988, p.28). Absent a belief that education would naturally correlate to economic equality, these institutions employed the classical approach to higher education in order to introduce African American students to the best intellectual traditions of the day. Despite some concern that the classical approach was simply mimicking the practices of white universities, the fact that the curriculum was taught in many cases by and for a people who had personally experienced slavery, meant that the material and the way that it was taught and received naturally took on a flavor unique to African American experiences of the era.

As black higher education progressed and its relationship to the white power structure changed, the courses of study of the schools that emphasized industrial education started to reflect a more academic curriculum. We state this to highlight the fact that in many ways African American supporters of the industrial model of education were not unaware of the shortcomings associated with assuming a position in favor of industrial education alone. They, like the supporters of a more progressive vision of African American education, did not possess naïve understandings about the benefits and challenges associated with their approach. They instead made pragmatic decisions that they felt were the best for establishing a foundation for a better future for black people in America. Proof of this can be found in the fact that, despite Tuskegee's reputation as primarily an industrial school under Washington's leadership, it produced more teachers than any profession (Anderson, 1988). Further, the fact that Washington served on the board of trust for Fisk University, provided financial assistance to the school, and sent his children to Fisk, suggests that, regardless of his public rhetoric, Washington apparently saw the utility of both systems of education.

WHERE DOES BLACK EDUCATION STAND NOW?

The public debate between key segments of the black and white communities over the development of black higher education led to the establishment of extraordinarily successful institutions for educating African Americans. Regardless of which educational mantra guided each university's founding immediately following the Civil War, during the Jim Crow era, and in the present, their contributions to American society as a whole have been substantial. In *Problems in race, political economy, and society how capitalism underdeveloped black America* (2001), Manning Marable provided a brief discussion of the contributions of Fisk University as an illustration of the types of individuals HBCUs produced;

> Fisk was home for a major number of black intellectuals during the era of segregation: Dubois, historian John Hope Franklin; sociologist E. Franklin Frazier; artist/novelist Nikki Giovanni, John Oliver Killens, and Frank Yerby. A number of other Fisk alumni joined the ranks of the Black elite in the 20th century as decisive leaders in public policy, representing a variety of political tendencies: U.S. Representative William L. Dawson; Marion Barry, mayor of Washington. . . . Other Fisk graduates moved into the private sector to establish an economic program for Black development along capitalist lines, such as Maceo Walker, President of Universal Life Insurance Company. And within the professions, one

out of every six Black physicians, lawyers and dentists in the United States today are Fisk graduates. A similar profile could be obtained from Atlanta University, Morehouse College, Tuskegee Institute, Howard University, and other
black institutions of higher learning (p. 217).

The accomplishments of HBCU alumni, as documented by Marable in the
prior passage are many. Despite the original intent to use education in order to
trap African Americans forever on the margins, HBCUs have instead played a
major role in bettering black economic standing. Nor have their contributions
been singularly relegated to advancing black participation in American market
culture. Black universities have also had a significant impact on black participation in political affairs often in opposition to the dominant political order.

Examples of the impact of black universities on black social and political
progress are found in black college student activism during the Civil Rights
and Black Power movements. Students from HBCUs provided unsurpassed
leadership, grounding, and support for challenging racially based social injustices. Their support of the Freedom Rides, lunch counter boycotts, and
other forms of violent and non-violent protest against racism vividly demonstrate how far many of these schools have wandered from the original intent
of their white benefactors. Yet we cannot overlook the conservatism of many
black colleges and their administrators in the past and present. This conservative influence has forced many black colleges to operate under rigid constraints of race/class tyranny monitored by administrators selected by white
trustees and state governments. Despite these conditions, Marable went on to
describe HBCUs as:

> creating the intellectual and social space necessary for the development of mil-
> itant political reformers, dedicated public school teachers, physicians, and other
> skilled professionals within the black community. Without which the nightmare
> of Jim Crow might still exist, and the material conditions of the Black ghetto and
> working class would unquestionably be worse (Marable, p. 217).

Therefore, the mission of black schools has drastically evolved from its initial
aims of preparing African Americans to be politically disenfranchised workers
in an industrialized nation. Now higher education for blacks reflects enhancements in academics, political consciousness, and economic opportunity.

THE KNOWING THAT COMES FROM DOING

At this point, after advancing our argument by exploring the evolution of
thought concerning the historic design and vocation of HBCUs, we now fo-

cus on the study of contemporary higher education. Our purpose in advancing chronologically is to consider the quality and utility of HBCUs in the present, by documenting the practical knowledge that has resulted from their unique histories, and to explore the creative potential for addressing the disparities in wealth and race that we believe HBCUs possess.

Despite the desegregation of white universities, both private and public black institutions continue to serve a large percentage of blacks seeking college or professional training. Twenty-five percent of all blacks in higher education attended 35 state-supported black colleges. Sixty-two percent of all Black M.D.'s and 73 percent of all black Ph.D.'s are products of black colleges (Marable 2000, p. 218). These numbers represent the current success of these institutions in providing educational opportunity to African American students. However, despite this success, for those blacks and whites who are not students of African American higher education these numbers might be surprising. In fact, many HBCUs are constantly faced with defending their existence in post-Jim Crow era America, instead of publicizing and benefiting from these positive institutional characteristics.

Continuing our focus on race and wealth disparities and their relationships to higher education, if HBCUs represent centers of expertise for successful educational attainment for African Americans and consequently suggest better opportunities for financial stability, then why is the need for historically black colleges still questioned? The short answer lies somewhere between a lack of information about the success of black universities and the constant budget constraints that federal, state, and local branches of government experience when attempting to finance higher education. Therefore, one of the goals of this chapter is to help spark a wider range of discussion about the success and utility of HBCUs. However, regardless of financial constraints, history reminds us that racism likely undergirds these silences about black universities' successes. Questions regarding HBCUs are often posed using the premise that America's educational system has overcome the effects of racism and HBCUs are no longer needed. Obviously, as the previously referenced statistics concerning the graduation and retention rates and quality of experiences by African Americans at PWIs suggest, American higher education has not yet achieved any level of racial equality.

To this point we have primarily focused on the success of and the challenges to African American higher education and its relationship to disparities in wealth in broad systemic terms. However, we also believe that there is value in examining these interlocking systems as they occur in smaller social networks, such as in a specific college, in a specific classroom, and even on individual levels between professors, administrators, and students. Through this more micro-social perspective we are better positioned to see the significance of exploring the practical knowledge that comes from the actual teaching, learning, and administration of black colleges. Our goal for the concluding sections of this chapter is to document the knowledge that comes from the practice of providing effective service to students at HBCUs through the Carnegie Foundation's scholarship of teaching model.

THE SCHOLARSHIP OF TEACHING

This portion of the chapter presents discussions drawn from a larger research project involving over forty professors. The study looks across various disciplines and institutional types to document and examine the knowledge that informs teacher practice. This particular segment of that study focuses on the experiences and understandings that underlie the practice of educators at historically black colleges. Through their reflections, this set of discussions seeks to be part of an emerging conversation about college-level teaching and learning known as *the scholarship of teaching*. Forwarded most visibly by the Carnegie Institute for the Advancement of Teaching and Learning, the scholarship of teaching seeks to document, critically review, and publish professors' practical knowledge about teaching in their disciplines (Hutchings and Shulman, 2000). Mary Huber and Sherwyn Morreale (2002) define the scholarship of teaching as an invitation to faculty to treat teaching as an inquiry into learning, to share research and to critique and build on one another's work. This critical analysis of an educator's practice seeks to envision the way that pedagogy is improved when teachers look closely at their own teaching practices and share their findings with their colleagues (p. 12).

Traditionally, scholarship of teaching research has focused on the influence of disciplinarity on teacher practice (Boyer 1990, Huber and Hutchinson 2004, Huber and Morreal 2002, Shulman 1987, 2004, Shulman and Mesa-Bains 1993). In this study, we look at the influence of cultural and racial identity on both teachers' practice and teaching research. Consequently, our engagement of the scholarship of teaching literature seeks to push the conversation toward an analysis of how interactions between teachers and students are mediated by the educator's reflections on personal and student racial and cultural identity (Mitchell and Rosiek in press), in the context of institutions that are situated to challenge racially based social inequality.

Our data in this study and in previous work suggest that there is no simple correlation between students and faculty sharing the same racial identity and forming an automatic connection. Nor have we found the converse, i.e. no relationship between students and professors being members of the same racial groups and consequently having shared points of connection. Instead, what we found was a much more complex and nuanced functioning of racial and cultural identity that informed the success educators associated with HBCUs in educating African American students. Hence, our overarching aim for examining the practice of educators at HBCUs through the scholarship of teaching model is to get at the underlying epistemologies that guide these teachers' practice.

Regardless of the value of understandings of cultural and racial difference on teacher practice, as the scholarship of teaching literature suggests, this knowledge is rarely if ever documented or discussed in broader academic contexts. Therefore, through this merger of scholarship of teaching research with inquiry on knowledge claims from educators at HBCUs, we are intent on publicizing some of America's best-kept secrets for shrinking gaps in wealth along racial lines from those who have had over a century of proven success in battling this pervasive set of societal problems—Educators at HBCUs.

A SCHOLARSHIP OF TEACHING GLEANED
FROM HISTORICALLY BLACK COLLEGES

The insights that were discussed as informing the practice of educators at HBCUs through our use of the scholarship of teaching research model can be roughly organized into two interrelated categories. The first set of responses took account of the context in which learning occurs at HBCUs, and the second set of responses examined the countervailing influences of class and economic standing in those contexts.

As our earlier section on the evolution of African Americans education showed, the education of blacks in the United States has always occurred in a racially, politically, and economically contested sphere. There is little doubt this contestation continues to influence the ways educators at HBCUs think about their practice and engage their students. In our interviews with forty African American professors, these influences were demonstrated in the ways the professors at HBCUs described their expectations for their students. They spoke of expectations that their students would not only graduate, but would also take measured steps toward continuing their academic and professional careers, with a particular emphasis on further training beyond the bachelor's degree.

These ideas of presumed achievement and advancement are particularly provocative when juxtaposed against our informants' conception of black students at PWIs as un-welcomed visitors who receive sub-par service. In these notions of our participants, black students were characterized as attempting to acquire education in environments that assume that black students should remain inconspicuously present, instead of expecting exemplary service, opportunities for full participation, and academic and professional mentoring. Our participants identified these attitudes as institutional impediments to academic success for black students at PWIs that are absent at HBCUs. Further, they believed that these perceptions drastically hinder the ability of black students at PWIs to focus on the business of learning. This way of framing comparisons between learning opportunities for black students at HBCUs and PWIs bolsters claims for the importance of HBCUs and demonstrated a praxis-oriented reflection by our participants on the way racial difference influences the learning outcomes for African American students.

Regardless of the validity of these depictions of black student experiences at PWIs, in these and similar comments, our participants demonstrated specific beliefs that greatly influenced their practice. First, they believed that their students would naturally succeed in both their classes and at navigating their institutions. And second, they believed that an undergraduate degree was the beginning of their students' tenure in higher education as opposed to its completion. There is significant research about the effect of expectations and perceptions by teachers (and society as a whole) on student performance and outcomes that lends credence to our participants' remarks.

The expectation of success for African American students discussed by our participants is in direct contradiction to what educational psychologists and theorists refer to as "stereotype threat" (e.g., Aronson et al., 1999; Aronson et. al.1998; Steele, 1997; Steele and Aronson, 1995) among some African American students in white settings. Aronson, Fried and Good (2001) describe this phenomenon as a social psychological predicament rooted in the prevailing American image of African Americans as intellectually inferior. Further, in *Reducing the effects of Stereotype threat on African American students by shaping theories of intelligence* (2001), Arson et. al. described this phenomenon in detail as being experienced in:

> [S]ituations where a stereotype about a group's intellectual ability is relevant— taking an intellectually challenging test, being called upon to speak in class, and so on—Black students bear an extra cognitive and emotional burden not borne by people for whom the stereotype does not apply. This burden takes the form of a performance-disruptive apprehension, anxiety about the possibility of confirming a deeply negative inferiority—in the eyes of others, in one's own eyes, or both at the same time (p.114).

The educators whom we spoke with at HBCUs neither perpetuated nor allowed these perceptions about their students to influence their practice. In fact, a central part of the communal understandings that HBCUs were established upon were in direct contradiction to pseudo-scientific essentialist critiques of black intelligence. Consequently, the professors whom we interviewed had access to a broad reservoir of institutional and socio-cultural discourses from which to debunk discussions, theories, and practices founded in black intellectual inferiority. They described their students as brilliant and intentionally engaged them in a manner appropriate for developing emerging intellectuals. Their explicitly stated expectation was of student academic success as opposed to one of implicit intellectual failures and deficiencies attributed to racial identity.

This approach to engagement led to their next expectation, that the bachelor's degree would be the beginning of a pathway to further education as, when for example, one of our participants proudly stated that nearly 75 percent of his majors go on to graduate and professional schools. Some explanations for this phenomenal success rate are presented in colloquial African American community discourses. In an anecdotal way, some segments within the black community would say that to compete with whites in education, in the market place, and in society in general, blacks need to be 200 percent better prepared. While this is clearly speculation, the pervasiveness of injustices like racism lend some credibility to this anecdote for groups that historically have been disenfranchised. In fact, we found that in some ways the underlying principles that govern this type of thinking did influence the mentoring that some of the professors we interviewed provided when they advised their students to aspire for advanced graduate and professional degrees. Hence, the completion of an undergraduate degree was lauded as not enough for success in a competitive job market that is still significantly influenced by racism, sexism, and other persistent social injustices.

Beyond this anecdotal explanation, other professors at HBCUs also prescribed the high percentage of their students that went on to pursue advanced degrees to very practical and historically grounded factors. As one of our participants remarked, "Historically speaking, until fairly recent years, not many Fortune 500 companies visited career days or recruited heavily at HBCUs." With this as a mediating factor, graduate and professional schools offered a venue to better improve the standing of HBCU graduates when entering the job market. In this scenario, we see the effect of racist employment practices that, no doubt, have historically influenced disparities in wealth between blacks and whites. However, we also see ingenious and resourceful responses to these impediments that are characteristic of the evolution of HBCUs and African American education in general. In fact, through this situation we were provided insight into the ontological experiences that informed the anecdote that blacks may have to be 200 percent better prepared to respond to these racial disparities in wealth.

THE LEGACY OF CLASS AT HBCUS

The second category that emerged from our discussions of the understandings that influence the practice of educators at HBCUs concerned the influence of class and economic status on institutional cultures at HBCUs. This set of discussions prompted deep reflection and insightful comments by several of our participants, with one in particular referencing the way Booker T. Washington's experiences and educational opportunities at The Hampton Institute left a lasting imprint on student perceptions of financing degrees from HBCUs. These remarks focused on the way that Washington arrived at Hampton penniless, but with an extreme desire to both study hard and work tirelessly, and yet he enrolled. And in response to his willingness to work the institution made it possible for him to receive an education that established the platform for his meteoric rise in educational, political, and social significance. The positive effect of idealizing Washington's "will work for education experience before federal work-study programs existed" is that the school and overall community, regardless of the financial hardships, considered education as such a vital asset that it was willing to do all it could to support industrious students like Washington. However, the problem with this approach to education is that for institutions which have historically (as well as in the present) operated in the red, these economically unsound business practices, albeit altruistic, are perceived as having contributed to a legacy of financial struggles.

Washington's experiences were not uncommon for students at HBCUs during his era. Among our participants, who did not directly reference this approach as influencing student views about financing their educations, there were ongoing discussions about its influence upon the institutional cultures and financial stability of their universities. An unforeseen consequence of this legacy of inclusion (some may consider to a fault) has been a different kind of diversity at HBCUs. So, in addition to their legacy of providing opportunities for participation in higher education to students whose race has historically impeded their participation in higher education, HBCUs also have a legacy of providing greater access to students who would have been excluded as a result of their class and economic status. Consequently, regardless of the actual data behind these perceptions, and the legacy that they helped to establish, our participants believed that the range of wealth between students on campus at HBCUs was smaller than that which exists between black students at PWIs and their white peers. In their opinion, this combination of institutional/communal dedication and to some extent similar class standing and aspiration among their students facilitates a greater sense of connection, affiliation, and comfort by students at both ends of the economic spectrum.

When discussing class, our participants also discussed the role of aspirations for economic advancement as significantly influencing their campus cultures. We found this to be particularly interesting, in that even individuals who lacked the actual material markers of middle/upper class group membership were in many cases perceived as being granted membership into this group, based upon their aspirations, subsequent work, and the possibility of future economic advancement. In many ways, our participants conceived of these notions as a re-fashioning of the "American Dream" uniquely formulated within and to support the missions of HBCUs. They also considered an integral part of shaping that vision was the participation and visibility of their influential alumni. In many cases, they were the physical representation that these aspirations can be realized, and once they are realized, individuals are called upon to maintain a relationship with the source that afforded possibilities for that success.

The importance of perceptions of staying connected with alumni by HBCUs was observable in professional, civic, and political arenas, from Southern University's commemoration of its alumnus and celebrated NBA head coach Avery Johnson to Morehouse University's well-profiled relationship with Dr. Martin Luther King, Jr. The celebration of these alumni is proof and product that HBCUs were successful at the turn of the 20th century and remain extremely successful today at providing the type of skills that allow students full participation in American professional life. These individuals are also important because they help establish norms and expectations for success that are not readily available in U. S. society for African American students.

WHAT HAVE WE LEARNED?

From our interviews with teachers/scholars in black colleges and universities we learned that the knowledge that influenced the practice of the educators we studied was intimately connected to the broader societal meanings and purposes ascribed to education. Our participants did, indeed, consider education to be a vital aspect of addressing disparities in wealth and race — in that education provides better employment opportunities and participation in mainstream society. But they advocated for a critical education, not just any education. Critical education takes into account the role education has historically played in reproducing many of the social injustices that have disenfranchised African Americans. Therefore, they believed that their practice should be informed by a critical consciousness of the taken-for-granted notions that have led to resource access in American society being determined by a rigidly defined racial hierarchy. One of our participants summed up these beliefs by succinctly commenting, "Education lacking a sense of critical thought, grounded in an understanding of the political economy of race in the U.S., leads to slavery."

In a much broader sense, the knowledge that framed the way they thought about their practice also was described as "the embodiment of a meshing of higher education discourses with the *truth talk* or communal wisdom of the black community." Consequently, from their beliefs about their students' academic abilities to the significance of a continued relationship with alumni, they described how profoundly their practice was informed by an explicit faith in insights gained by a people with over 400 years of experience in challenging racially based injustice in America. These insights were evident in their belief that all students can learn and it was their responsibility to establish the best possible environment for that learning to take place.

Establishing such an environment has often occurred with limited resources, causing the need for sacrifices from the students, the institution, its teachers and the community. Our participants spoke of this history of sacrifice as shaping a central part of the missions of HBCUs—a central mission founded in a history of service and openness described as "a spirit of never being exclusive," as HBCUs have never had racially nor economically established boundaries to enrollment. These universities have successfully educated millions of students with, for the most part, limited access to financial recourses. These characteristics of racial and economic diversity have established a distinct set of institutional norms that in many ways mirror the strained relationship of the broader black community to wealth in the United States. Consequently, regardless of how much or little the community had, the pursuit of education was considered paramount. The community in its many forms struggled to make higher education as available as possible to all who wanted to participate.

The survival and continued vitality of HBCUs was demonstrated in our informants discourses through their articulated longstanding belief that education is a significant part of combating poverty in the black community. Our participants spoke of HBCUs as existing with a sense of pragmatically grounded ethics. The pragmatic ethics they referred to meant that HBCUs operated with an awareness of the bottom line (in an often-antagonistic environment), while still maintaining an existential acknowledgment that their aims transcended the commodification of education. There were constant references to a *purposeful urgency* inherent to the functioning of HBCUs: If students are not allowed to receive this type of education here, where else can they find institutions with a concentration of beliefs centered on the unique experiences of blacks in America?

We highlight these ideas with an explicit understanding that not all black students want to nor should attend HBCUs. However, we are arguing, in response to our original discussion of the relationship between wealth and race, that HBCUs have historically played an integral role in assisting African Americans' participation in mainstream American life. We also believe that this participation by blacks in mainstream America, as a result of the unique legacies of HBCUs, is not simply greater access to life as cogs in a machine. Instead, we believe that the education provided by HBCUs creates critical participants in society who have influenced the workings of that machine in significant social and political ways and will continue to do so in future generations.

CONCLUSION: HISTORICALLY BLACK COLLEGES AS CENTERS WITH SPECIFIC EXPERTISE

Based upon the success of HBCUs in producing numerous African American intellectuals, entrepreneurs, and professionals, we would like to advance the case that HBCUs be considered centers of expertise for addressing problems associated with race and wealth. Our thought behind this proposal is straightforward and sums up the line of inquiry we have outlined throughout this chapter. First, that higher education is essential to providing greater access to better-paying jobs, which increases one's opportunity to acquire wealth. Second, that African Americans historically have been disenfranchised from access to higher education (or provided an inferior form of that education), and this unequal access to higher education is a significant factor in the gap that exists in wealth between whites and blacks in America. Third, that HBCUs have exhibited from their early days to the present an extraordinary ability to offer African Americans opportunities to excel in social, political, and economic arenas. Last, regardless of the end of Jim Crow and other legally sanctioned restrictions, African Americans still face serious obstacles in PWIs, in the job market, and in society in general.

As a result of the racial gaps in education and wealth, the hostile environments in white universities, and the profound history of accomplishments at HBCUs, we believe that questions associated with whether America still needs HBCUs are better directed to how we can better fund HBCUs in order to afford them the resources required for even greater success in educating African American students. Through this proposition we are not necessarily advocating that there should be an explosion of new HBCUs, but that the ones that already exist should be better supported. We specifically mean supported in their traditional missions, as well as in collaborating with PWIs so that

PWIs can take note of (and attempt to implement) some of the practices referenced by the educators we interviewed. We are well aware that ours is a very limited study to support such broad funding and so we believe that other studies must follow in order to corroborate our findings and serve as catalysts for a more-focused approach to structuring areas within PWIs and HBCUs that are best suited to mine and disseminate the knowledge of how to enrich the black community through higher education.

The scholarship of teaching model would be useful here, because it calls for educators to not only think about their own practice but to document and share its results with others for further refinement and implementation. Our belief is that, as a result of the number of students and educators at PWIs who have had some contact with HBCUs, the seeds for this type of practice already exist at PWIs and need only be nurtured in order to be fully recognized and appreciated. This nurturing of knowledge calls for a greater working relationship across institutional types in order to further the educational opportunities for each. This should not be a daunting task, particularly in cities across the South such as Nashville, Atlanta, Birmingham, and Baton Rouge, where HBCUs and PWIs with large student populations would benefit greatly from a systemic approach to improving higher education. Through this vision of shared knowledge, when a black person asks the question, "Where would I be or what would I have if I were white?," the range of answers changes because, white or black, education becomes informed by critical perspectives of American political and economic life so that the acceptance that the race and wealth gap must shrink is acknowledged, regardless of race. Does understanding and commitment automatically ensure the rapid closure of disparities between race and wealth in America? No, but it does provide a different-yet-familiar starting point with a proven record of success for addressing the challenge of race and wealth disparities.

REFERENCES

Anderson, J. (1988). *The Education of Blacks in the South 1860–1935*. Chapel Hill and London: University of North Carolina Press.

Aranson, J., Fried, Carrie and Catherine, Good. (2002). Reducing the effects of stereotype threat on African American students by shaping theories of intelligence. *Journal of Experiential Social Psychology, 38*, 113–125.

Basinger, J. (2003). Closing in on $1–million. *Chronicle of Higher Education,* p. s1

Banks, J. (1998). The lives and values of researchers: Implications for educating citizens in a multicultural society. *Educational researcher, 27*, 7, 4–17.

———. (1988). *Multiethnic Education: Theory and Practice,* (2nd ed.). Boston: MA: Allyn and Bacon.

Banks, J., Banks, C. (2001). *Handbook of Research on Multicultural Education* (2nd ed.). San Francisco: Jossey Bass.

Black Issues in Higher Education. (1999). Mississippi's Big Three Getting The Big Bucks—university president salaries. Retrieved July 10, 2006 from http://www.findarticles.com/p/articles/mi_m0DXK/is_17_16/ai_57745851.

Bontemps, A. (1972). *Young Booker: Booker T. Washington's early days*. New York: Dodd Mead.

Bowles, S., and Gintis, H. (1976). *Schooling in Capitalist America: Educational Reform and the Contradictions of Economic Life*. New York: Basic Books.

Boyer, E. (1990). *Scholarship Reconsidered Priorities of the Professorate*. Princeton: NJ: The Carnegie Foundation for the Advancement of Teaching.

Brubacher, J. S., and Rudy, W.(1976). Higher Education in Transition: A History of American Colleges and Universities, 1636–1976. New York: Harper and Row.

Burrell, L., and Trombley, T. (1983). Academic advising with minority students on predominantly white campuses. *Journal of College Student Personnel, 21,* 121–126.

Collier, M. (1988). Competent communication in intercultural unequal status advisement context. *Howard Journal of Communication, 1,* 3–22.

Cornett-Devito, M., and Reeves, K. (1999). Preparing students for success in a multicultural world: Faculty advisement and intercultural communication. *NACADA Journal, 19*(1), 35–44.

Crockett, D. (1985). Academic advising. In L. Noel, N. Levitz, D. Saluti, and Associates (Eds.), *Increasing Student Retention: Effective Programs and Practices for Reducing Dropout Rates*. San Francisco: Jossey-Bass.

Crookston, B. (1972). A developmental view of academic advising as teaching. *Journal of College Student Personnel, 13,* 12–17.

Cross, T. (1997). Black graduation rates at nation's highest-ranked colleges and universities. *The Journal of Blacks in Higher Education, 15,* 53–55.

Darity, W., Myers, S. (1998). *Persistent Disparity: Race and Economic Inequality since 1945*. Chetenham: UK: Edward Elgar.

Dubois, W. (1928). *The Souls of Black Folks* (7th ed.). Chicago, IL: A.C. McClurg and Co.

Day, J. and Newberger, E. (2002). *The big payoff: Indicate Attainment and Synthetic estimates of work life earnings*. D.C.: U.S. Department of Commerce Economics and Statistics Administration U.S. Census Bureau.

Dyson, M. (2002). *Open mike: Reflections on racial identities, popular culture and freedom struggles*. New York: Basic Civitas Books.

Gilbert, J. (2001). From Stereotypes to Sociotypes: The Impact of Multicultural Education. Journal on Excellence in College Teaching, 12(2), 55–76.

Gilroy, P. (2000). *Against Race: Imagining political culture passed the color line*. Cambridge: Harvard University Press.

Gordon, D. (2003). *Black Identity Rhetoric, Ideology, and Nineteenth-Century Black Nationalism*. Cabondale and Edwardsville: Southern Illinois University Press.

Huber, M. and Hutchings, P. (2004). *Integrative learning mapping the terrain*. Washington: Association of American colleges and universities and the Carnegie Foundation for the advancement of teaching.

Huber, M., Morreale, S. (Ed.). (2002). *Disciplinary Styles in the Scholarship of Teaching and Learning: Exploring Common Ground.* Merrifield: VA: AAHE Publications.

Inside Higher Ed (2005). The rich get richer. Retrieved August 4, 2006 from http://inside highered.com/news/2006/01/23/nacubo.

Liston, D. (1988). *Capitalist schools: Operation and ethics in radical studies of schooling.* New York: Routledge.

Marable, M. (2000). *How capitalism underdeveloped Black America.* Cambridge, MA: South End Press.

———. (2002). *The Great Wells of Democracy The Meaning of Race in American Life.* New York: BasicCivitas Books.

Maxwell, B. (2003). *We're in this struggle together.* Retrieved July 7, 2006 from http://www.jou.ufl.edu/rolemodels/publisher/struggle.shtm.

McIntyre, A. (1997). *Making meaning of whiteness.* Albany, New York: State University of New York Press.

Mesa-Bains, J. S. a. A. (1993). *Diversity in the classroom: A case book for teachers and teacher educators.* Hillsdale: Research for better schools and Lawrence Erlbaum Associates Inc.

Miller, L. S. (1995). *An American imperative accelerating minority educational advancement.* Binghamton, NY: Vail-Ballou Press.

Mills, C. (1997). *The Racial Contract.* New York: Cornell University Press.

Mitchell, R., and Rosiek J. (in press). Professor as embodied racial signifier: a case study of the significance of race in a university classroom. *The Review of Education, Pedagogy, and Cultural Studies.*

Nettles, M. (1995). The emerging national policy agenda on higher education assessment: A wake-up call. *Review of Higher Education, 18,* 293–313.

Ogbu, J. (1992b). Understanding cultural diversity and learning. *Educational Researcher, 21*(8), 5–14.

Rosenberg, P. M., (1997). Underground discourses: Exploring whiteness in teacher education. In M. Fine, L. Weis, L. C. Powell, and L. M. Wong (Eds.), *Off white: Readings on race, power, and society (pp. 78–89).* New York: Routledge.

Shabazz, A. (2004). *Advancing Democracy African Americans and the Struggle for Access and Equity in Higher Education in Texas.* Chapel Hill, NC: University of North Carolina Press.

Shulman, J., Mesa-Bains, A (Ed.). *Diversity in the classroom: A case book for teachers and teacher educators.* Mahwah, New Jersey: Lawrence Earlbaum Associates.

Shulman, L. (1981). Discipline of inquiry in education: An overview. *Educational researcher, 10*(6), 5–12.

———. (1987). Knowledge and teaching: Foundations of the new reform. *Harvard educational review* (57), 1–22.

———. (2000). *From minsk to pinsk: Why a scholarship of teaching and learning.* Retrieved October 12, 2002, from www.iusb.edu/%7Ejostl/contents.v2htm.

———. (2004). Teaching as Community Property: Essays on Higher Education. In P. Hutchings (Ed.), *Lamark's Revenge:Teaching among the scholarships.* San Francisco: Jossey Bass.

Steele, C., Aronson, J. (1995). Stereotype Threat and the Intellectual Test Performance of African Americans. *Journal of Personality and Social Psychology, 68*, 797–811.

Sue, D. (1990). *Counseling the culturally different: Theory and practice* (2nd ed.). New York: John Wiley and Sons.

———. (1991). A model for cultural diversity training. *Journal of Counseling and Development, 70*, 99–105.

Thelin, J. (2004). *The History of American Education*. Baltimore and London: Johns Hopkins University Press.

Tozer, S., Senese, P., and Guy, C. (2002). *School and Society Historical and Contemporary Perspectives* (4th ed.). New York: McGraw-Hill.

U.S. Department of Education, National Center for Education Statistics; NCES Common Core of Data (CCD); Projections of Educational Statistics to 2013. From Digest of Education Statistics 2003.

Vine, P. (1976). The social function of eighteenth century higher education. *History of Higher Education Quarterly, 16*, 409–424.

Wade, S., Thompson, A., and Watkins, W. (1986). Beliefs, ideology and history texts. In R. Gardner, Alexander, P. (Ed.), *Beliefs About Texts and Instruction with Texts* (pp. 265–293). Hillsdale: NJ: Erlbaum.

West, C. (1999). *The Cornel West Reader*. New York: Basic Civitas books.

———. (1990). *Race Matters*. Boston, MA: Beacon Press.

Wheeler, E., Ayers, J. , Fracasso, M. , Galupo, M. and Rabin, J. (1999). Approaches to Modeling Diversity in the College Classroom: Challenges and Strategies. Journal on Excellence in College Teaching, 10(2), 79–93.

William, W. (2001). *The White Architects of Black Education Ideology and Power in America 1865–1954*. New York: Teachers College Press.

Winston, R.B., and Miller T.K., (1987). *Student developmental task and lifestyle inventory manual*. Athens, GA: Student Development Associates, Inc.

Chapter Eight

Wealth Whiteout: Creative Writers Confront Whites' Downward Mobility in America's Newest Gilded Age

Cecelia Tichi

> Poor medical care, job insecurity, the bane of old age, lack of proper education, and that nagging sense of mistrust of a society in which you are a productive member who does not seem to share in the fruit of that production—these issues pervade every cultural group, creed, race, and religion.
>
> Walter Mosely, *Workin' on the Chain Gang*, 2000

At the turn of the twenty-first century, the African-American novelist, Walter Mosely, published an extended essay that particularly challenged its white audience with this provocative title: *Workin' on the Chain Gang*. The author of a popular series of detective novels, notably *Devil in a Blue Dress*, and of science fiction too, Mosely had become best known for his black sleuth, Easy Rawlins, who solves crimes in racist L.A. of the 1950s.

At the approach of the year 2000, however, Mosely's fury at broad-based socioeconomic inequity prompted his move into a different literary genre. Responding to a publisher's invitation, he agreed to contribute to a series of short books constituting a "Library of Contemporary Thought." Taking leave of fiction, he temporarily dispensed with the novelist's stock-in-trade—plot, character development, the shaping of a story in a particular location, and so on—in order to craft his social critique in the direct address of the essay, a form prominent in the U.S. literature from the earlier nineteenth century of Ralph Waldo Emerson through W. E. B. Du Bois and beyond. Mosely's personal expository essay was meant to disclose the bases of deteriorating socioeconomic conditions for multitudes of whites as well as people of color in contemporary America.

Workin' on the Chain Gang explicitly evokes the image of shackled (i.e., enslaved) black men in prison stripes toiling in blazing heat—a historically familiar, racialized image. Mosely, however, added this twist: he now insisted that his U.S. white readers, male and female, try on this image of the chain gang and recognize how well one-size-fits-all at the turn of the new millennium. The image of enslavement, Mosely argued, could no longer be relegated to history nor confined solely to the experience of African-Americans. Nor was the novelist-turned-essayist simply exercising literary license, much less trivializing the one-syllable word for human property. Mosely responded, instead, to a new buccaneering capitalism reminiscent of the late nineteenth century's Gilded Age but now reemergent in the later twentieth century to straiten masses of Americans. Mosely understood that the entire middle class was now newly victimized under this regime. Now vast numbers of whites, along with blacks and browns, were dehumanized by "the juggernaut of capitalism" in which "the value of life itself fluctuates according to the cost of production" (11).

Mosely's essay is particularly apt for a humanistic inquiry into the ways by which creative writers engage social crises. The race-based disparity, in America, of wealth between and among groups became Mosely's topic and the incentive for the *Chain Gang* project. The novelist's segue from fiction to the essay shows formal flexibility and a strategic gauging of audience receptivity at a pivotal historic moment: "the end of the century [which] can be perceived as a border, a milestone, a marker for the human race" (3).

Workin' on the Chain Gang belongs in a particularly American subgenre of the essay: the jeremiad, named for the lamentations of the Old Testament prophet Jeremiah who voiced the Lord's wrath at Israel's despoiling of a plentiful land and its cities. Originating in literature of seventeenth-century New England Puritans, who took as their colonial identity a New English-American Israel, the jeremiad became a recurrent form in American literature. Its writers periodically excoriated a nation understood to have regressed from its spiritual ideals and obligations. The American jeremiad simultaneously exhorted audiences to renewed commitments to the attainment of those ideals. The long-term tradition of the jeremiad has been recognized in varied authors, including Jewish- and African-American ones (for instance Richard Wright). Mosely's secular *fin de siecle* American jeremiad decries a world in which "decisions are made by governments in concert with corporations that are designed to increase profit and influence, not to advance humanitarian ends" (5). The persona of the essayist is fired by emotional intensity along an axis of righteous anger and awe. The sheer tenacity of human survival over millennia prompts Mosely's reverential awe. But he hastens to address the human depredation of recent history: "the shackles of slavery, the constraints of capitalism, the corruption of idealistic systems, and the iron convictions of hatred, prejudice, and ignorance—these are our baggage" (5).

If tempted to identify that statement as politically Marxist, one ought first to ask a different question: Who are the "we" whom Mosely cites? Who are the shackled, the constrained, the casualties of corrupted ideals? What U.S. group(s) are referenced? Given Mosely's title, one first thinks: African-Americans, for the history of a once-enslaved people is undeniably the primary reference of the title. "Over hundreds of years," Mosely writes, "black people developed identities designed to deal with the tyranny of capitalism in its most naked state: slavery" (11). Mosely, in fact, tells readers that his initial plan for the centenary essay was an attack on ongoing U.S. racism, which had become obscured, he felt, by such public rituals as commemorations of the achievements of the Civil Rights movement. Meanwhile, as Mosely planned to argue, racism remained virulent in the underemployment and imprisonment of black men, and in the extremes suffered by black women who are then praised for their strength.

Whites, however, are emphatically included in *Workin' on the Chain Gang* because Mosely realized that the core issues of his project—poor medical care, job insecurity, insufficient education, exclusion from the benefits of high productivity—"pervade every cultural group, creed, race, and religion" (11). When Mosely writes that "we" have been "shanghaied. . . drugged and chained and made into property" and that he fears a future in which "the majority of citizens will be beasts of burden," the essayist thus refers to whites as well as people of color (6, 7).

The opening pages of *Workin' on the Chain Gang* make clear the parameters and rationale for Mosely's "we." Quite simply, the terms of historicized slavery and of its aftermath of social and legal oppression serve to frame an argument on conditions now besetting once comfortable whites in a newly brutal economy. Initially intending to write about race, Mosely finds his true subject to be class in contemporary America, itself now a binary society of fewer and fewer haves *v.* multitudes of have-nots. He engages a class division which the social critic Barbara Ehrenreich says is "defined solely by money—who has it and who doesn't" (201). Mosely laments the shared experience of ethnic-racial entwining in a rising misery quotient affecting all racially categorizable groups:

> In their various groups white Americans might feel that they belong, that there is a group spirit that looks out for them. But individually they suffer the barbs of bureaucratic indifference and the vicissitudes of corporate whims like everyone else. At the group level a white man might identify with the white, male, Christian president. But that identification means very little on the unemployment line or when the HMO refuses to supply possibly life-saving technology (14).

Mosely's "barbs" and "vicissitudes" cover joblessness and the denial of health care in the era of for-profit medicine, but his statement implies the cascade of socioeconomic travails that have filled the public record since the late 1970s: the decline in U.S. social services as state budgets are slashed nationwide, the depression of middle and working class incomes, the instability and degradation of work, which has moved into the contingent status of temping, contract and part-time employment. The "barbs" and "vicissitudes" also indicate the upsurge in need for donated food, the stripping away of employees' insurance, pension, and medical benefits, the lack of affordable housing and of childcare for parents working outside the household, in addition to the steep increases in costs of preschool and post-secondary education (and imposition of stiff fees for extracurricular activities of middle and high schoolers whose districts are strapped for money).[1] These and other signs of social crisis now afflicted whites, Mosely asserted, just as they long had impacted blacks. The "race to the bottom" had become an equal opportunity plunge. Equality found its basis in mutual deprivation. At the turn of the new century in America, Mosely argued, whites had become the new people of color. Whites were now the new blacks.

Contemporary American writers' literary record of whites' downward mobility as delineated in *Workin' on the Chain Gang* is apparently spare—or so it seems at first. The Gilded Age of the late nineteenth and early twentieth century had provided memorable literary white characters who tumbled from middle-class prosperity to depths of degradation and despair, and their precedent is instructive. Among numerous texts, one might single out the 1899 appearance of Frank Norris's fictional San Francisco dentist, McTeague, the title character whose life ends in a brutal fight in Death Valley, or of George Hurstwood in Theodore Dreiser's *Sister Carrie* (1900). A onetime Chicago manager in custom tailored suits and calfskin shoes, Hurstwood dies destitute on the New York city streets, his final despairing utterance—"What's the use?"

Where, however, are the counterparts of these characters in contemporary fiction of the late twentieth- and early twenty-first centuries? Who are Walter Mosely's chain gang whites in recent novels? Mosely chose the essay to express the impact of contemporary economic conditions, but who among his literary cohorts has executed this idea in fiction? Tom Wolfe's bestselling novels, *Bonfire of the Vanities* (1987) and *A Man in Full* (1998), might seem to provide notable examples, both books featuring wealthy "Masters of the Universe" who are felled by hubris, the first a Wall Street top bond salesman, the second a construction magnate.

In each novel, however, the protagonist's ruin is spectacular, literally a spectacle because it is exceptional. Both novels, that is, present their protagonists' financial collapse as anomalous rather than representative of a wider social trend.

Mosely's *Chain Gang*, however, affirms the presence of a downwardly mobile group in its collective noun, "gang." Given the massive layoffs in the much vaunted "lean-and-mean" corporate restructuring from the 1980s through the opening years of the new century, one expects to find a fictional character who is representative of this huge group of the "downsized." Literary history of the twentieth century, in fact, provides a lesson on how socioeconomics correlates with literary production. In Arthur Miller's post-World War II drama, *Death of a Salesman* (1949), Willy Loman embodied the white middle class American striver who is crushed when his sales career founders. At mid-twentieth century, playwright Miller's protagonist exposed the hypocrisy of the American theology of career success and its destructive power. It was understood that countless Willy Lomans dotted the American landscape.

Years earlier, the Joad family of John Steinbeck's *The Grapes of Wrath* (1939) had likewise dramatized the human costs of American aspirations in collision with savage socioeconomic conditions. The Joads' great migration from Dustbowl Oklahoma to California showed American family disintegration under horrific economic pressures of the Great Depression. Though characterized as poor white "Okies," the Joad family actually struck an empathetic chord among middle class readers because the values of the fictional characters exactly mirrored the readers' own: family cohesion, a strong work ethic and the goal of home ownership, which is itself a material symbol of stability, respectability, and self-worth—in short, the American Dream.

Steinbeck's Joads, in fact, might serve as a guide in a search for contemporary literature's response, in this historical moment, to what Walter Mosely's jeremiad terms "the juggernaut of capitalism" in which "the value of life itself fluctuates according to the cost of production." The Joads, that is, arrived camouflaged as "other." Their hillbilly vernacular, their rusticity, their social marginality served to distance them from middle class readers. At this level, the "Okie" Joads are exotics. At another level, however, they are kindred spirits of Steinbeck's readers, who became engrossed in their story in large part because readers saw their own most cherished values mirrored in those of the characters. Steinbeck idealized this salt-of-the-earth populace (as had the Russian writer Leo Tolstoy), but his decision to cast the Depression epic as an "Okie" tale of exile and cross-country quest no doubt minimized readers' own anxieties. Depression-era middle class readers, deeply fearful about their own socioeconomic status, needed the "otherness" of the Joads. Why?—because years of bank failures, job losses, foreclosures on homes, and so on were the atmosphere in which they approached the novel. The Joads' exotic "otherness" provided a mental and emotional safety cushion against a heightened consciousness of the readers' own jeopardy in the worst economic downturn the nation had suffered.

The class difference between the Joad family and the readers whose embrace put *The Grapes of Wrath* on the bestseller list proved to be strategically brilliant, if uncalculated, on Steinbeck's part. The "exotic" Joads opened access to a narrative whose dark socioeconomic message otherwise might have been too frightening to confront directly.

In the era of *Workin' on the Chain Gang*, contemporary American literature includes a similarly camouflaged but equally revealing novel. A bestseller, this new book dramatizes the issues which Mosely addresses, issues which are undergirded by the public record of job loss, health care woes, and so on. Just as *The Grapes of Wrath* reached the U.S. public at first as fiction and, in 1940, as a feature motion picture, so Americans in very recent years experienced a reprise of this pattern. In 1999 and '03, respectively, U.S. readers and moviegoers found their contemporary moment starkly represented by Andre Dubus III's *House of Sand and Fog*.

It is useful briefly to trace this synergistic interplay of multimedia publicity, promotion, and marketing to indicate the extent of U.S. public exposure to *House of Sand and Fog*. The point here is to map the presence of the novel and film in the U.S., a national narrative playing to a national audience. The novel far surpassed literary coterie success, though some readers knew Dubus as a 1985 winner of prestigious Pushcart Prize for fiction and as finalist for the 1994 Prix de Rome, sponsored by the American Academy of Arts and Letters. In 1999, *House of Sand and Fog* became a finalist in a far more widely publicized U.S. prize competition, the National Book Award for Fiction, which thus officially certified the literary high status of the author and the book. This was a sort of successful peer review certain to garner readers who were self-identified as persons of discerning taste. Newspapers nationwide reviewed the novel favorably, including *The New York Times*, the *Los Angeles Times* and *The Philadelphia Inquirer*, as did leading magazines read by the affluent and highly educated (*The New Yorker*, *Mirabella*).

In popular circulation, *House of Sand and Fog* was to gain tremendous exposure when Oprah Winfrey selected it in 2000 for her nationally televised Oprah's Book Club, thus guaranteeing bestseller status. The *Oprah* certification would mean literally just that: "Oprah's Book Club" stickers would appear on the cover, and the novel would be prominently displayed in customers' high traffic areas in national chain bookstores, notably Barnes & Noble and Border's Books.

The public circulation of *House of Sand and Fog* intensified with the film version of 2003, which closely paralleled the book and brought the added luster of two Academy Award winning actors in leading roles, Jennifer Connelly and Ben Kingsley, who was himself nominated for a second Oscar for his role in the film, as was an actress in a supporting role (Shohreh Aghdashloo) and also the composer of the soundtrack (James Horner). The film was duly promoted in reviews on TV and the web (for instance, on *CNN*, *E!* and *E! Online*) and in print nationally (*Hollywood Reporter*, A. O. Scott in *The New York Times*).

The pre-Academy Award publicity on TV and in prime-market newspapers also generated attention for the film, which was screened nationwide in general release from December '03 through early winter '04. The DVD version went on sale in March, '04, displayed in Blockbuster stores and discounted at Wal-Mart and Target stores and including the now-customary special features, such as filmed scenes which were deleted in final editing, together with commentary by author Dubus. The new paperback edition matched the DVD packaging in front photographs of Connelly and Kingsley. Their pictures on the front of the book were artfully positioned beneath a banner strip proclaiming NATIONAL BESTSELLER and a gold medallion which read "NOW A MAJOR MOTION PICTURE." The opening pages contained blurbs from reviews and prominent authors.

Just as Walter Mosely's stature as a popular novelist served to attract reviewers to *Workin' on the Chain Gang*, so Dubus's credential as a prize winning fiction writer stimulated initial interest in *House of Sand and Fog*. The multiplier effect, however, of *Oprah*, the film, the Academy Award nominations and the rest put *House of Sand and Fog* in what must be called public consciousness. This meant that many who did not actually read the novel or see the movie might well know something about it (in the way in which Steinbeck's Joads circulate in popular culture irrespective of whether one reads the novel or sees the John Ford film).

Whether *House of Sand and Fog* proceeds to take its place on school reading lists and to endure in general knowledge cannot now be known, any more than the long-term reputation of *The Grapes of Wrath* could have been predicted in 1939–40. What can be said is that in the opening years of the twenty-first century, *House of Sand and Fog* became a story well situated in national circulation and imprinted across genres. It became a story disseminated throughout print and visual media and repeatedly summarized, blurbed, referenced. It gained both prestige and traction and, equally important for this discussion, can be considered cultural capital.

What is this story? What is the basis of its appeal? How does *House of Sand and Fog* exemplify the "Chain Gang" crisis of a contemporary white U.S. population? As readers and moviegoers know, Dubus weaves a grim, destructive tale from disputed ownership claims on a beach-town bungalow in the San Francisco Bay area. The house itself is a modest suburban dwelling, a typical middle class American house of the mid-late twentieth century even though the novel presents it as well-maintained, the film as rundown and cluttered. In both versions, the glimpse of the Pacific from its rooftop mocks the notion of an ocean view.

The bungalow, however, takes on epic importance for the disputants who battle for its possession. The antagonists are a former Iranian air force colonel and a Boston-area young woman who inherited the West Coast house from her father and has lived there first as a newlywed, then as a single woman whose husband has left her. The plot is set in motion when sheriff's deputies arrive to evict her for nonpayment of property taxes. Vacated, the house is scheduled for sale at public auction, and the colonel, seeing the newspaper notice of the sale, recognizes a business opportunity: to buy the property, to install his family briefly in the bungalow, then to resell it at three or four times the auction purchase price and reinvest in other profitable ventures. For the colonel, the house represents the immigrant's opportunity to leverage the American dream. For the evicted woman, the bungalow represents a family tie to her late father—more, it is incontestably her home, an American woman's American home.

In both fiction and film, the sequence of scenes, the dialogue and the characterizations are closely paralleled, as is Dubus's alternation of viewpoints presented in voices of Colonel Massoud Behrani, and of the woman, Kathy Nicolo. Other characters coming into play include Colonel Behrani's wife, Nedereh (Nedi), his young teen son, Ismail, and a recently-married daughter, Soraya, who is just arriving back from her wedding trip.

For her part, Kathy is too ashamed to tell her Boston-area family that the husband whose absence she mourns left for good months earlier in the couple's newly-purchased second car. Though the novel presents Kathy's eviction to be the result of a mistake by the county tax office, and though the film shows her ouster as caused from long disregard of the envelopes containing her tax bills, the end result is the same. Locked out of the house, alone and friendless in cheap motels and then in her car, Kathy turns her attentions to a sheriff's deputy, Lester Burdon, who had proven helpful during her eviction and who turns up, not-so-coincidentally, at odd moments. Married with two children, Lester becomes Kathy's lover and self-styled champion, plotting how she can regain ownership of the house when Kathy's Legal Aid attorney seems stymied by legal restrictions and by the colonel's stubbornly exorbitant price—the going market price—set for transfer of the house to the county and then to Kathy.

The plot (which moves in the film on rails of ominous music) takes on a dreadful air of inevitability. In several exchanges, Kathy and the Colonel confront one another at the house, and his fierce pride and intransigence are a match for her increasingly desperate, erratic, self-destructive behavior. Both individuals are single mindedly bent on securing the house, whatever the cost—and both pay with their lives, as do the colonel's wife and son. Lester, too, becomes a casualty of sorts.[2]

Critics can consider whether *House of Sand and Fog* is a modern tragedy or melodrama, but our interest lies in its representation of the predicament of "chain gang" whites as defined by Mosely. How, we ask, does *House of Sand and Fog* serve to dramatize whole populations of whites now experiencing severe downward mobility in the contemporary moment? What are the techniques of the novelist? To approach this question, we need first to consider how this story is conducted so that its readers and viewers, a largely white audience, can feel sufficiently separate or detached to enter into its story without undue anxiety of self-identification with the specific plight of the characters.

The narrative, first of all, encourages an appreciation of the "otherness" of Colonel Behrani, whom Dubus portrays as an émigré who consciously sets himself apart from American culture despite his naturalized U.S. citizenship. The colonel's contempt for most things American—tourists, coffee, revealing clothing worn by women in public—all set him apart, as does his disdain for what he sees as Americans' irresponsibility and lack of discipline.

Other narrative techniques also mark him as foreign, such as the Farsi terms which Dubus disperses amply throughout the colonel's thoughts, and also the diction and syntax which reveal Behrani as a non-native speaker of English. Readers consistently encounter phonetic spellings of Farsi words within the mind of a high-caste Persian whose formality of dress and manner, whose taste in furnishings and food differentiate him from the America where he lives in exile following the 1978 Iranian revolution. These techniques of fiction are revealed, for instance, when Dubus presents Behrani's cherished identity in recollection of "the perfectly tailored uniform of an honorable colonel, a genob sarhang in the King's Air Force, the King of Kings, Shahanshah Reza Pahlavi, who three times in my career his hand I kissed" (22). Massoud Behrani is in, but not of, America. The very notion of assimilation to its ways, readers and viewers realize, would horrify him. American readers and moviegoers thus can observe him as though through a one-way cultural mirror.

The character of Kathy Nicolo, too, is exoticized in ways that distance her from readers and viewers of *House of Sand and Fog*. Dubus evokes empathy for her loneliness, for her grief over her failed marriage, for her yearning to be grounded in life and perhaps to have a child. But the author also presents Kathy as a chronically backsliding addict. The prefatory term, "recovering," is a euphemism in her case, which is precisely DuBus's point: as a character, Kathy Nicolo verges on being a pathological case study, especially in the novel version, in which her addictions are multiple—to tobacco and alcohol, to cocaine, to "chain-watching" movies. DuBus presents her thoughts as an allegorical battle against the enemy within:

> I lit a cigarette and blew the smoke out the window. In the program, they'd tell you at these times to HALT. If you're Hungry, Angry, Lonely, or Tired—any of these—you should slow down and watch your step. I happened to be all four, I

knew it, and the last thing I felt like doing was facing the B.E.A.S.T. in the air and recognizing the enemy voice in my head so I could start accusing it of fucking malice (86).

The "enemy voice" speaks often and insistently in Kathy's mind, the term subsequently capitalized in the novel as a dialectical demon: Enemy Voice. The woman who copes with estrangement from her family and the loss of her marriage is also sufficiently pathologized that readers and viewers experience her as distinctly discontinuous from themselves.

How then does Dubus's narrative engage the issues of whites' socioeconomic crisis in the late twentieth and early twenty-first centuries? How do a swarthy Persian and a troubled female addict represent a crisis of lowered social status and of much-diminished wealth among a population racialized as white and heretofore held to represent a stable norm of U.S. prosperity? How, in short, can the two principal characters of *House of Sand and Fog* be regarded in Walter Mosely's terms as typical of an entire class of whites who are now "workin' on the chain gang?"

The *House* of Dubus's title is the crucial starting point. Ownership of the house, which each character claims obsessively—and by law—is a primary route to the crisis of middle and upper-middle class American whites. True to Dubus's title, the modest California bungalow is the central symbol of the novel and film. Overriding the colonel's Persian identity and Kathy's addiction, the house represents the American core value of home ownership, and most reviewers have remarked on this point, for instance Bill Gallo, who observed, "The house comes to mean everything—a sense of root and anchor, the pride of self-worth, the very notion of home and stability. . . . This is. . . emotional merchandise. . . not mere boards and bricks" (*Dallas Observer*, Dec. 25, 2003). As a recent study of American family finances states, "The home is the most important purchase for the average middle-class family. To the overwhelming majority of Americans, home ownership stands out as the single most important component of 'the good life.' Homes mark the lives of their children, setting out the parameters of their universe" (Warren and Tyagi, 20).

The centrality of the house in Dubus's project in fiction correlates with its prominence in contemporary work in social science. The foundation of the middle class American dream, the house is nonetheless increasingly out of reach and, if attained, only temporarily occupied by owners in these years of crushing credit card debt and a high divorce rate. Virtually a middle class entitlement from the post-World War II era of U.S. economic expansion, the ownership of an American home in recent years has become an unattainable goal and a site of demographic risk. "Home foreclosures have more than tripled in less than 25 years," as documented by the Mortgage Bankers of America and the Federal Housing Administration (FHA) (Warren and Tyagi, 7, 194). Studies show the foreclosures to accord with bankruptcies in an era of deregulated credit in which aspirant home buyers are lured into the market with sub prime and other loans which far exceed the borrowers' ability to re-pay, with numerous fees and with high credit insurance premiums added on.

As Elizabeth Warren and Amelia Warren Tyagi write in their 2004 study of the financial crises now besetting American families, "Many of the 'house poor' are middle-class families that overextended themselves in a desperate effort to find a home" (Warren and Tyagi, 133). Personal bankruptcies, they find, often are spurred by home foreclosures, and evidence suggests that this topic is circulating in anxious informal discussions among friends and neigh-bors nationwide. In April, 2004, an Associated Press reporter filed a story on Americans' major concerns across state and region, from small-town Min-nesota to Dubuque, Iowa. He found the possible loss of the home to be a para-mount expressed worry: "I'm worried about losing my house. . . I'm tired of worrying about it. . . . If a family is barely surviving on two salaries, what happens if they lose one?. . . The house goes back to the bank. [sarcasm here] Isn't that the American way" (Fournier). As the anthropologist Katherine K. Newman writes, "Home ownership is America's most visible measure of eco-nomic achievement. Adults who have lost their homes—to foreclosure or dis-tress sales—have truly lost their membership card in the middle class" (102).

As novelist, Dubus converts this dictum and the data from the Mortgage Bankers and FHA into his central symbol of the novel. The symbol produces the same message as the economic and anthropological data. The American home, in Dubus's terms, has lost its firm foundation. It has been destabilized and shrouded in a chill, opaque vapor. Symbolically and actually, the home dwelling is no longer a widely attainable American dream for an economi-cally pressured white middle class. It has become, instead, a house of sand and fog.

To revisit Kathy Nicolo in this context is to see beyond the troubled addict to a cultural template of the white American single woman, post-divorce, struggling to make ends meet in the house vacated by the second income earner, an ex-husband. Working as a house cleaner for a set fee or hourly wage, Kathy typifies the American female worker without insurance, pen-sion, or health care benefits. (When she steps barefoot on a nail and suffers a deep puncture wound, over-the-counter ointment is the treatment; a visit to a doctor is out of the question.) The novel and film use unpaid back taxes as the springboard for her eviction, but data show that demographically speaking, Kathy Nicolo typifies a sizable population of downwardly mobile white women who are blindsided by their financial crises. When the dazed Kathy seeks help from a Legal Aid lawyer, she is a version of a national middle-class pattern identified by Warren and Tyagi, who write of the bankruptcy data they and a research team analyzed from the Harvard University Consumer Bankruptcy Project, begun in 2001. "Most people who filed for bankruptcy never even met a lawyer until the mortgage company sent a foreclosure notice, at which point they hired someone whose ad appeared in the yellow pages or on late-night television" (79).[3]

Dubus reflects yet another dimension of the single woman's peril. Deciding to make Kathy childless, the novelist streamlines his plotline, but Kathy Nicolo's age is noteworthy and significant. At thirty-six, she is the age of the mature American single mother, a point surely not lost on that particular demographic of women readers and viewers of *House of Sand and Fog*. The jeopardy of a single mother of Kathy's age is indeed dire, for 200,000 single mothers go bankrupt each year, and "if current trends persist, more than one of every six single mothers will go bankrupt by the end of the decade" of 2000–'10." Put in relative terms, "Single mothers are now more likely than any other group to file for bankruptcy—more likely than the elderly, more likely than divorced men, more likely than minorities, and more likely than people living in poor neighborhoods" (Warren and Tyagi, 104–05). In a poignant moment, Kathy Nicolo voices the hope and yearning of this broad demographic of the women she typifies: "I was starting to feel like anything was possible again . . . the feeling that we could start out new again, clean, all our debts cleared" (174). The reality, however, is that "losing" the house "had been the final shove in a long drift to the edge" (181).

If Kathy Nicolo represents the white lower middle class, Dubus's Colonel Behrani is her counterpart in the American upper middle class. Kathy typifies the plight of those struggling to avoid destitution, but Dubus's colonel represents the downward mobility besetting those of upper-middle-class privilege. Barely escaping revolutionary Iran with his life (and recalling the murder of his closest friend and his family), Behrani occasionally indulges his nostalgia for the old pre-revolutionary days when his family lived so well in Tehran within their enclosed garden walls, motoring about the city in his Mercedes with a personal driver and ushered with his family to the head of lines at theatres and restaurants.

Behrani, however, is now in a crisis mirroring that of American professional- and managerial-class males whose careers have ended abruptly and prematurely with layoffs from corporate downsizing, mergers, and the outsourcing of positions since the 1980s. An educated, well-traveled careerist ("we are an educated family; we do not need to live as the peasant class"), Massoud Behrani had risen through the military ranks. As a senior officer, he negotiated complicated sales of fighter jets from Boeing to the Iranian Imperial Air Force. (Dubus pointedly makes him a noncombatant in the officer corps). In rank, the colonel is the equivalent of a corporate senior manager or vice-president, and his values are those of corporate America: loyalty and dedication to the organization and its success, pride in his abilities and achievements, appreciation of the material good life afforded as the reward for his efforts. As anthropologist Newman says, this sort of figure is "a well-educated, skilled professional, accustomed to power, to deference, to middle-class norms of consumption" (10)

Yet the colonel is now living a lie—or as he puts it, "lying and play-acting," a "charade" (56, 164). In public in America he can pass as a businessman in fine tailored suits, dress shirts, silk neckties. In actuality, since arriving in the U.S. with $280,000, he has failed to find a managerial position in the industry he knows intimately, aerospace and defense contracting. Though maintaining a luxurious Bay Area apartment to "keep up appearances" until he can marry off his daughter into the Iranian émigré upper-class (a *fait accompli* as the novel and film open), the colonel finds his finances now to be so dire that he tries to staunch the outflow of money by working two low-wage jobs. By day, he is a highway roadside trash pickup crewman, by night a convenience store clerk (18). He admits to a succession of such jobs "in a tomato cannery, an auto wash, a furniture warehouse, a parking lot, two gasoline stations" (48). In utilitarian terms, his work life is indistinguishable from Kathy Nicolo's for all his self-confessed "mask" of "pride and vanity" (164).

Always careful to dress in business attire when leaving or entering his household, Behrani keeps his wife and children ignorant of his secret life and their financial predicament—just as numerous displaced American executives have done, according to Newman's study of middle-class downward mobility and a *New York Times* report, *The Downsizing of America* (1996). When Behrani buys Kathy Nicolo's bungalow at auction and leaves the high-rise apartment, he is down to $48,000 and "fears to lose it all, to become bankrupt like so many Americans" (20). The colonel thus occupies and typifies what the anthropologist Newman calls "the troubled world of the financially distressed, the dispossessed, and the realm of low-level occupations" (10). She explains, "Downward mobility is not merely a matter of accepting a menial job, enduring the loss of stability, or witnessing with dismay the evaporation of one's hold on material comfort; it is also a broken covenant" (230).

The dramatization of the colonel's fall makes *House of Sand and Fog* an allegory of the heretofore privileged U. S. white male professionals and managers now in free fall as careers are destroyed by circumstances beyond any individual's control. The colonel's struggle, replicated widely throughout corporate America, includes family support and the education of his son in a context of drastically diminishing savings and the specter of looming poverty. Newman calls this "falling from grace" and sums up the predicament: "one can play by the rules, pay one's dues, and still be evicted from the American dream [because] there simply is no guarantee that one's best efforts will be rewarded in the end" (229). Indeed, this is the stark message of *House of Sand and Fog*. Its grim conclusion shows no exit, no bounce back in this relentless "fall from grace" because the condition is terminal.

To return to *Workin' on the Chain Gang*, however, is to encounter a different message. In synchrony with Dubus on the conditions now faced by middle-class whites, Walter Mosely nonetheless posits a different future. Mosely's essay avoids race-based *schadenfreud* or anodynes on "what goes around, comes around" in the face of ongoing socioeconomic stress among U.S. whites. On the contrary, *Workin' on the Chain Gang* signals an urgent need for remedial action. It does so in a remarkable subtitle: *Shaking Off the Dead Hand of History*.

A break with the past, Mosely argues, is possible and crucial for a viable U.S. future. The plan of action requires, first, a social inclusiveness across racial lines. Mosely thus extends to whites a welcome into the confraternity of those with greatest experience and expertise in survival of dire economic conditions over long periods of time, namely, people of color. Whites are the new blacks (or "neoslaves" in Mosely's term) and thus can learn a great deal from the historical experience of the oppressed minority. African-American history, in short, is the data base and guide to the future for newly downsized whites.

The groundwork for change has already been laid, Mosely explains, urging recognition that in recent years blacks with whites have mixed as "neighbors, coworkers, and cousins" (10). He notes that the historically racialized separation of people of color from whites—via differentiation by class, culture, speech dialect, etc.—has largely come to an end. Decades of black-white racial interaction, some coerced, some volitional, in a context of mass media and popular culture has resulted, he has found, in both races being now "intertwined" (10).

The cross-racial kinship and entwining is no cause for lamentation and submission, but rather the basis for implementation of a vision of a more equitable future. *Workin' on the Chain Gang* exhorts Americans across the color line to recognize mutual self-interest to be gained in joining together to demand equal rights and an economic "fair share." To "shake off the dead hand of history" means a major redirection of the corporatized socioeconomic order in the U.S. In this, says Mosely, African American history is vitally important for whites:

> The black American experience is a subject that is supremely American. It is the history of a centuries-long war in which one group of people strove for justice, for a fair share. Relegating black history to an elective or a ghetto or a moment

in the past holds us all back. Black history is a torch that can lead us out of the darkness. In order to find the way, we have to work together and follow one another's strengths (53).

Mosely's is the voice of the orator, his tone righteous anger, his message both invocation and exhortation. Admitting the effort might feel Sisyphian, Mosely also acknowledges that "to imagine the impossible" is the prerogative of the fiction writer. "Pushing ideas to their limits is what I'm expected to do—*in fiction.*" But he calls it a "small step from fiction to nonfiction in this world of technology and change" (103). Vis-a vis himself and his fellow citizens in a world of corporate and military chains, Mosely warns, in effect, that the death trip of *House of Sand and Fog* is the American dystopia to be repudiated by civic action. "Make no mistake," says the novelist, "we *all* need to resist if we want to survive intact" (53).

REFERENCES

The Downsizing of America. New York: Times Books, 1996.

Dubus, Andre III. *House of Sand and Fog*. 1999. Reprint. New York: Vintage, 2003.

Ehrenreich, Barbara. *Fear of Falling: The Inner Life of the Middle Class*. New York: Harper Collins, 1989.

Fournier, Ron. "Anxious Americans Trying to Decide." *The Tennessean*. April 25, 2004: 23A.

Mosely, Walter. *Workin' on the Chain Gang: Shaking Off the Dead Hand of History*. New York: Ballantine, 2000.

Newman, Katherine S. *Falling from Grace: The Experience of Downward Mobility in the American Middle Class*. New York: Free Press, 1988.

Warren, Elizabeth, and Amelia Warren Tyagi. *The Two-Income Trap: Why Middle-Class Mothers and Fathers Are Going Broke*. New York: Basic Books, 2003.

NOTES

1. In December, 2002, the U. S. Conference of Mayors would underscore the food-and-shelter crisis of the opening years of the twenty-first century, reporting a 19% increase in demand for food aid over the previous year for working families and stating that "the lack of food and adequate shelter for the working poor is becoming an endemic problem" (*New York Times*, Dec. 18 '02: A18). On the U.S. mainland, between 1979 and 1996, U. S. Department of Labor statistics show that "more than 43 million jobs have been erased in the United States," with victims of layoffs outnumbering victims of violent crime by fifty per cent (this according to *Times* analysts.) In the opening years of the new century the layoffs continued in relentless, numbing numbers,

with the *Times* reporting on December 30, 2001, that "corporate America announced roughly a million layoffs in 2001," an unprecedented scale of downsizing. At "Motorola, 40,000 jobs, at Boeing, 30,000, at American and United Airlines, 20,000 each." Wall Street jettisoned 43,000 jobs in the financial industry, and Dell Computer had its first-ever layoffs, 5,400. From October, 2000 to '02, the number of Americans left newly jobless reached 2.3 million. By August '02, one million additional workers had lost jobs, and *The Wall Street Journal* reported that the U. S. Bureau of Labor Statistics disclosed in August '02 that 8 million applicants were competing for 3.5 million available jobs: "This time the data suggest that millions couldn't get a job even if they moved, upgraded their skills or took a job they once thought beneath them." Newspapers and business magazines in the opening months of 2004 reported that businesses were "outsourcing" or "off shoring" jobs that could be done via fiber optic cable, especially those in information technology, engineering, basic research, and financial analysis (see *BusinessWeek*, Feb. 3, 2003 and March 1, 2004; see also *The Economist* Feb. 21–27, 2004).

The Congressional Budget Office found that in 2001, adjusted for inflation, the families in the middle of the U.S. income distribution rose from $41,400 in 1979 to $45,100, a 9% increase. Meanwhile the income of families in the top 1% rose from $420,200 to $1.016 million, an increase of 140%. In April, 2002, two research groups, the Economic Policy Institute and the Center on Budget and Policy Priorities, examined household incomes at the peak of each of three income cycles—the late 1970s, late '80s and late '90s—and found that in forty-four states, the gains in the top twenty per cent of households outstripped that of the bottom twenty per cent. In September, 2002, the U. S. Census Bureau reported, according to *The New York Times*, that the "most affluent fifth of the population received half of all household income [in 2001], up from 45 percent in 1985," while "the poorest fifth received 3.5 percent of total household income, down from 4 percent in 1985." The "increases in poverty [in 2001] were concentrated in the suburbs, in the South, and among non-Hispanic whites" (Sept. 25, 2002: A1, A19).

In February, 2002, the *New York Times* reported unprecedented requests by "hard-pressed" middle- and upper-middle income parents for tuition refinancing for their children's college educations. The article quotes a representative of a company which assists colleges and universities with billing: "People are saying that they're being laid off, their stocks are down, and they're looking for ways to pay the bill." A study commissioned by the National Center for Higher Education, supported by the Ford Foundation and the Pew Charitable Trusts, also reported in 2002 that "state spending on higher education and financial aid lagged behind steep rises in tuition," that poor families were spending 25% of their annual income for their children to attend four-year public colleges in 2000, compared with 13% in 1980. Middle-class families' tuitions costs had nearly doubled from 1980, from 4% to about 7%. "For the wealthiest families, there was no increase from the 2% spent in 1980." In January '03, *The Wall Street Journal* reported that "families in record numbers—having maxed out on federal student loans—are turning to private lenders such as Citibank and Sallie Mae to cover tuition payments." Private borrowing, the *Journal* reported, "jumped to about $5 billion in the 2001–02 school year, a 39% increase from the year earlier and up from $1 in 1995–96" (Jan. 8 '03: D1, D3). *The New York Times* reported in the same month that "student borrowers now amass an average of $27,600 in educational debt, more than three and a half times what they compiled a decade ago in unadjusted dollars." The *Times* reported that the percentage of graduating seniors who had taken out education loans had jumped from 46 to 70 in a decade and that "the growing debt has begun to encroach on other major purchases like homes (Jan. 28 '03: 1A). A *Times* editorial of April, 2004, stated, "Faced with soaring tuition and dwindling aid, record numbers of students who would excel at college are no longer applying. If the trend continues, this country could easily return to the time when the poor were locked out of higher education and college was hardly a given for middle-class families ("Week in Review," April 25, 2004: 14).

2. Dubus recounts the sources for *House of Sand and Fog*. According to the online archive of Oprah's Book Club, the characters are based on: 1) a woman whom Dubus had read about in the newspaper, wrongfully evicted from her house and forced to live in her car, and 2) a college friend's father who had been a colonel in the Iranian air force and could only find menial jobs after fleeing to the United States.

3. Warren and Tyagi write, "When we analyzed data from the Department of Housing and Urban Development, we found that among single parents who had purchased a home in the 1980s with a mortgage backed by the Federal Housing Administration (FHA), more than *one in ten* had lost their home by 2002 because of foreclosure" (105). It is noteworthy that Warren and Tyagi address particular loan and credit practices which impact minority citizens, such as sub prime loans (see pp. 136, 147, 149, 159–60).

Chapter Nine

Selling Identities: A Cultural Approach to Race and Identity Politics in the Postmodern Age

Edward Fischer

When asked to write about anthropological approaches to a given topic (be it religion, economics, or, in this case, race), I approach the assignment with trepidation. On the one hand, I believe that my discipline has a lot to offer the study of these subjects and that it is important that our insights enter into academic and public dialogues. On the other hand, as an insider, I am acutely aware of the great diversity in the field of cultural anthropology and the folly of trying to sum it all up in a neat, balanced account. What I offer here, therefore, should be taken as an anthropologist's perspective on race rather than the anthropological perspective on race. For the later (or as close as it comes), the reader is directed to the American Anthropological Association's (1998) "Statement on Race."

My argument is that multiculturalism–that favorite child of liberal sensibilities—can act to hide and even exacerbate the situation of wealth inequality in the United States. This may seem like an odd thing for an anthropologist to argue, and indeed many of my colleagues in the discipline would probably accuse me of sedition. Nonetheless, I will show how identities–racial and otherwise–are produced, sold, and consumed in the current era of globalized capitalism in ways that reinforce long-standing inequalities.

I begin with a brief discussion of anthropological approaches to "race." I then look to the economic context of late twentieth-century capitalism and the ways that identities have been commodified. I then turn to a number of advertising campaigns that portray Native Americans and African-Americans in order to impart to products a patina of authenticity. I conclude by looking at the situation of wealth inequality in the United States and arguing that the multiculturalism found in advertising acts to turn attentions away from pressing material inequalities that plague our society.

ANTHROPOLOGICAL PROBLEMS WITH "RACE"

There is often confusion outside the discipline about just what is anthropology (literally, "the study of humanity"). Anthropology in the United States is divided into four subfields: biological anthropology, archaeology, linguistics, and cultural anthropology. (I am a cultural anthropologist and I focus here on cultural explanations of racial categories.) The man who gave us these four subfields was Franz Boas, generally considered the "father" of modern U.S. anthropology. As a German Jewish immigrant, Boas was quite sensitive to the notions of racial determinism. He refuted the prevailing racist ideas of the time with his conception of cultural relativity—that no culture was superior to another but rather the result of a unique historical trajectory. He argued that it is learned culture, not racial heritage that determines thought and behavior (for a summary of this line of thought, see the essays in Boas 1940). Boas' notion of cultural relativity has become the core concept of anthropology, and has been widely influential throughout the social sciences and humanities.

Anthropology is an interdisciplinary discipline. It seeks to understand the human condition not by focusing on one aspect (psychology, economics, religion) but at the complex interrelations between such domains through a more holistic approach. The academy has, in recent years, caught up with anthropology in this regard. Even as academic fields become increasingly specialized, we have come to realize the value in interdisciplinary approaches, acknowledging that no one field has a monopoly on the truth. Indeed, the present volume is a testament to the value of interdisciplinary studies: striving for a more holistic view by approaching a topic from various angles. This is a very anthropological approach.

In turning to genetics over the last two decades, biological anthropologists have begun to reject the concept of "race." It turns out that genetic variation is greater within populations ("races") than between them. This is to say that, at the genetic level, "race" as a subspecies category of Homo sapiens is virtually meaningless. Such a perspective plays neatly into our modern, Boasian, liberally humanistic understanding of equality: all humans are fundamentally alike. This is the very basis for our understandings of human rights and civil rights.

Granted, racial differences are very visible differences: skin color, facial geometry, body proportions, eye and nose size and shape, and so on. We use these–in conjunction with speech, dress, and other visible markers–to categorize individuals in terms of their culture. They can be handy symbols of origins–biological origins for sure, and to the extent that these overlap cultural origins as well. Yet, we must keep in mind that the phenotypic traits of race are nothing but symbols for a cultural identity, invoking cultural preconceptions that we inscribe onto racialized bodies.

Thus, *race is a particular discourse on identity* but one that cloaks itself in natural, biological associations. Racial categories are the basis of discrimination, but they can also provide the basis for political activism. We must keep in mind that racial categories, like all categories, are too neat to represent real world reality (witness the proliferation of multiple hyphenated identities). Such categories are homogenizing, containing much diversity, and can be confining. Race is a social and cultural category–not biologically meaningful– and the term "race" is commonly used as a code for "culture." It is a meaningful category–it motivates action and so has real world consequences–but it is "real" only to the extent that we agree it is, which is to say that it is a social construction.

LATE CAPITALISM AND CONSUMING IDENTITIES

The scope of anthropology (studying humanity) offers a great deal of intellectual freedom, and in my own work I draw heavily on the tradition of political economy. I look at how culture influences political and economic decisions. I spend most of my time studying the impact of globalization on Maya peoples in Guatemala, but this has led me to examine the workings of capitalism in the United States as well. In this paper I offer some reflections on race in the context of what has been called the "late capitalist" age of American society.

David Harvey (1989) dates the beginning of late capitalism to the launch of the first communications satellites in the early 1970s. Yet, it involves much more than just technological change: the late twentieth century also witnessed a massive social and economic restructuring accelerated during the 1990s after the fall of the Berlin Wall and the triumph of neoliberal capitalism around the world.

A key element of late capitalism is neo-liberalism. In some quarters, a neoliberal belief in the virtues of the free market has become a sort of religion that calls for Adam Smith's invisible hand to work its magic without the meddling interference of the state. Related to this is globalization as empirical reality (not as ideology)—the observable and documentable fact that falling transportation and communication costs and increasingly sophisticated technologies have brought the world virtually closer together. Finally, there is the rise of post-Fordism through the post-industrialist turn in the U.S. and other developed economies: a move to the "knowledge economy" (and the less exalted service economy) in the more developed world, leaving industrial production and assembly for the so-called Third World (the *maquilas* in Mexico and sweatshops in China that fill our insatiable desires for cheap consumer products).

Post-Fordism, like many recent terms, is defined by what it comes after (Fordism). Fordism (a term coined by Antonio Gramsci [1971]) denotes the mass-production model Henry Ford employed to change the automobile industry in the early 1900s–breaking down the assembly process into its smallest components and assigning each to a worker who would do the same repetitive task over and over again. In Marxist terms, this greatly increased worker alienation—alienation not only from their means of production but also from the fruits of their labors.

Great strides in improving the human condition have been made through the efficiencies of Fordist mass production techniques. This is the promise of liberal capitalism: greater efficiencies mean that more people can buy more stuff, raising everyone's standard of living. Indeed, as prices for mass produced products fall because of increased efficiencies, they become within the reach of greater and greater numbers of people down the economic ladder. This happened with sugar in England around the turn of the 19th century: a product at first enjoyed only by aristocracy and wealthy merchants gradually entered the diet (along with tea) of commoners. Then textiles. Then cars. Then all sorts of consumer devices. More stuff for everybody–the dream of free market optimism. And mass produced affluence seemed to buy off the American worker for much of the twentieth century: tract housing for everyone (unless, of course, you were black and wanted to move into a white neighborhood), refrigerators, televisions, and telephones—why overthrow a system that produces such affluence?

In the words of the French philosopher Jean Baudrillard (1998), we ceased to define ourselves through production and began to see ourselves as primarily consumers–and this is a very ephemeral basis for identity. Yet today we are no longer satisfied with mass-produced, white-bread affluence. As a consequence, in this late-capitalist, post-Fordist age, we want to de-alienate our consumption. Despite rising standards of living, we are more alienated than ever–what my colleague Cecelia Tichi calls the culture of "Fortress America"–and even the wealthy yearn to get out of their McMansion fortresses and connect with something more real, more authentic. If we are to define ourselves through what we consume, then we must have great variety–no more of Henry Ford's "any color you want as long as its black" mentality. Corporate America has become very adept at selling us authenticity–which, of courses, ceases to be authentic once it is mass-marketed, and so the cycle of "innovation" (usually in style more than substance) has accelerated to breakneck pace. We have an insatiable appetite for the authentic, but, of course, the paradox is that as soon as we begin to consume something "authentic" it ceases to be authentic.

Actually, it is unclear if we really want the "real thing" (unless it is a comfortably familiar Coca-Cola)—we often prefer a sanitized, sterilized version

(see Žižek 2000; Dougherty 1969). We create simulacra (copies with no originals) by imaging an idyllic past for ourselves and we try to replicate that
imagined past in an illusory present in which we live and believe to be real.
We want to go to neighborhood coffee shops–but rather than chance dirty
bathrooms or stale coffee we opt for a sanitized Starbucks, a coffee shop that
tries to recreate the neighborhood hangouts of New Orleans, San Francisco,
and Seattle with its calculated hipness, but also with the comfortable, conservative consistency of a big corporate brand. We build gated communities in
the style called "New Urbanism", trying to reengineer "community" (almost
half of all new house constructions in California are in some sort of gated
community.) We buy retro automobiles like the PT Cruiser and the new Thun-
derbird and the MiniCooper (now made by BMW) and the new Beetle. On
television we see a deep nostalgia for the 1950s and the comfortably less
ironic and un-subversive family and social structures. But, of course, we
imagine the past as more idyllic than it was. We should not need Trent Lott to
remind us that all was not hunky dory in the 1950s and before.

SELLING IDENTITIES

How, then, does the move toward consumptive identities affect our understandings of "race"? Racial and ethnic identities, in the late capitalist context,
become commodfied, reduced to an image that can be manipulated and
bought and sold. Paul Gilroy (2000:249) notes that "the fruits of alterity have
acquired an immediate value even where the company of the people who har-
vested them is not itself desired." Through multicultural advertising and multicultural consumption we create false (seemingly anthropological) identifi-
cations with an Other. These make us feel good about ourselves. Our
cosmopolitan multicultural sensibilities force our gaze away from the very
real material inequalities that plague our society. Advertisers consciously play
on these self-perceptions.

Those of a certain age probably remember the famous "Crying Indian" television advertisement produced by Keep America Beautiful and shown for a
number of years in the mid 1970s (see Elliot 1998). In it, we see a native
American man dressed in buckskins and a feather in his hair, set off in his
leather canoe. As he paddles unhurriedly across the water he passes floating
trash, a plant with smokestacks billowing out fumes, and he winds up alongside a road where a passing car throws out a fast food bag. The camera zooms
in close to his face and a single tear can be seen streaking his cheek.

This sums up a common romanticized view of Native Americans in which
all indigenous peoples live in harmony with their environment, with Mother

Earth. In a way this is empowering for Indians–they are not brutish savages, the enemies of the good cowboys, but noble savages who have important lessons to teach us today. And we are able to demonstrate our openness and sensitivity by gladly and masochistically consuming an Indian's message, telling us what we want to hear: the oppressed Indian telling us how bad we are. While such representations are infinitely better than the Tonto character of the Lone Ranger series, they are confining in other ways, setting up a romanticized vision of what Indians should be.

Consider the American Indian College Fund's marketing campaign of the late 1990s–misty, sepia toned prints of young Native Americans that appeared in *The Atlantic, Harper's, The New York Times Magazine*, and other such media outlets. These images overtly play to romanticized and wistful views of noble savages (whom we call Native Americans to highlight their stoic authenticity and our multicultural sensitivity). As the ads make clear, these are not professional models or actors, but *real* Indians, a fact that burnishes the patina of authenticity. They are shown in various states of traditional dress (or undress) in idealized traditional tableaus (such as bathing with a horse). These representations play to our notions about what modern Indians should be like. But the story does not end there: these young Native Americans want to go to college, to better themselves, to live out their own vernaculars of the American Dream. They are ideal poster children for a campaign that plays to the guilt and to the fantasies of an affluent liberal class. To add yet another layer of empirical and ethical complexity: these are self-representations. The American Indian College Fund is run by Indians. In this light they represent the agency and intentionality of native peoples and their savvy adoption of identity politics. In a more sinister way, however, such representations also reflect the sort of "discipline" that Michel Foucault (1977) writes about: the internalization of categories and stereotypes imposed through hegemonic power masquerading as liberal multiculturalism.

We find a similar situation with many rap musicians—selling authenticity in a winner-take-all market so that a handful get super-rich while the vast majority, who live the urban, inner-city life glamorized by the stars, get left behind.

In 2003, Dr. Pepper unveiled a new ad campaign, "Be You" (PR Newswire 2002). The irony is apparent: "Be You" by buying a product of a multinational conglomerate (Dr. Pepper is produced by Dr.Pepper/7-Up, Inc., a subsidiary of London-based Cadbury Schweppes, LLP). But beyond this glaring paradox, there are many cultural messages to be gleaned from this campaign. The ads consist of various celebrities looking back to their inspirational *originals*. In the most popular segment, LL Cool Jay pays tribute to Run DMC as pioneers of rap. Young and Rubican, the advertising agency that developed the campaign (and a subsidiary of London-based WPP Group, the world's largest ad firm) wanted the ads to stress "originality, individuality, and creativity."

The stress on authenticity and originality is revealing—this is not Coke, this is Dr. Pepper, more original, more authentic, more in touch with gritty inner-city life. So we have two London-based multinational conglomerates conspiring with African-American rap stars to make their product appear more authentic, more singular (Kopytoff 1986) in order to sell that product to their target audience, which is not so much African-American rappers, but white under-35s. Adding a whole other tragically fortuitous layer of authenticity is the fact that Run DMC member Jam Master J was shot dead at his studio in October 2002 (Newman 2002), and this advertisement was his last taped performance—what better way to prove the links to a romanticized "gangsta" lifestyle.

But Coke does not want Dr. Pepper to steal all of this gritty, inner-city authenticity. Its subsequent campaign was called "Real" (Day and Eliott 2003), and in one spot the socially-conscience rapper Common storms out of a meeting in which a corporate suit proposes a Common action figure—his rapped response "the real cannot be bought or sold, taught or told / the boy tried to keep it but he lost his soul" (Coca Cola 2003). "Common and what he stands for aren't for sale" is the message that presumably seeks to say the same thing about Coke–but of course Coke is for sale. Yet, somehow, through the alchemy of marketing, it is the "real thing" (Leith 2003). "Coke is it"—but really it is not "it" precisely because it is as empty as all of the other products, from cosmetics to cars, that seek to sell us self-identity and self-worth as well as more clear-cut utilities. The insidious fact of capitalism is that it is a treadmill, the end is never reached. Marx recognized this when he noted the switch from use values to exchange values. As Žižek (2000: 21–23) points out, the slogan "Coke is it" is appealing because it is contradictory: Coke is never simply 'it' "precisely insofar as every satisfaction opens up a gap of 'I want More!'"

The Coke brand Sprite has taken this concern even further. In a series of ads that ran in 2001–2002, titled "Voices of the Street" (Parpis 2001), people give seemingly impromptu raps about the dangers of being fake. The ads are shot in a calculated, informal, almost amateurish style. They seem like one-take shots. One ad features a young woman dubbed Crystal who raps to an erstwhile boyfriend, "you might fool others but you ain't foolin' me," exhorting viewers to "see through it" (Coca Cola 2001) There is no product identification until the very end, when the "Obey your thirst" tagline appears onscreen. Image is nothing, taste is everything.

Nike, too has hopped on the authenticity bandwagon. Notably, a number of their recent ads have featured street ball players (Elliott 2001). These are not big stars getting paid millions to sell a product, just some guys playing basketball. The products are not conspicuously highlighted. They do not need to be, as Nike is selling an idea as much as a material object. Such slick marketing hides the exploitative labor that goes into producing Nike shoes–the factories and sweatshops of young women in Taiwan working for $2 a day and often enduring sexual harassment of a sort that is off-the-scales by U.S. standards (Kristof and WuDunn 2000). Even the quality of the shoe, the objective reasons we should want to buy it–quality and price–are ignored. They are selling an image, but it is an image that pretends to not be an image: Just some young black men, living in a big city, going out to shoot hoops because they love it.

One of Nike's most successful ad campaigns ("Freestyle") interspersed NBA and WNBA stars with street ball players and their fancy, more authentic moves, and an infectious beat provided by hip-hop grandfather Afrika Bambaataa and Steven "Boogie" Brown using the sounds of ball bounces, squeaks, and grunts (Nike 2001). Like the American Indian College Fund ads, the Freestyle spot tames (in a Foucauldian sense, disciplines) the Otherness (and authenticity) of street ball players, making this exotic cultural form palatable to white, mainstream American culture and allowing it to be co-opted to sell overpriced shoes.

The problem in analyzing much contemporary advertising is that one is never quite sure when irony is being invoked. Clifford Geertz (1973) once noted that anthropologists are supposed to tell winks from twitches. But with these ads, one can never be sure what are self-parodying, ironic winks to the viewer and what are grotesque twitches of a capitalist system trying to sell its products.

Frantz Fanon (1963) argues that the oppressed must identify an oppressive archetype in order to overcome histories of suppression. This is to say, that consciousness must be raised before a revolution is possible. But, what of the current situation in which the oppressive archetype is composed of iconic elements of the oppressed culture? *This* is where cultural, political, and economic hegemony can work most efficiently: effectively blocking opposition by adopting it. A little multicultural advertising and consumption inoculates us against wider, more revolutionary changes. It allows the insidious distancing in the form of appearing to commune with an Other: of course I'm concerned, I always buy Free Trade coffee; how could we possibly be racist, our kids only listen to rap music. In fetishizing aspects of African-American culture we come, as Marx would have predicted, to overvalue the object while divorcing it from the person who produced it.

RACE AND WEALTH INEQUALITIES

The boom of the 1990s saw the creation of much new wealth, but it was highly unevenly distributed. It is revealing to look at trends in income between 1950 and 1980 compared with those from 1980–2001 (see Ginsburg 2003). In the earlier period we find a situation of highly equitable income growth–that age of industry, cars and steel, unions and large corporations with an ethos of long-term stability. But over the last twenty years, income growth has been highly inequitable, with the poorest quintile's income growing by only 7.5% as compared to the top 5%'s 96.8% increase. Broken down by racial variables, the situation looks encouraging for black households, although their incomes still lag far behind those of whites. The median income for black families in 2001 was 38% below white family income and Hispanic income was 36% below white income.

In late capitalism the material bases of the economy have been subsumed to culture. There is an increasing investment in fictitious capital as opposed to real, or productive, capital (see Friedman 1994). Original art is the classic example of fictitious capital: a painting might increase in value, but this value is not based on any sort of material utility.

In 2000, 1.9% of the United Sates' Gross Domestic Product (GDP) was spent on entertainment and another 1.1% on printing and publishing (a total of 3% of GDP); in contrast agriculture accounts for 1.4% of GDP and automobiles for 1.2% (see Nichols 2003). The U.S.'s largest export sector is entertainment. Now, we may receive a great deal of utility (that slippery economic term that seeks to encompass so much cultural stuff) from entertainment–and arguably such compressed leisure time makes us more productive (and this is an irony of late capitalist affluence–we do not have more leisure time). But, this is not the Wealth of Nations that Adam Smith envisioned; it is rather built on Marx's fictitious capital (See Friedman 1994): Adam Smith envisioned that production efficiencies would lower prices and increase the material standard of living for everybody: sewing machines make clothes assembly quicker and so more people can afford to buy clothes. Contrast this with Nike, whose business model is not really built on technological innovations–although this does play a role, and was important in the companies early rise with the pump and other technological advances–but on marketing that is image creation and maintenance.

Thorsten Veblen (1899), that scholar of the first gilded age, who gave us such terminology as "conspicuous consumption" and what is known as the "Veblen effect" (where a price increase results in higher demand, in contrast to the expectations of classic supply and demand but perfectly in line with an ethos that values conspicuous consumption as a way of validating social role), has been largely dismissed by a generation of economists for placing moral values on consumer choices. It goes again to the free-market dogma of letting the invisible hand do its work–who are we to decide what is a good utility versus a bad utility? But, of course, we do already make these valuations–the utility of a $20 rock of crack cocaine is not the same as a $20 pair of shoes. We do make societal valuations of what is good and what is bad.

Consumer culture–the predominance of fictive forms of capital–turns our attention (with its opiate qualities) and resources away from pressing material inequalities in our society. Rather than rewarding companies for coming up with clever marketing campaigns, why not reward them for developing ecologically sound industrial agriculture, why not invest in affordable housing, and education?

CONCLUSION

Anthropologists have traditionally sought to explain how culture influences human behavior. In recent years, anthropologists have focused on how culture is constructed, represented, and increasingly commodified. While popular advertisements are not the usual subject of anthropological analysis, I have shown how they illustrate and manipulate changing cultural conceptions of race. Large corporations seek out the authenticity of racialized experience to burnish the aura of their mass produced products. This allows geographically and socially distant consumers to imagine a communion with an Other that stymies the need for more radical contact.

I have argued that cultural aspects of "late capitalism" exacerbate wealth differences in the United States. Late capitalism is marked by increasing investment in "fictitious" capital. On the surface fictitious capital looks and acts like "real" (or productive) capital: investment produces returns, money begets new money. And yet fictitious capital is more ephemeral than real capital: it is made up of ideas, symbols, art, and culture rather than new machinery or factories or other material inputs. This new sort of capital investment tends to reinforce class and racial stratification in a much more subtle and yet much more effective way than the old pillage and plunder sort of capitalist expansion. Our multiculturalism seeks to manage Otherness to create understandable, manipulable sort of hybridities that subverts the very progressive intentions of the concept.

REFERENCES

American Anthropological Association. 1998. Statement on "Race". http://www.aaa net.org/stmts/racepp.htm
Baudrillard, Jean. 1998. *The consumer society: Myths and structures*. London: Sage.
Boas, Franz. 1940. *Race, language and culture*. New York: Macmillan.
Coca-Cola Company. 2001. "See Through It." Television advertisement. Produced by Lowe, Lintas & Partners.

———. 2003. "Real Music." Television advertisement. Produced by Burrell Communications Group, directed by Malik Hassan Sayeed.

Day, Sherri and Stuart Elliot. 2003. "Advertising: Coca-Cola goes back to its 'Real' past in an effort to find some new fizz for its Classic brand." *The New York Times*, 10 January 10, p. C4.

Dougherty, Philip H. 1969. "Getting 'Real Thing' for Coke." *The New York Times*, 17 November, p. 77.

Elliot, Stuart. 1998. "Advertising: An environmental campaign is 'Back by popular neglect." *The New York Times*, 22 April p. D6.

———. 2001. "The Media Business: Advertising; Nike Makes a Commercial that Resembles a Music Video, and Hopes it is Viewed as such." *The New York Times*, 10 April 10, p. C8.

Fanon, Frantz. 1963. *The wretched of the earth*. New York: Grove.

Foucault, Michel. 1977. *Discipline and Punish: The Birth of the Prison*. New York: Pantheon Books.

Friedman, Jonathan. 1994. *Cultural identity and global process*. London: Sage Publications.

Geertz, Clifford. 1973. *The interpretation of cultures*. New York: Basic Books.

Ginsburg, Woodrow L. 2003. *Income inequality and poverty*. Washington: Americans for Democratic Action.

Gramsci, Antonio. 1971. *Selections from the Prison Notebooks of Antonio Gramsci*. Quintin Hoare and Geoffrey Nowell Smith, ed. and trans. New York: International Publishers.

Harvey, David. 1989. *The condition of post modernity*. Oxford: Basil Blackwell.

Kopytoff, Igor. 1986. The cultural biography of things: commoditization as process. In *The social life of things: Commodities in cultural perspective*, Arjun Appadurai (ed.). Cambridge: Cambridge University Press, pp. 64–91.

Kristof, Nicholas and Sheryl WuDunn. 2000. "Two Cheers for Sweatshops." *The New York Times*, 24 September, p. SM170.

Leith, Scott. 2003. "Coca-Cola to launch new ad campaign." *The Atlanta-Journal-Constitution*, 9 January, p. E1.

Newman, Andy. 2002. "D.J. for Rap's Run DMC is shot to Death in Queens." *The New York Times*, 31 October, p. B1.

Nichols, Bonnie. 2003. *The arts in the GDP*. Washington: The Nancy Hanks Center.

Nike, Inc. 2001. "Freestyle." Television advertisement. Produced by Wieden & Kennedy, directed by Paul Hunter.

Parpis, Eletheria. 2001. "Teen Voices." *Adweek* 42(12): 16.

PR Newswire. 2002. "Popular Dr. Pepper 'Be You' Ad Campaign Hits Second-Year Stride in 2003." *PR Newswire*, 30 December, p.1.

Veblen, Thorstein. 1899. *The theory of the leisure class : An economic study of institutions*. New York: Macmillan.

Žižek, Slavoj. 2000. *The fragile absolute—Or, why is the Christian legacy worth fighting for?* London: Verso.

Chapter Ten

The "Currency" and "Purchase"
of Literary Criticism

Dennis D. Kezar

Friedrich Engels famously claimed that he had learned more about post-revolutionary French society from Balzac than from "all the professed historians, economists, and statisticians of the period together." While appreciative of his interdisciplinary generosity, I do not share Engels' absolute confidence in literature's socially revelatory analytical powers. Nor do I think literary critics can make literature socially revelatory without borrowing liberally and opportunistically from "historians, economists, and statisticians." Nevertheless I will make certain claims about the analytically specific and special offerings of literary analysis to a volume such as this one. And they will be claims in which disciplinary pride is balanced by coextensive admissions that what makes literary studies special also makes it/them deeply limited.

This is not a chapter on *Race and Financial Disparity*, in other words, but a chapter on what literary criticism can and cannot do with analytical categories such as "race" and "financial disparity"; and it is a chapter addressing a readership imagined as interdisciplinary but also as comprised of professionals in identifiably different academic fields. What do we (literary critics) do that distinguishes US from YOU? The question is complicated by the fact that English departments have proven themselves increasingly appropriative and accommodating of other disciplines, and by the fact that many other disciplines are happy to return the mutually beneficial if not sustainable favor. And it's a question complicated by the rubric of this volume: literary critics, traditional inhabitants of English departments, were among the first in the humanities to assimilate economic analysis (or at least some form of Marxism or its free market reactions) to their critical practice; and literary critics have been just as attuned to critical and professional opportunities afforded by race and culture. But, it will be my contention in the pages that follow, literary critics—insofar as WE are literary critics and not something else—mean something very different by categories such as "race" and "financial disparity" than YOU do (insofar as you are something other than a literary critic).

For literary critics, categories such as "race" and "wealth" exist first and foremost as tropes, as rhetorically interesting and rhetorically useful and viable objects of analysis. For literary critics, there is nothing *real* that is ontologically anterior to the rhetorical conception of such categories, because for us literature is not only the site of reality's constitution but also the substance. I make this claim not only as a professor of Renaissance English literature, but also—much more generically and offensively—for all professors of literature and its criticism. And I do so expecting that many of my colleagues would disagree with this claim and even condemn it—because one might conclude from this claim that I mean literary criticism is radically insincere and socially irrelevant; or because one might conclude from this claim that literary criticism has been inaccurately conflated with literature as such.

I do not intend such conclusions by the above claim. I do not doubt that literary critics can be just as committed to the understanding of race and financial disparity as any other profession; I argue simply that literary criticism is not the way to understand such topics. Accordingly, I want us all to acknowledge the limits of literary criticism, in the realm of interdisciplinary study of the social realm, before we proceed toward my slightly positivist claims for the discipline. Those limits can be quickly established. Literary criticism has no language of "the real" that is comprehensible to any of you anywhere else on the spectrum determined by interdisciplinary inquiry. "The real," "the *ding an sich*," "things," "the body," "technology," "science," all these terms are tropes we use to invoke interdisciplinary relevance while we—sometimes surreptitiously—go about our disciplinary business. The same is true of terms like "race" and "economics."

Literary criticism, along with its invocation of literary theory, continues not to have very much of a problem being relevant in a limited and shifting sense. Let me give an example that will, I hope, eventually make sense to those of you in other disciplines. It is an example having to do with literary criticism's perennial problem with the relationship between *relevance* (defined as the capacity to sell an idea in whatever marketplace one chooses to inhabit) and *reference* (defined as one's capacity to invoke the real, the tangible, the direct object, the other, that to which all words refer, and so on). In 1979, Paul de Man (an important guide for several generations of literary critics and theorists) described the general direction of the literary-critical *zeitgeist* in oppositional terms that today's literary critics can only read as synonyms:

> We may no longer be hearing too much about relevance, but we keep hearing a great deal about reference.

In the year before the publication of a very important book in my own field and in literary criticism more broadly (Stephen Greenblatt's *Renaissance Self-Fashioning*), "relevance" meant *the value of "intrinsic literary form,"* and "reference" meant (at least to de Man) an extrinsic interest in *a "nonverbal 'outside.'"*[1] Arguably the huge institutional success of Greenblatt's program (sometimes called "new historicism," sometimes "cultural materialism") reversed de Man's hierarchy by replacing his relevance with his reference—by making the socially real the arbiter of analytical effectiveness.

There is a long history leading up to the limited success of literary criticism's "new historicism" and "cultural materialism" that extends even to their offshoots ("queer theory," "postcolonial theory," "race theory," and so on). To oversimplify radically but fairly the received genealogy that has brought us to our current state of the critical art: a group of "New Critics" once celebrated literary form (de Man's "relevance") as a kind of objective science while at the same time injecting their critical work with what in retrospect appears a conservative agenda celebrating received canons and received authors; this cloying *formalism* eventually produced a reaction in which the text was understood as instead a *ding an sich*, composed of various articles and strands of deterministic language (thus the *deconstruction* propounded by de Man was born); after deconstruction, however, the search for relevance (as de Man's passage suggests) quickly ramified from the text to the surrounding context—culture, things, and so on.

This theoretical trend would seem to position the discipline of literary criticism (as distinguished from *interdisciplined* literary criticism) right in the path of a volume such as ours. But if you look carefully at the critical products of this trend—a trend increasingly moving analysis toward the material and allegedly toward the socially real—you will see that this is not the case. Let me give as an example a book that is at present hugely successful in the discipline of literary criticism, Bill Brown's *A Sense of Things: The Object Matter of American Literature* (2003). This book, which I very much admire, does not so much depart from the stated goals of new historicism/cultural materialism. It attempts to *actualize* them even more:

> However much I shared the new historicist 'desire to make contact with the 'real," I wanted the end result to read like a grittier, materialist phenomenology of everyday life, a result that might somehow arrest language's wish, as described by Michel Serres, that the 'whole world . . . derive from language.'[2]

But as some critical readers of Brown's book have noted, his critical attempt to make literature more real—more material, gritty, and thus more relevant—is troubled by the fact that Marxism (at least for the current state of the art in literary criticism) no longer has any analytical purchase (nor does Francis

Fukuyama, I would add as consolation). For Brown, there is no "economy of the real" beyond metaphor. This is why his only reading of Marx has to do with that strange moment in *Capital* when a table stands on its head; this is why his book never mentions the institution of slavery (despite the fact that the book focuses upon late nineteenth-century American literature), other than to note Mark Twain's comfortably metaphoric complaint that his thing-filled home had subjected him and his wife to a life of "house-keeping slavery."[3]

Let me provide another, more detailed example of literary criticism's analytical difficulty with the category of the real. Elaine Scarry's fascinating and occasionally mystifying essay, "The Made Up and the Made Real," appears in a collection that, had we enough time and space, I would reproduce here. That collection is *Fieldwork: Sites in Literary and Cultural Studies*, and is edited by Marjorie Garber (once a Renaissance literary scholar and now a broader "cultural critic"), and two former graduate students.[4] There is something brief but useful to say about the context in which Scarry's essay appears. Note the volume's title and its apparent appeal to anthropology (and indeed anthropology is economically represented in the collection: two of its contributors are the real deal [Michael Herzfeld and Mary Steedly]). But the main title ultimately bows to the more accurate subtitle: of the remaining twenty-nine authors (most of the essays are quite brief), nineteen are professors of English, African-American, and/or Comparative Literature; four are professors of languages not anglophone; three are professors of Art History; two are professors of Law; and one is a political scientist.

Let me italicize Scarry's two central claims, and emphasize their departure from most of the interdisciplinary claims one finds in the law-lit movement and indeed in the broader world of cultural studies:

> *"The recognition of the kinship between the once solitary realm of art and the capacious realm of artifacts has not worked to the advantage of either."*

The logic of interdisciplinarity almost invariably requires that one or more disciplines realize "advantage" as a result.

> *"The difference between art objects and other objects can . . . be understood as follows: both undergo creation, but almost all artifacts other than art undergo a second stage of creation to which art is never subject. . . . In the overtness of its fictionality (rather than its fictionality), art is exceptional."*

Whereas most, if not all, interdisciplinary endeavours involving the humanities claim or assume an ontological and epistemological equivalence between *the apparently real* (science, law, economics), and *the overtly fictional* (music, sculpture, literature), Scarry argues that such equivalence is a mistake—for the very fact that the arts announce their fictionality while the sciences seek to hide it.

It should be plain that Scarry's thesis, if tenable, poses certain limitations on a literary analysis devoted to the concerns of this volume. "Race" and "wealth," like her examples of made things invested in naturalizing their construction (nation-states, quarks, fire, the body, gender), would seem to be on some important level more *real* than *The Merchant of Venice* or *Their Eyes Were Watching God*, if we look at these texts for race/wealth revelations. We could of course blur this difference with a "contextual" analysis of both texts — paying attention, perhaps, to the socio-economic status of 16th century Venetian Jews, or to the marketing and publication history of Hurston's novel. But would we, in such cases, be operating as literary critics? Not, Scarry would say, as long as we failed to acknowledge the barrier art builds between itself and the "real world"; and not as long as we imperturbably conducted our analysis as though both interpretive realms could be made — through the voodoo of interdisciplinarity — entirely equivalent or commensurate.

But Scarry's thesis also points us, perhaps inadvertently, to certain strengths offered by literary analysis to a study of race and wealth. The analysis of overt fictionality, for instance, can direct scholars in other disciplines (let us call them scholars of covert fictionality) to some of the phenomenon of fiction, and to some of the strategies by which fiction can be hidden. While of course Scarry is sensible to say that not all fictions can be profitably exposed, one can certainly imagine wishing to do so in important cases. Overt fictionality therefore provides a model of skepticism and analysis for those disciplines interested in discovering the relevant constructedness of their own objects of study. The analysis of overt fiction can also provide a vocabulary through which covert fiction can be described. And Scarry's wide-brushed line between overt and covert fictionality should suggest to us, perhaps most importantly, that neither kind of fiction (and therefore neither disciplinary genre) exists in an absolutely pure state: no art announces itself as only art, and no "fact" exists without a certain liability to fiction (just as no sunset can't be painted).

In literary study, recent critical modes have made increasingly bold claims for the continuities between literary language and "the real world" of physical and social consequence (speech-act theory, cultural studies), and for a chiastically implicated relation between text and real world context (New Historicism). While Scarry's warning about the mutual disadvantage of this recognized "kinship" between "the once solitary realm of art" and "the capacious realm of artifacts" is bracing, her larger claims about the peculiarity of art direct us to the usefulness — for other disciplines — of its critical vocabulary and method.

As both a defense of Scarry's central thesis and an example of some of the pressures it faces from today's established literary-critical practice, I quote excerpts from Henry Louis Gates' *The Signifying Monkey: A Theory of African-American Literary Criticism.*[5] In the following passages, Gates would seem to read *Their Eyes Were Watching God* as only a literary critic can. His claims about personhood and identity, for instance, arise from his (sometimes quite technical) analysis of text and the construction of voice; his claims for the social consequence of Hurston's novel arise from an awareness of canon formation; the "real world" of his reading is not the world of Hurston, so much as the world of her characters.

With Scarry's distinction between the literary "made-up" and the socially "made-real" in mind, let us consider some of the larger claims Gates makes for the text:

> Zora Neale Hurston is the first writer that our generation of black and feminist critics has brought into the canon, or perhaps I should say the canons. For Hurston is now a cardinal figure in the Afro-American canon, the feminist canon, and the canon of American fiction, especially as our readings of her work become increasingly close readings, which Hurston's texts sustain delightfully. The curious aspect of the widespread critical attention being shown to Hurston's texts is that so many critics embracing such a diversity of theoretical approaches seem to find something new at which to marvel in her texts.
>
> My own method of reading *Their Eyes Were Watching God* stems fundamentally from the debates over modes of representation, over theories of mimesis, which as I have suggested form such a crucial part of the history of Afro-American literature and its theory. Mimetic principles can be both implicitly and explicitly ideological, and the explication of Hurston's rhetorical strategy, which I shall attempt below, is no exception. I wish to read *Their Eyes* in such a way as to move from the broadest notion of *what* it thematizes through an ever-tighter spiral of *how* it thematizes, that is, its rhetorical strategies. I shall attempt to show that Hurston's text not only cleared a rhetorical space for the narrative strategies that Ralph Ellison would render so deftly in *Invisible Man*, but also that Hurston's text is the first example in our tradition of "the speakerly text," by which I mean a text whose rhetorical strategy is designed to represent an oral literary tradition, designed 'to emulate the phonetic, grammatical, and lexical patterns of actual speech and produce the 'illusion of oral narration.' The speakerly text is that text in which all other structural elements seem to be devalued, as important as they remain to the telling of the tale, because the narrative strategy signals attention to its own importance, an importance which would seem to be the privileging of oral speech and its inherent linguistic features. Whereas Toomer's *Cane* draws upon the black oral voice essentially as a different voice from the narrator's, as a repository of socially distinct, contrapuntal meanings and beliefs, a speakerly text would seem primarily to be oriented toward imitating one of the numerous forms of oral narration to be found in classical Afro-American vernacular literature. [p. 180–181]

There are of course *real* social claims subtending these passages (not just the claims for canon formation but also the teleological claim that Hurston has effectively created rhetorical opportunities for other writers working in her tradition). But Gates' analytical energy, as he notes, is not "thematic" (concerned with what is being said in the text) so much as mechanical (concerned with how its effects are achieved). And the terms of his formal analysis would seem to match up fairly well with Scarry's: Hurston's "speakerly text" is allegedly unique because, by focusing so much on the mimesis of orality, it hides more conventional narrative structures (rendering their fictions more covert). In other words, Hurston's novel achieves something like the "made-real" by obscuring many of the devices by which stories are told, though its mimesis of orality can never be more than a self-announcing "illusion."

That literature can approximate the "made-real" through formal and cultural analysis is at the heart of Gates' reading of Hurston's own theory of African-American literature. In a remarkable passage, Gates repeats with approval Hurston's equivalence of such literature with money:

> Hurston is one of the few authors in our tradition who both theorized about her narrative process and defended it against the severe critiques of contemporaries such as Wright. Hurston's theory allows us to read Their Eyes through her own terms of critical order. It is useful to recount her theory of black oral narration, if only in summary, and then to use this to explicate the various rhetorical strategies that, collectively, comprise the narrative strategy of Their Eyes Were Watching God. Hurston seems to be not only the first scholar to have defined the trope of Signifyin(g) but also the first to represent the ritual itself. Hurston represents a Signifyin(g) ritual in Mules and Men, then glosses the word signify as a means of "showing off," rhetorically. The exchange is an appropriate one to repeat, because it demonstrates that women most certainly can, and do, signify upon men, and because it prefigures the scene of Signification in Their Eyes that proves to be a verbal sign of such importance to Janie's quest for consciousness:

> 'Talkin' bout dogs,' put in Gene Oliver, 'they got plenty sense. Nobody can't fool dogs much.'
>   'And speakin' 'bout hams,' cut in Big Sweet meaningly, 'if Joe Willard don't stay out of dat bunk he was in last night, Ah'm gonter springle some salt down his back and sugar-cure his hams.'
>   Joe snatched his pole out of the water with a jerk and glared at Big Sweet, who stood sidewise looking at him most pointedly.
>   'Aw, woman, quit tryin' to signify.'
>   'Ah kin signify all Ah please, Mr. Nappy-Chin, so long as Ah know what Ah'm talkin' about.'

> This is a classic Signification, an exchange of meaning and intention of some urgency between two lovers.

I use the word *exchange* here to echo Hurston's use in her essay, "Characteristics of Negro Expression." In this essay Hurston argues that 'language is like money,' and its development can be equated metaphorically with the development in the market place of the means of exchange from bartered 'actual goods,' which 'evolve into coin' (coins symbolizing wealth). Coins evolve into legal tender, and legal tender evolves into 'cheques for certain usages.' Hurston's illustrations are especially instructive. People 'with highly developed languages,' she writes, 'have words for detached ideas. That is legal tender.' The linguistic equivalent of legal tender consists of words such as 'chair,' which comes to stand for 'that-which-we-squat-on.' 'Groan-causers' evolves into 'spear,' and so on. 'Cheque words' include those such as 'ideation' and 'pleonastic.' *Paradise Lost* and *Sartor Resartus*, she continues, 'are written in cheque words!' But 'the primitive man,' she argues, eschews legal tender and cheque specifically, she concludes, black expression turns upon both the 'interpretation of the English language words; he 'exchanges descriptive words,' describing 'one act . . . in terms of another.' More in terms of pictures' and the supplement of what she calls 'action words,' such as 'chop-axe,' 'sitting-chair,' and 'cook pot.' It is the supplement of action, she maintains, which underscores her use of the word 'exchange.' [pp. 196–197]

"Language is like money." We would seem to be very close here to the rubric of this volume and its analytical advertisements of social relevance, the real, the meeting of rubber and road. But I wish to digress once more—and one final time—in order to establish my thesis: that literary analysis must always digress and substitute when confronted with such a rubric. I want to suggest one other, major limitation that confronts literary criticism in its attempts to analyze something like the relation between race and financial disparity. That limitation arises from *our* disciplinary difficulty in analyzing material causality, and this difficulty arises from our habituated need for materialist and historicist criticism.

Our last twenty years, as literary critics, have been ruled by a conflicted post-Marxian moment in which material causality (the idea that money and things and clothes really make culture happen) is viewed with what I would call practical skepticism (a skepticism produced by the fact that our analytical training cannot prove or disprove the efficacy of material objects). At the same time, our last twenty years have celebrated things and *the real* (race and money have certainly been included in this celebration) as metaphorically engaging tropes. To distort Gates, money for us has always been language, and language has always been our analytical money. There are signs, such as that evinced by Brown, that we may be turning more directly toward the real and toward a more responsible analysis of how things really participate in a world of social causality. If people like Greenblatt have obscured this line of analysis for the last twenty years—dismissing the analytical habits of a Frederic

Jameson (an unreconstructed Marxist-materialist critic)—perhaps even people like Greenblatt are realizing the limits of this approach. This is at least suggested by a recent overview of Greenblatt's development:

> In "Towards a Poetics of Culture" Stephen Greenblatt criticized [Frederic] Jameson's reductiveness [ascriptions of cultural phenomena to material causes], and in Marvelous Possessions he referred to "wonder" as an element situated partly in economies that nonetheless "seems to resist recuperation." Yet in Practicing New Historicism, cowritten recently with Catherine Gallagher, he modified these claims and echoed Jameson's statement about sequences, saying we now need "a wholly integrated and sequential account of causes and effects."

But if these are signs of a broader trend in literary criticism, they are also signs of literary criticism's lack of a coherent disciplinary identity, and signs of its analytical poverty in an increasingly interdisciplined academy. Our future relevance may only lie in becoming more like the social sciences.

This conclusion might sound depressing for my discipline, and frustrating to those in my discipline committed to the idea that their work can do something real and effective with subject matter such as race and wealth. Nevertheless the above critique could be applied to most of the prominent works, from my profession, that attempt to deal with such subject matter (Eric Lott's acclaimed *Love and Theft* and Walter Benn Michaels' magisterial *The Gold Standard* come to mind).[6] But a depressing and quietist note is not quite the sound on which I wish to end. We who profess English literature (or the literature of the third world, or the literature of the Americas), can do something better than other professions. We can pay attention to literary (as opposed to legal) language, even if we conceive that language *only* as rhetoric, and can argue that that language does have social consequences. If proof of this claim is required of a skeptic, we can point (if we can point to nothing else) to the existence and even prominence of English departments in today's academy. And we can point to our class enrollments. I realize that this is not an entirely satisfying proof, but it does indicate at least an institutional faith in the teaching of literature's capacity to change behavior and thought. There is no necessary reason why we could not some day analyze a topic such as race and wealth with the same efficacy as you do—other than the fact that we simply treat language differently than you do. And when we try to treat language as you do, we are relinquishing our professional identity. Resistance to this relinquishment is everywhere apparent in our critical practice and theoretical difficulties. But in the teaching of literature that matters to us, and in the persuasion of our students that it should matter to them, we occupy a position that permits the practice of concerns such as that implicit in the title of this volume. The gap between that potential practice and the inarticulate consciousness of my profession has been my concern in the preceding pages.

NOTES

1. This and the previous citation appear in Paul de Man, *Allegories of Reading: Figural Language in Rousseau, Nietzsche, Rilke, and Proust* (New Haven: Yale University Press, 1979), 3.

2. Bill Brown, *A Sense of Things: The Idea of Things and the Ideas in Them* (Chicago: University of Chicago Press, 2003), 3. Here Brown cites Michel Serres, *Statues* (Paris: Francois Bourin, 1987), 111.

3. See Brown, 24, and 21–43.

4. Those former students are Rebecca Walkowitz and Paul Franklin. The volume was published by Routledge in 1996. Elaine Scarry, "The Made-Up and the Made-Real" in *Field Work: Sites of Literary and Cultural Studies*, Eds. Marjorie Garber, Paul Franklin, and Rebecca Walkowitz (Routledge: New York and London, 1996) p. 214–224.

5. New York: Oxford University Press, 1988.

6. See Eric Lott, *Love and Theft: Blackface Minstrelsy and the American Working Class* (New York: Oxford University Press, 1993), and Walter Benn Michaels, *The Gold Standard and the Logic of Naturalism: American Literature at the Turn of the Century* (Berkeley: University of California Press, 1987). It can only be irresponsible to address these two important books in such a brief way, but were there space to develop an argument about them—in relation to my thesis—it would look like this: Lott's book illustrates a tremendous faith in the efficacy of literary criticism to address cultural appropriation as a social phenomenon; Lott's book believes, finally, that literary criticism can redress social policy by recording acts of linguistic and performative theft. Michaels' book, by contrast, is much more circumspect and modest (and, in my view, accurate) in its assessment of the limitations of literary criticism and theory; in his analysis, all we really have to deal with is language, and language is all we can change.

Chapter Eleven

Race and Wealth Disparity: The Role of Law and the Legal System

Beverly Moran and Stephanie M. Wildman

Many of the Chapters in this text assume that law plays some role in the creation and maintenance of wealth disparities based on race.[1] Yet many lawyers, judges, legislators, professors, and law students would strongly dispute this view. Many legal workers, like other Americans, believe in an American legal system that aspires to, and often achieves, neutrality in matters of class and equality in matters of race. They do not view law and the legal system as one way that American society polices race and wealth disparities. Because American law seems removed from race and wealth concerns, legal workers see no place for considerations of race and wealth disparities in their education or practice.

In response to the view that American law and legal institutions are class and color blind, this chapter provides examples of how legal institutions sometimes create and maintain racialized wealth disparities. The chapter offers examples of this phenomenon by examining a sequence of federal judicial decisions, the federal taxing statutes, the role of legal education, and access to legal services. These examples are instructive because they cut across a broad spectrum of the American legal system. By revisiting issues of race and wealth in different legal settings from the constitution to federal cases, the tax system, and legal education and practice, this chapter confirms that race and wealth are both involved in legal outcomes and ignored by legal actors and institutions in a systematic way. Legal actors and citizens of all vocations need to look more critically at the American legal landscape and critique the influence of race and wealth.

America's foundational aspirations toward equality and neutrality allow legal actors to ignore the effect that race and wealth disparities have on law and the legal system, even when those actors acknowledge how often law fails to achieve these ideals. Legal realists,[2] critical legal theorists,[3] critical race theorists,[4] feminist theorists,[5] and others have noted the contradiction between legal doctrines and legal realities. Yet, despite its contradictions and failures, the urge towards equality and neutrality creates opportunities for change. As E.P. Thompson observed:

> [P]eople are not as stupid as some . . . suppose them to be. They will not be mystified by the first man who puts on a wig.[6]

For Thompson, claims to neutrality and equality provide opportunities to redress an unequal class system even while these concepts also protect ruling class interests. Thompson reasons that a "partial and unjust" law cannot gain popular support and so is not useful in maintaining class hierarchy. Thus the aspiration for universality and equity can sometimes force law to follow its "own logic and criteria of equity."[7]

THE AMERICAN CONFLICT BETWEEN EQUALITY, NEUTRALITY, AND ASSIGNED RACE ROLES

From its beginnings, the American legal system has articulated two distinct, yet contradictory, views of human relations. The Declaration of Independence aspires to equality among people and neutral application of law.[8] Yet, at the same time, Article I, section 2 of the United States Constitution provides that the census shall count:

> . . . the whole number of free persons, including those bound to Service for a Term of Years, and excluding Indians not taxed, three fifths of all other Persons[9]

This constitutional provision allocates roles by race for the construction of political rights: Indians outside American society, Black slaves, and White male full citizens.

Ironically, neutrality and equality can support subordination and hierarchy. Anatole France illustrated this point when he sarcastically applauded the majestic equalitarianism of the law, which "forbids the rich as well as the poor to sleep under bridges, to beg in the streets, and to steal bread."[10]

In 1943, Robert Hale echoed Anatole France's sentiment, as he wrote about the law's role in creating unequal bargaining relationships and unequal wealth effects. Hale explained that wealth gives its owner control over his or her own life and leisure and over other people's lives as well.[11] Hale illustrated this control of the wealthy over the working classes through the greater bargaining power that capital has over labor, especially low-skilled workers. This unequal bargaining power leads to inequitable distributions of wealth as those with control over capital can extract work from others without just compensation. As seen in Hale's work, legal neutrality claims that law has no effect on this wealth distribution. Instead, law simply protects property rights and freedom of contract. Under this concept of legal neutrality, other institutions, for example the market, fuel the wealth distribution occasioned by unequal bargaining power.

Hale rejected the claim that legal neutrality has no wealth effects. Rather, Hale pointed out that legal rules lead to particular wealth distribution patterns and that different legal rules would create different wealth distribution patterns while still protecting property rights and freedom of contract.[12] For Hale, the allegedly neutral system of American property and inheritance laws does more than merely protect private property and freedom of contract; these laws also give property owners power over workers to the detriment of most Americans.

Sixty years after Hale, Stephen J. Rose, in a book and poster depicting the interrelationships of income, wealth, occupation, race, gender, and household type, showed that five percent of the United States population owns fifty-nine percent of the nation's wealth.[13] Using an icon representing 190,000 people as its primary unit, the left side of the poster portrayed the American population by income up to $150,000. Ninety-two percent of the American population earned at or below this $150,000 in combined household income. Ninety-two percent of the American population is able to fit within the physical frame of the approximately two by three foot poster. In order to expand the chart at the same 190,000 people per icon scale and include those who earn combined incomes of up to $300,000, the poster must add eight feet in height. The number of icons needed to represent the remaining population who earn more than $150,000 annually is both small and dramatic. In order to reflect the 20,000 households with more than $10 million in yearly income, the poster must grow twenty stories high.

Although Rose's poster tells a different story, the American myth perpetuates the idea that anyone can climb those twenty stories in one lifetime. This belief coexists with public rules and private practices that have tied wealth to race for generations. As a result, non-whites are even less likely to move out of poverty than whites.

The disparate, distributional result that ties race and wealth was supported throughout American history by government programs. The United States began as a slave nation and the end of slavery did not break the tie between race and wealth. Most people are aware of the failures of the post-Civil War Reconstruction and the emergence of the Jim Crow system of segregation.[14] Few are as aware of how the liberal New Deal tied race and wealth. The New Deal introduced the notion of an economic safety net into American politics. As such it pulled millions of Americans from poverty. But the New Deal also excluded agricultural and domestic workers from that economic safety net because those occupations served as a "neutral" proxy for race.[15]

After World War II, the government continued to enrich its citizens based on race through the Federal Housing Administration, which made home ownership available to working class whites, while excluding black buyers through redlining and other exclusionary practices.[16]

These government programs increased white family well-being significantly while systematically excluding blacks, Indians and others. Yet, because each program based exclusions on seemingly neutral factors, many whites have never understood the role their race played in their rise from poverty to middle class status.

Hale argues that contract law is driven by bargaining power and made up of seemingly class neutral rules that actually shift bargaining power to owners of capital and away from labor. Favoring the wealthy over workers is not the stated justification for these rules. Instead, proponents justify these rules as the most efficient means of supporting an important social goal called freedom of contract. The rules ignore the fact that, without true bargaining power, there can be no freedom of contract. Thus the rich and the poor share in the same freedoms which somehow mysteriously tend to favor the wealthy. The New Deal developed seemingly race-neutral rules that actually shifted wealth away from blacks and towards whites. These rules were not presented as part of an effort to bring the white working class into the middle class while leaving black America in Depression conditions for another forty years. Yet, by restricting benefits to whites either explicitly—as in the federal home mortgage arena—or implicitly—as in Social Security—these government programs helped ensure that government benefits would enforce an income and wealth gap between white Americans and their non-white counterparts. These gaps, first between the wealthy and everyone else (which is enforced by contract law among other legal rules) and between black wealth and white wealth (perpetuated by historical gaps in government benefits) occur in a wide range of assets, including access to education.

FACIAL NEUTRALITY REINFORCING HIERARCHY IN JUDICIAL DECISION-MAKING

Two judicial decisions announced twenty-five years apart illustrate how equality and neutrality can veil the reinforcement of existing wealth inequities. *Rodriguez v. San Antonio School District*[17] and *Hopwood v. Texas*[18] both concern the Texas public education system. *Rodriguez* dealt with elementary and secondary education;[19] *Hopwood* grappled with higher education in the state's premier law school.[20]

Rodriguez challenged the practice of funding local school districts through property taxes. In a property tax system, rich school districts are able to raise more funds through taxation than poor districts. Paradoxically, because rich districts have land and buildings with higher property values, these districts are able to raise greater funding while putting less tax burden on each taxpayer within the district. As Douglas Reed explained:

> . . .property-rich districts could generate significant revenues for education (at relatively low tax rates), while property-poor districts could produce only very small amounts of revenue (while taxing themselves at comparatively high rates).[21]

This uneven and unequal funding scheme led three law professors to argue that state wealth, rather than school district wealth, was a better measure of funding per student.[22] The professors urged:

> children are classless ; . . . no child of tender years is capable of meriting more or less than another.[23]

The Edgewood school district's budget, where Mr. Rodriguez's children attended school, spent only two thirds per student as compared to the Alamo Heights school district's per student expenditures.[24] The residents of the Edgewood district were predominantly Mexican-American; in contrast, the residents of Alamo Heights were predominantly "Anglo."

Although the factual record fully apprised the Supreme Court concerning the wealth and ethnic differences between the Edgewood and Alamo districts, the majority explicitly rejected a link between the "property-poor districts" and race. Instead the majority declared:

> Nor does it now appear that there is any more than a random chance that racial minorities are concentrated in property-poor districts.[25]

Citing a Connecticut-based study, the majority also rejected associating economic disadvantage and "property-poor" districts.[26] In ruling against the funding challenge the majority wrote:

> In sum, to the extent that the Texas system of school financing results in unequal expenditures between children who happen to reside in different districts, we cannot say that such disparities are the product of a system that is so irrational as to be invidiously discriminatory . . . The complexity of these problems is demonstrated by the lack of consensus with respect to whether it may be said

with any assurance that the poor, the racial minorities, or the children in over-burdened core-city school districts would be benefited by abrogation of traditional modes of financing education.[27]

Thus, in 1973 the Supreme Court let Texas fund its school districts through property taxes, thereby ensuring that rich school districts would spend more on their elementary and secondary school systems than poor school districts. The Court refused to find any connection between wealth and race or ethnicity, nor did it find a connection between wealth and educational resources.

In 1996, the Fifth Circuit decided *Hopwood v. Texas*, a challenge to the admissions policy at the University of Texas School of Law.[28] Children who attended kindergarten in Texas at the time *Rodriguez* was decided were 25 years old when the *Hopwood* litigation began. Thus Texans who were in the applicant pool to attend the University of Texas Law School grew up in an educational system that allowed vast differentials in their publicly funded education because of *Rodriguez*. In addition, these Texan applicants grew up shortly after the University of Texas desegregated although, for the vast majority of its history, the University of Texas was a segregated institution.[29]

Even though the University of Texas and its law school had ended *de jure* segregation, enrollment at the University of Texas remains predominantly white. During the *Hopwood* era, the law school embarked on an affirmative action plan meant to address this *de facto* segregation.

In *Hopwood,* the Fifth Circuit characterized the question before it as whether:

> in order to increase the enrollment of certain favored classes of minority students, the University of Texas School of Law discriminates in favor of those applicants by giving substantial racial preferences in its admissions program.[30]

The court rejected the University of Texas Law School's admission policy as unconstitutional because it produced an entering class containing students who did not meet a supposedly neutral and objective standard of merit.[31] The court's reliance on supposedly neutral tests did not reflect the race and class issues inherent in the Texas public school system.

Both *Rodriguez* and *Hopwood* reflect a kind of neutrality. As Anatole France might have said, in *Rodriguez* the law is equalitarian and neutral when it allows all parents to spend whatever funds they want on their children's education, so long as they have the money to do so. Further, the law remains neutral when the graduates of under-funded schools are subjected to the same tests as graduates of well-funded schools in order to gain admission to the state university's law school. Each decision reflects a theoretical neutrality that together created a real world differential in access to public education at the primary, secondary, and graduate levels.

The law acknowledges that a rule allowing only whites to enter the University of Texas is not neutral.[32] But the Fifth Circuit employed the shield of neutrality by demanding that the University of Texas employ an admission policy for local Texas residents that heavily relies on test scores. Many view the use of test scores as neutral, even though the judges received evidence of these tests' race and class bias.[33] Further, the differences in educational opportunity on the primary and secondary level meant that there would be different test scores by race even if the tests themselves contained no racial bias.

From a doctrinal perspective, *Rodriguez* and *Hopwood* illustrate Hale's two observations that (1) neutrality can mask redistributive effects and (2) different rules could create different wealth effects without harming fairness, freedom of contract, or property ownership. Read together, *Rodriguez* and *Hopwood* offer a microcosmic view of children denied educational opportunities under the guise of neutral law.[34]

STATUTORY LAW: RACE, WEALTH, AND TAXES

As the discussion of *Rodriguez* and *Hopwood* above illuminates, American legal institutions sometimes create seemingly neutral rules that actually enforce race and wealth roles. For example, access to education is a type of wealth.[35] The *Rodriguez* and *Hopwood* decisions each articulate neutral rules that, when combined, distribute public education in skewed ways. Yet, as Hale pointed out, the unequal distribution of wealth is hard to detect exactly because neutral rules serve to mask unequal wealth distribution and to make the skewed distribution possible. Until now this chapter has looked at a series of rules and government policies that purported to be race and class neutral, such as freedom of contract and law school admissions. This chapter now turns to a law that does not purport to represent class neutrality: the federal tax code.

There are a number of reasons to consider tax laws as statutes with both race and wealth effects. The first and most obvious reason for considering that the United States tax system might have both race and wealth effects is that the system clearly implicates both income and wealth distribution. For example, at its most basic level, the gift and estate tax laws explicitly tax large estates as they pass from generation to generation and the income tax uses progressive rates as income rises.

A second reason for expecting to see differences based on race and wealth in the United States taxing statutes is that both the income and the wealth gaps between blacks and whites are dramatic in this country.[36] Because both the income and wealth gaps are so extreme by race, effects of the intersection of race and wealth might appear more readily in a statute that deals directly with income and wealth.

The observations contained in the paragraphs above argue that the American tax system is both race-neutral as written and race- and wealth-sensitive as structured. In fact, as one would expect, it turns out that the United States tax system does have a series of rules that result in blacks and whites at the same income, education level, marital status, number of children and region of residence, paying very different amounts of federal income tax with blacks paying more.[37] This differential by race is achieved through a number of mechanisms. One way that the distribution is achieved is through the technical rules and how those rules interact with how people live. Another way the distribution is achieved is by the silence that allows the rules to play out differently by race without any movement toward reform. A third factor that helps maintain wealth distribution by race is the shaping of public opinion so that Americans accept rules that favor the wealthy as neutral rules that favor us all.

Technically the distribution of tax benefits to whites and away from blacks is achieved through a series of credits, exclusions and deductions that all work so that the greatest benefits go to people who fit a white profile and the lowest benefits go to people who fit other profiles.[38] A quick example of this phenomenon are the bundle of benefits that apply to home ownership.

A vast gap in home ownership exists between whites and blacks.[39] The gap in home ownership is a direct result of a wide range of government policies from the creation of the Republic to date. Thus, it can hardly be argued that home ownership is a voluntary act or that black people have purposefully eschewed home ownership. Instead, black people are now, and have been, consistently shut out of the home ownership market by a series of laws, rules and private policies.

The Internal Revenue Code gives tremendous benefits to home ownership. The cost of financing a home is completely deducible for most Americans. Property taxes that support local schools are also deductible. If the house goes up in value, the owners can draw money out of the house through borrowing, not pay any tax on the receipt of the borrowed funds, and get a deduction on the payment of mortgage interest. When the owner sells the home, the gain realized from any increased value or equity is usually received completely tax-free.

The combination of the tremendous tax benefits for home ownership combined with the practices and policies that kept blacks from home ownership shows how the intersection of a neutral law with a race-charged situation compounds race effects. The intersection of the law and the reality of how people live allows the "neutral" law to change wealth outcomes by race.

As E.P. Thompson might tell us, the intersection of race and wealth in the United States tax laws is best achieved if the law is supported by public opinion. For example, support for such concepts as freedom of property and freedom of contract helps mask how the law is used to create wealth based on bargaining power. In the case of tax legislation, manipulation of public opinion and societal ignorance of racial hierarchy both contribute to attitudes that veil recognition of the tax law's role in maintaining wealth disparities.

One illustration of how public relations can manipulate public opinion for political ends in federal tax legislation is provided by Marjorie Kornhauser. Kornhauser examines the use of public relations to manipulate public opinion for political ends in federal tax legislation.[40] Her article presents an early example of the still current political phenomenon of small, well-financed groups influencing tax legislation through lobbying, the media, and rhetorical appeals to the "common man." Kornhauser shows Americans reacting completely outside their class interests when dealing with tax policy.

Kornhauser's work concerns the repeal of certain public reporting requirements that made information on wealthy taxpayers' income accessible to the general public. Kornhauser opines that the average American had nothing to lose from the public reporting requirement. In contrast, wealthy Americans felt vulnerable in the face of public revelations of their holdings. Even though they represented a numeric minority, the campaign the wealthy mounted against the disclosure rules gained wide popular support. The wealthy were able to construct a tale that resonated with average Americans who came to identify with those wealthy taxpayers who were actually harmed by the provision.

Contemporary debates over the estate tax present a more current example of the same identification phenomenon. The estate tax is nothing if not a tax that directly targets upper class families seeking to make intergenerational wealth transfers. Yet, even when commentators assure the public that only one percent of the population would ever confront the gift and estate tax, a mass abolition movement arises against the "death" tax.[41]

What Professor Kornhauser's work illustrates and what the public outcry against the "death tax" reflects is how the great American cultural urge toward neutrality and equality masks, as Hale and France both suggested, a tremendous class-based privilege. The cultural concern for equality and neutrality serves as both a strength and weakness. In its best light, the culture fosters empathy with those less fortunate and a willingness to sacrifice for the greater good. At its worst, it supports a type of silence that prevents Americans from seeing, and therefore discussing, ways to actually achieve that neutrality and equality. This silencing dynamic is evident in federal courts and their contribution to public education policy, common law contracts rules and federal statutes and legal education.

LEGAL EDUCATION: TRAINING GROUND
FOR CONTINUED SILENCE

Wealth disparities and race both play marginal roles in the law school curriculum.[42] Although all first year law students study subjects that raise wealth
and race issues, legal educators rarely teach those subjects in ways that raise
those concerns. Instead, legal pedagogy adopts a mode of "perspectivelessness," reinforcing the ideal that legal discourse is objective and analytical.[43]
Perspectivelessness supports the myth of legal neutrality. Although legal
scholars like Hale have been very explicit about the role of wealth in American law[44] and critical race theory has been equally explicit about the role race
plays in American legal institutions,[45] both topics remain relegated to bou-
tique seminar courses. Students can, and often do, study law for three years
without ever considering either wealth or race as legitimate topics of study.

The omission of race and wealth disparities from the core law school curriculum reinforces its invisibility in other parts of the profession thereby supporting the kinds of judicial decisions and statutes discussed in the preceding
sections. As E.P. Thompson observed "class is something which in fact happens."[46] When class just "happens" in the law school classroom without any
study or comment, legal educators train the next generation of lawyers to ignore these fundamental issues of fairness and their implications for democracy.[47]

A student writing exercise provides one example of the absence of basic
knowledge about wealth disparity within the context of legal education. Upon
finishing a unit on work and care giving, which included readings on the
United States' economy and how it is managed to ensure unemployment, students taking a Social Justice Law class spent three minutes on a free write exercise answering the question: "What is class?" Several essays discussed
physical classroom space. Other students wrote about "class" as conduct, in
the sense of classy, or snobby, or being embarrassed by a lack of "classiness."
Thus, even in the context of readings and discussions of wealth disparity,
these students' first-reaction to the term "class" was to envision meanings disconnected from wealth. When asked whether they spoke much about class
and wealth disparity in law school, the students answered "No."

The silence on wealth and class in law school is not limited to one school
or one classroom.[48] Indeed, that silence is so pervasive that it impacts student
career choices and reduces the number of law students who aspire to work for
social justice. Several studies of legal education note that students enter law
school with a desire to work in the public interest.[49] Yet by the time these
same students graduate, they have changed their vision of success toward a
corporate practice devoid of social justice issues.[50]

Class implicates relationships and power so that, while social stratification statistics give us a snapshot of one aspect of class or wealth, these statistics fail to convey the ways people experience class, how they identify themselves and others, or how power structures become replicated.[51] Wealth's invisibility in legal education is part of how class "happens." When class just "happens," the failure to pay attention replicates and reinforces existing structures.[52] The replication and reinforcement of these existing structures influences the development of law, legal theory, and the next generation of legal professionals.

Income and wealth inequalities exist for many reasons; law is only one of those reasons. Yet, as this chapter shows, law is not a trivial reason. In many ways, legal rules, especially those rules that purport to support equality and neutrality, can mask the means for supporting wealth and power differentials of all sorts. Legal education disserves the very people who need to understand both how law supports and undercuts equality and neutrality. Legal education ignores the issues of race, class, and inequality through the silence on these issues that permeates many classrooms. As a result, future leaders lack the training that they need to even imagine how law supports or undercuts true equality, much less how to address those issues in any serious way.

ACCESS TO LAWYERS AND THE LEGAL SYSTEM: A FORM OF WEALTH

This chapter offers different definitions of wealth. Some view income as a proxy for wealth. The discussion of the racial roles assigned by the Constitution makes race a type of political wealth. The discussion of *Rodriguez* and *Hopwood* addressed education as a form of wealth. The racial allocation of government benefits in the discussion of the federal tax laws illustrates how tax laws are structured. These tax laws create wealth transfers from blacks with less wealth to whites with more wealth and the public financing of housing does the same by reducing blacks' access to the funds needed to purchase housing and other types of wealth.

Access to lawyers and the legal system is another form of wealth. A typical view of the provision of legal services would see legal services as a value-free commodity that is governed by the market. But as Hale pointed out, legal rules have tremendous impact on the protection of property rights, the creation of bargaining power, and the determination of wealth distribution. Just as legal rules concentrate other types of wealth, such as education, housing, and tax benefits, legal resources are yet another type of wealth that remains unevenly distributed by class and race. Reginald Heber Smith decried the notion of "one law for the rich and another for the poor."[53] Smith viewed freedom and equal access to justice as inextricably intertwined.[54]

Like Smith, President Jimmy Carter charged that legal resources are inappropriately apportioned. The President complained that 90% of lawyers served only ten percent of the population.[55] In a recent study by the National Legal Aid and Defenders Association, researchers found that in California alone there was roughly one legal aid attorney for every 10,000 economically disadvantaged Californians.[56] Equal justice under law is a disregarded ideal when access to lawyers is so skewed.[57]

The availability of lawyers to bring social justice cases on behalf of individuals and communities affects both the nature of cases that are brought into court and the legal rules that prevail. Cruz Reynoso provides an example of the importance of lawyers for the protection of wealth with his description of a New Mexico program established to increase Native American lawyers.[58]

> Soon we started seeing cases coming out of Arizona . . . in which Native American tribes sued to receive water that they were entitled to under treaties. Rights mean nothing if nobody enforces them.[59]

Access to lawyers empowered the Indian community and allowed it to achieve rights that were previously not enforced because of a lack of legal resources. In New Jersey, it is estimated that less than one percent of all tenants have lawyers to help them in landlord tenant court.[60] How different would landlord tenant relationships look in New Jersey, or any state, if the parties approached the court with equal resources?

The United States spends only 300 million dollars on legal services to serve over forty million poor citizens.[61] By contrast, "A single law firm, which represents maybe a hundred or so corporate clients, earned . . . [one billion dollars]."[62] The total profits of a half dozen law firms exceeds the total federal, state, and local expenditures for legal representation for the poor.[63]

CONCLUSION

Louis Brandeis once warned that: "We can have democracy; in this country; or we can have great wealth concentrated in the hands of a few, but we can't have both."[64] In the United States, race and wealth are so intertwined that the wealthy few are also almost invariably white. If Brandeis is correct, and democracy cannot exist alongside concentrated wealth, then perhaps wealth concentrated by race presents an even greater threat than wealth that is concentrated through more random means.

Most disciplines seem to believe that law plays a role in creating and maintaining wealth and race disparities. This chapter shows that, from the origins of the nation when the United States Constitution explicitly established racial roles to the present, government policy often directed wealth from Indians and blacks towards whites. This chapter discussed one ironic aspect of legal method that helps legal institutions and doctrines play their role in maintaining race and wealth hierarchy—the aspiration to equality and neutrality. The examples of seemingly neutral rules having race and wealth effects included: Texas public education as sustained by *Rodriguez* and *Hopwood*; the color-blind federal tax laws; the law school classroom and its replication of silence on matters of class; and access to justice as measured by the availability of lawyers' services.

This chapter reflected different definitions of wealth. Human beings held as slaves provided a form of wealth to their owners,[65] access to education which develops human capital,[66] home ownership, and access to legal services. While other disciplines have a more focused definition of wealth, the legal landscape invites a more encompassing view.

This chapter began by noting the influence law has over other disciplines. That insight came from this text's invitation to its authors to self-consciously examine their discipline and how that discipline studies race and wealth disparities. In turn, this text invites its readers to use that self-conscious review as an introduction to each discipline's method. Legal method includes case analysis and textual analysis. Critical race theory has influenced legal method and other disciplines by recognizing that racism and racial hierarchy is the norm and that whites have little incentive to change that reality.[67] This chapter employed those legal methods in reviewing judicial decisions and statutes. The chapter also utilized a number of techniques borrowed from other disciplines. It applied sociology in its examination of tax statutes as well as literary theory and participant observations in looking at the law school classroom. Thus other disciplines draw on law and legal analysis, in turn, draws on many methods as well. Legal scholars see this aspect of the discipline of law as one of law's strengths.

Richard Delgado urges those in the academy to learn from other disciplines in their effort to promote social change. He notes, for example, that post-colonial literature, searching for ways to oppose imperial forces in Africa, Asia, and Latin America developed chronologically parallel to the civil rights tradition in the United States, but "without much interchange between the two."[68] Law and legal institutions need assistance from other disciplines to reveal the inconsistencies contained in the legal system and ultimately to hold that system accountable.

NOTES

Another version of this chapter appears as an article in the Fordham Urban Law Journal.

1. Most of the chapters in this text touch on law. See for example, Collins and Margo (laws that prohibited blacks from owning property), Kirkland and Peters (laws that enforced segregation), Brown and Cornfield (laws effecting unionization), Wong (No Child Left Behind federal legislation), Mitchell and Mitchell (public education laws and segregation), Tichi (bankruptcy and property taxation).

2. Karl N. Llewellyn, Jurisprudence: Realism in Theory and in Practice (1962); Max Radin, Law as Logic and Experience (1940).

3. For more information on critical legal studies, see Mark Kelman, A Guide to Critical Legal Studies (1987); Gary Minda, Postmodern Legal Movement: Law And Jurisprudence at The Centuries End (1996).

4. For more information on critical race theory, see Critical Race Theory: The Cutting Edge (Richard Delgado & Jean Stefancic, eds. 2d ed. 2001); Richard Delgado & Jean Stefancic, Critical Race Theory: An Introduction (2001); Critical Race Theory: The Key Writings That Formed The Movement (Kimberlé Crenshaw et al. eds.,1995).

5. Patricia J. Williams, The Alchemy of Race & Rights (1996); Mari J. Matsuda, Where Is Your Body? And Other Essays on Race, Gender and the Law (1996); Catherine A. Mackinnon, Toward a Feminist Theory of the State (1989).

6. English judges wear wigs, so Thompson's reference is to the role of law in perpetuating or combating injustice. See E.P. Thompson, Whigs and Hunters: The Origin of the Black Act 262–263 (1975).

7. Id. Thompson allows that a legal system may not achieve neutrality and fairness: "It is true that certain categories of person may be excluded from this logic (as children or slaves), that other categories may be debarred from access to parts of the logic (as women or, for many forms of eighteenth-century law, those without certain kinds of property), and that the poor may often be excluded, through penury, from the law's costly procedures." Id.

8. "We hold these truths to be self-evident, that all men are created equal, that they are endowed by their Creator with certain unalienable Rights, that among these are life, liberty and the pursuit of happiness." The Declaration of Independence para. 2 (U.S. 1776).

9. U.S. Const. art. I, § 2, cl. 3.

10. Anatole France, Le Lys Rouge [The Red Lily], reprinted in John Bartlett, Familiar Quotations 655 (1980).

11. Robert L. Hale, Bargaining, Duress, and Economic Liberty, 43 Colum. L. Rev. 603, 626–28 (1943).

12. Id. at 628. "Bargaining power would be different were it not that the law endows some with rights that are more advantageous than those with which it endows others." Id. at 627–628.

13. Stephen J. Rose, Social Stratification in the United States: The New American Profile Poster 34 (2007). see also William J. Collins and Robert A. Margo, Racial Differences In Wealth: A Brief Historical Overview, supra, chapter II.

14. Angela P. Harris, Equality Trouble: Sameness and Difference in Twentieth-Century Race Law, 88 Cal. L. Rev. 1923, 1931–33 (2000).

15. See Ira Katznelson, When Affirmative Action Was White: An Untold History of Racial Inequality in Twentieth-Century America (2005) (reporting how U.S. social programs favored whites). William E. Forbath, Constitutional Welfare Rights: A History, Critique and Reconstruction, 69 Fordham L. Rev. 1821 (2001); Joel F. Handler, "Constructing the Political Spectacle": The Interpretation of Entitlements, Legalization, and Obligations in Social Welfare History, 56 Brook. L. Rev. 899 (1990). See also Martha R. Mahoney, John O. Calmore & Stephanie M. Wildman, Social Justice: Professionals, Communities, and Law 451-571 (2003) (for a discussion of livelihood and the economic safety net) [hereinafter Mahoney, et al.]

16. For more on the private and public practices that operated to deny black Americans home ownership see William J. Collins and Robert A. Margo, Racial Differences in Wealth: A Brief Historical Overview, supra, chapter II and Elizabeth Kirkland and Sheila R. Peters, "Location, Location, Location" Residential Segregation and Wealth, Disparity, supra, chapter III. See also, Sheryll Cashin, The Failures of Integration: How Race and Class are Undermining the American Dream (2004), Douglas S. Massey & Nancy Denton, American Apartheid: Segregation and the Making of the Underclass (1993), Melvin L. Oliver & Thomas M. Shapiro, Black Wealth/White Wealth: A New Perspective on Racial Inequality (1995), Margalynne Armstrong, Race and Property Values in Entrenched Segregation, 52 U. Miami L. Rev. 1051 (1998), Mahoney, Segregation, Whiteness, and Transformation, 143 U. Pa. L. Rev. 1659 (1995), Florence Wagman Roisman, Teaching About Inequality, Race, and Property, 46 St. Louis U. L.J. 665 (2002).

17. San Antonio Indep. Sch. Dist. v. Rodriguez, 411 U.S. 1, 12 (1973).

18. Hopwood v. Texas, 78 F. 3d 932 (5th Cir. 1996), cert. denied, 518 U.S. 1033 (1996).

19. See Kenneth Wong, Federalism and Equity: Evolution of Federal Educational Policy, supra, chapter VI for further discussion of elementary and secondary education.

20. Access to education provides a form of wealth See Roland Mitchell and Reavis Mitchell, History and Education: Mining the Gap, supra, chapter VII.

21. Douglas S. Reed, Twenty-Five Years after Rodriguez: School Finance Litigation and the Impact of the New Judicial Federalism, 32 Law & Soc'y Rev. 175, 175 (1988).

22. Edward B. Foley, Rodriguez Revisited: Constitutional Theory and School Finance, 32 Ga. L. Rev. 475, 481 (1998). John E. Coons, William H. Clune III & Stephen D. Sugarman, Private Wealth and Public Education 2 (1970).

23. John E. Coons, William H. Clune III & Stephen D. Sugarman, Private Wealth and Public Education 419 (1970).

24. Rodriguez, supra, note 17 at 11–12.

25. Id. at 57.

26. Id. at 23.

27. Id. at 54–55, 56.

28. Hopwood v. Texas, 78 F. 3d 932 (1996).

29. The famous Supreme Court decision in Sweatt v. Painter, 339 U.S. 629 (1950), challenged that segregation and served as one of the building blocks in the litigation strategy that led to Brown v. Bd. of Educ. of Topeka, 347 U.S. 483 (1954). See also, A'Lelia R. Henry, Perpetuating Inequality: Plessy v. Ferguson and the Dilemma of Black Access to Public and Higher Education, 27 J.L. & Educ. 47, 66–71 (discussing the cumulative negative effect Rodriguez, Hopwood and other "colorblind" holdings on higher education for black students).

30. Hopwood, supra, note 18 at 934.

31. In 1993 resident (Texan) white applicants had a mean GPA of 3.53 and an LSAT of 164. Mexican Americans scored 3.27 and 158; blacks scored 3.25 and 157. Id. at 937 n.7.

32. See Sweatt v. Painter, 339 U.S. 629, 634 (1950) ("It may be argued that excluding petitioner from that school is no different from excluding white students from the new law school. This contention overlooks realities.").

33. For more on testing and bias, see Daria Roithmayr, Deconstructing the Distinction Between Bias and Merit, 85 Calif. L. Rev. 1449 (1997); Nicholas Lemann, The Big Test: The Secret History of the American Meritocracy (1999) and William C. Kidder & Jay Rosner, How the SAT Creates "Built-in Headwinds": An Educational and Legal Analysis of Disparate Impact, 43 Santa Clara L. Rev. 131, 133–34 (2002) (describing how the process of selecting and developing SAT questions exacerbates that test's disparate impact on African-American and Chicano test-takers).

34. For further discussion of the race and class implications of Rodriguez, see Goodwin Liu, The Parted Paths of School Desegregation and School Finance Litigation, 24 Law & Ineq. J. 81 (2006) (arguing that Keyes v. Sch. Dist. No. 1., 413 U.S. 189 (1973) and Rodriguez together presented the opportunity to fuse school finance litigation and desegregation, though the Court rejected that opportunity); Paula J. Lundberg, State Courts and School Funding: A Fifty-State Analysis, 63 Alb. L. Rev. 1101, 1145 (2000) (arguing that the states which are less urban, have a higher per-capita income and, and greater state constitutional protection have been and will be more likely to reject of the Rodriguez holding and invalidate their own funding schemes); Denise C. Morgan, The Less Polite Questions: Race, Poverty and Space in Public Education, 1998 Ann. Surv. Am. L. 267 (1998) (arguing that to improve public education encourage litigation that, contrary to the traditional litigation preceding and including Rodriguez, is capable of fusing race, poverty and space); Michael Heisse, Equal Educational Opportunity, Hollow Victories, and the Demise of School Finance Equity Theory: An Empirical Perspective and an Alternative Explanation, 32 Ga. L. Rev. 543, 575 (1998) (discussing how Rodriguez forced proponents of school finance equity at the federal level into state court battles for adequacy); Susan H. Bitensky, We "Had a Dream" in Brown v. Board of Education . . ., 1996 Det. C. L. Rev. 1, 16 (1996) (arguing that Rodriguez must be overturned in order for the U.S. to realize the full promise of Brown).

35. For more on education as a form of wealth see Wong, Chapter VI and Mitchell and Mitchell, Chapter VII.

36. Rose, supra, note 13.

37. Beverly Moran and William Whitford, A Black Critique of the Internal Revenue Code, 1996 Wis. L. Rev. 751, 754 (1999).

38. The home mortgage interest deduction presents one example of this phenomenon. . Id. at 754; see also Beverly Moran, Setting an Adgenda for the Study of Tax and Black Culture, 21 U. Ark. Little Rock L. Rev. 779, 783 (1999); William C. Whitford, Remarkable, 76 N.C.L. Rev. 1639, 1645 (1998).

39. William J. Collins and Robert A. Margo, Racial Differences in Wealth: A Brief Historical Overview, supra, chapter II and Elizabeth Kirkland and Sheila R. Peters, "Location, Location, Location" Residential Segregation and Wealth, Disparity, supra, chapter III.

40. Marjorie E. Kornhauser, Shaping Public Opinion and the Law in the 1930s: How a "Common Man" Campaign Ended a Rich Man's Law (February 2006), Tulane Public Research Paper No. 06–02, available at SSRN: http://ssrn.com/abstract=880383.

41. "The estate tax currently affects less than 1 percent of families, and it is the most progressive tax in the country because its impact is almost entirely on the nation's richest families. . . At the moment, the government imposes a tax of about 46 percent on estates worth more than $2 million, or more than $4 million in the case of couples." Edmund L. Andrews, G.O.P. Fails In Attempt To Repeal Estate Tax, N.Y. Times, June 9, 2005 at C1.

42. bell hooks describes class in America as the subject the culture does not address. "Nowadays it is fashionable to talk about race or gender; the uncool subject is class." bell hooks, Where We Stand: Class Matters vii (2000) (grieving that greed sets "the standard for how we live and interact in everyday life"). Her comment is reminiscent of Patricia J. Williams description of race as the elephant in the room that gets tiptoed around, also not discussed. Patricia J. Williams, The Alchemy of Race and Rights: Diary of a Mad Law Professor 49 (1991). Although both wealth and race tend to be ignored in law school classrooms, several good casebooks are available on these subjects, including Emma C. Jordan & Angela P. Harris, Economic Justice: Race, Gender, Identity and Economics (2005); Juan Perea, Richard Delgado, Angela P. Harris & Stephanie M. Wildman, Race and Races: Cases and Resources for a Diverse America 2d (2007); and Derrick Bell, Race, Racism and American Law (5th ed., 2004).

43. Kimberlé Williams Crenshaw, Foreword: Toward a Race-Conscious Pedagogy in Legal Education, 4 S. Cal. Rev. L. & Women's Stud. 33, 35 (1994).

44. See, e.g., Cass R. Sunstein, Why Does the Constitution Lack Social and Economic Guarantees?, 56 Syracuse L. Rev. 1, (2005) (supporting the idea that the Nixon appointments to the Supreme Court removed the potential for a progressive understanding of wealth distribution).

45. Critical Race Theory: The Cutting Edge (Richard A. Delgado and Jean Stefancic eds., 2d ed. 1999); Critical Race Theory: The Key Writings That Formed the Movement (Kimberlé Crenshaw et al. eds.,1996).

46. E. P. Thompson, The Making of the English Working Class 9 (1964). See also Martha R. Mahoney, Class and Status in American Law: Race Interest and the Anti-Transformation Cases, 76 S. Cal. L. Rev. 799, 805 (2003) (arguing that "when law ignores class while claiming to protect white workers, it gives authority to the claim that whites are harmed by the advent of people of color").

47. See Stephanie M. Wildman, Democracy and Social Justice: Founding Centers for Social Justice in Law Schools, 55 J. Legal Educ. 252, 255–56 (2005) (describing the connection between democracy and social justice issues like class and race).

48. Margaret Montoya illustrates another example of missed learning opportunities for the whole class, because prevailing assumptions in the classroom prevented the recognition of wealth disparities. See Margaret E. Montoya, Mascaras, Trenzas, y Greñas: Un/Masking the Self While Un/Braiding Latina Stories and Legal Discourse, 17 Harv. Women's L.J. 185 (1994).

49. Robert Stover, Making It and Breaking It: The Fate of Public Interest Commitment During Law School (1989) (Reporting that 1/3 of beginning first-year law students said they hoped to work in public interest jobs and 1/6 of graduating third years expressed the same hopes; the number of students who expressed commitment to public interest jobs dropped by half during law school.); Robert Granfield, Making Elite Lawyers: Visions of Law at Harvard and Beyond 3 (1992) (describing student's changing view of career goals).

50. Id. Note, however, that corporate law practice need not be disconnected from social justice work. Bob Egelko, 14 S.F. Law Firms Pledge Free Work for Poor Clients: Judicial Nudge Prompts Commitment, S.F. Chron., Dec. 15, 2000, at A.26 (describing the successful effort of Chief Judge Marilyn Hall Patel, U.S. District Court in San Francisco, and Chief Justice Ronald George, California Supreme Court, with the Bar Association of San Francisco to encourage law firms to commit a percentage of attorney time to pro bono work).

51. Martha R. Mahoney, Class and Status in American Law: Race Interest and the Anti-Transformation Cases, 76 S. Cal. L. Rev. 799, 805 (2003).

52. Id.

53. Reginald Heber Smith, Justice and the Poor 3 (1919).

54. Id.

55. Robert Granfield, Making Elite Lawyers: Visions of Law at Harvard and Beyond 4 (1992).

56. Jose Padilla, Surviving 40 Years of Poverty Law Practice: Salvaging Justice, Address at Santa Clara University Law School (Oct. 16, 2006); Deborah L. Rhode, Access to Justice, 69 Fordham L. Rev. 1785, 1786 (2001).

57. A study released by Legal Services of New Jersey on October 13, 2006 finds that over the past year nearly 120,000 low-income New Jerseyans attempted to receive free legal assistance, but were turned away due to a lack of resources. Legal services providers are worried that the data under-represent the problem because many low-income people do not attempt to receive legal services when they need them. The report, "People Without Lawyers: New Jersey's Civil Legal Justice Gap Continues," also found that 99 percent of defendants in landlord-tenant eviction cases at state courts were not represented by a lawyer. Kate Conscarelli, Poor Jerseyans Have Limited Access to Legal Aid, Study Finds, The Star Ledger (New Jersey), Oct. 13, 2006.

58. Cruz Reynoso, Educational Equity, 36 UCLA L. Rev. 107 (1988).

59. Id. Lawyers are not, however, a panacea for the ailments of disempowered communities. Marc Galanter, in a classic article, explains how the legal system is stacked against the "have-nots" in society. Marc Galanter, Why the "Haves" Come

Out Ahead: Speculations on the Limits of Legal Change, 9 Law and Soc'y Rev. 95 (1974).

60. Kate Conscarelli, Poor Jerseyans Have Limited Access to Legal Aid, Study Finds, The Star Ledger (New Jersey), Oct. 13, 2006.

61. Justice Earl Johnson, Jr., Equal Access to Justice: Comparing Access to Justice in the United States and Other Industrial Democracies, 24 Fordham Int'l L.J. S83, S83–S84 (2000).

62. Id.

63. Id.

64. Joseph R. Conlin, The Morrow Book of Quotations in American History 48 (1984).

65. Anthony Paul Farley, Accumulation, 11 Mich. J. of Race & Law 51 (2005) (urging that the rule of law supports the primal scene of accumulation).

66. Wong, supra, note 20 and Mitchell & Mitchell, supra, note 21.

67. See, Chapter V, Brown and Cornfield and Richard Delgado & Jean Stefancic, Critical Race Theory: An Introduction 6-9 (2001) (describing basic tenets of critical race theory).

68. Richard Delgado, Si Se Puede, But Who Gets the Gravy?, 11 Mich. J. of Race & Law 9, 19 (2005).

Another version of this chapter appears at 34 Fordham Urban Law Journal 1219 (2007).

Index

Abu-Lughod, Janet, 6
academic research, xi
Academy of Management, 44
accommodationism, 91
accountability, 77, 78–79
activism, 96
Adler, M. J., 45
admission policies, 153–54
advertising, xii–xiii, 131–34
Africans and the Industrial Revolution in England (Inikori), 7
American Anthropological Association, 127
American Apartheid: Segregation and the Making of the Underclass (Massey and Denton), 25
American Historical Review, 4
American Indian College Fund, 132
American Sociological Association (ASA), leadership in, 64
Anderson, James, 87, 91, 93–94
anthropology, 127–37; literary criticism and, 141
anti-poverty programs, 45–46, 76; accountability in, 77, 79–80; implementation of, 77–78
Aranson, J., 100
archaeology, 128
Armstrong, Samuel C., 88

Asia, history of, 4–6
Asian Age, 4–6
asymmetric social relations, 58
"Atlanta Compromise" (Washington), 91–92
authenticity, 127, 130–31, 131–34

Bambaataa, Afrika, 134
Bane, Mary Joe, 46, 47
bankruptcy, vii–viii, 120–21
bargaining power, 149–51
Barry, Bruce, x, xi, 41–56
Baudrillard, Jean, 130
Bell, Derrick, 65
"Be You" ad campaign, 132–33
bilingual education, 77
biological anthropology, 128
Black Issues in Higher Education, 83
Black Power Movement, 96
Black Wealth, White Wealth: A New Perspective on Racial Inequality (Oliver, Shapiro), 66–68
Blau, Francine D., 15
Blaut, J. M., 3
Boas, Franz, 128
Bonfire of the Vanities (Wolfe), 113
Boston Fed Study, 34
Bowie, Norman, 53
brain drain, 83–84

neo-liberalism, 129
net financial worth, 66–67
net worth, 66–67
New Critics, 140
New Deal, 150–51
new historicism, 140, 145
Newman, Katherine K., 120, 122–23
New York Times, 37, 125–26
Nike ad campaigns, 133–34, 135
Nkomo, Stella, 49–50
No Child Left Behind Act, xii, 77,
    79–80
Norris, Frank, 113
nostalgia, 130–31

Oates, J. F., 45
Oliver, Melvin L., 66–68
originality, 132–33
*Origins of Global Wealth Disparities:
    A World History Case Study* (Quirin),
    xvii

Parboteeah, K. P., 44
Peters, Sheila, xiii, 23–40
Peterson, Paul E., 78–79
Pfizer, 53
philanthropy: corporate, 47; education
    and, 91
Polikoff, A., 32
political science, on decentralization and
    inequity, 71–72
politics of education, 72–81
Pomeranz, Kenneth, 4
Porter, Michael, 47
Portera, Mack, 83
Portes, Alejandro, 61, 62
post-Fordism, 129–30
poverty: child, 43; corporatism and,
    42–44; education and, 104; global,
    43; legal system and, xiii–xiv;
    management literature on, 44–47;
    scope and persistence of, 42–43
"Poverty and Profits" (Hostetler, Kelso,
    Adler, Long, Oates), 45
Powell, G. N., 48
Powell, John A., 23

power: legal system and, 149–51;
    poverty and, 43; as wealth, xii
Prahalad, C. K., 46–47
Preston, Lee, 52
*Problems in Race, Political Economy,
    and Society: How Capitalism
    Underdeveloped Black America*
    (Marable), 95–96
promotion rates, 47–48
property values, 28–31, 37. *See also*
    home ownership
psychology, xiii
public opinion, 156
public relations, 156

Quinn, Dennis, 52
Quirin, James, x, xiii, xvii, 1–10

Rabe, Barry G., 78–79
race: advertising and, 131–34;
    anthropological views of, 127–37;
    critical race theory on, xi, 62–68;
    culture and, xx–xxi; Eurocentrism and,
    3–4; genetics and, 128; ideologies of,
    housing and, 28; interpretations of, x;
    in literary criticism, 138–47;
    management literature on, 47–50;
    models of, 49–50; problems in
    studying wealth and, xvi–xvii; roles,
    legal system and, 149–51; sociological
    perspectives on, 57–70; wealth gap
    and, explanations of, xvii–xviii
race relations, industrialization and,
    25–26
racism: critical race theory on, 65–68;
    sociological study on, 64–65
rap music, ad campaigns and, 132–33
rational choice theories, 50, 72–73
"Real" ad campaign, 133
real estate boards, segregation and,
    27–28
redistributive policies, 67; educational
    policy and, 71–81, 75–76
redlining, 29–31
*Reducing the Effects of Stereotype
    Threat on African American Students*

Biographies of Authors

Bruce Barry, Brownlee O. Currey Professor of Management; Professor of Sociology; Director, Ph.D. Program in Management, Vanderbilt University. B.A.(1980) and M.A. (1981) University of Virginia, Ph.D. (1991) University of North Carolina. Research interests include power and influence in organizations, the psychology of conflict and negotiation, workplace rights, business ethics, and public policy. Professor Barry has published over twenty articles and chapters on these subjects, and is a co-author of three books on negotiation.

Tony N. Brown, Assistant Professor of Sociology, Department of Sociology, Vanderbilt University, Adjunct Research Scientist, Research Center for Group Dynamics, University of Michigan; B.S. (1991) University of Maryland—Eastern Shore (Sociology); M.A. (1993) and Ph.D. (1998) University of Michigan, Ann Arbor (Sociology). Research interests include racial and ethnic relations, sociology of mental health, quantitative methodology, and survey methodology. Professor Brown has published eight articles.

William J. Collins, Associate Professor of Economics, Department of Economics, Vanderbilt University. A.B. (1993), A.M. (1995) and Ph.D. (1998) Harvard University. Professor Collins's general research interests include Economic History, Labor Economics, and International Trade. Professor Collins has written more than seventeen articles on the following topics: racial disparities in labor markets, housing markets, health, and education; the origins and impact of policy responses to discrimination; labor market integration in the United States and India; and international trade and capital goods prices.

Daniel B. Cornfield, Professor of Sociology, Vanderbilt University, B.A. (1974), M.A. (1977), and Ph.D. (1980) from University of Chicago. Research fields include: Diversity, Labor Sociology, Labor Unions, Unemployment, Minorities, Organized Labor, Labor Relations, Affirmative Action, Sociology of Work and Technology. Professor Cornfield has published five books and more than fifty articles and chapters.

Edward Fischer, Associate Professor of Anthropology, Director for Latin American and Iberian Studies, Vanderbilt University; B.A. (1989) University of Alabama at Birmingham, M.A. (1995) and Ph.D. (1996) from Tulane University. Research interests include political economy, globalization, development, Maya studies, identity, ethnicity and cognition. Professor Fischer has published five books, eleven journal articles, eight book chapters, six book reviews and other research works related to these fields.

Dennis D. Kezar, Associate Professor of English, University of Utah, B.A. (1990) University of the South (Sewanee), M.A. (1993) and Ph.D. (1997) from University of Virginia, Research Fields include: Renaissance drama, Shakespeare, Milton, Epic, Closet drama, and literature. Professor Kezar has published three books and ten articles.

M. Elizabeth Kirkland, Research Associate at the Race Relations Institute, Fisk University. B.A. (1982) Baker University, J.D. (1990) University of Missouri-Kansas City. Research interests include race relations, racial residential segregation, and housing policy. Ms. Kirkland previously practiced law in the areas of environmental litigation and criminal defense, and she has published work on racial discrimination in jury selection.

Robert A. Margo, Professor of Economics and of African-American Studies, Boston University, and Research Associate, National Bureau of Economic Research. A.B. (1976) University of Michigan, A.M. (1978) and Ph.D. (1982), Harvard University. Professor Margo has done extensive research and academic work both in Economics and History. Author of "Disenfranchisement, School Finance and the Economics of Segregated School in the United States South, 1890–1910," "Race and Schooling in the South, 1880 -1950: An Economic History," "Wages and Labor Markets in the United States, 1820–1860," and (with J. Perlmann) "Women's Work? American Schoolteachers, 1650–1920". Professor Margo has written more than 60 articles on topics such as women's employment history, new evidence on American slave nutrition and health, salaries for black and white teachers, the poor at birth, the history of wage inequality, racial differences in home ownership and microeconomic aspects of the Great Depression. Has written a series of work-ing papers for the National Bureau of Economic Research, for which he is a research associate. Research in progress focuses on the growth of manufac-turing in the 19th century.

Reavis Mitchell, Jr., Chair and Professor, Department of History, Fisk Uni-versity. B.A. (1969) Fisk University, Master of Science (1972) Tennessee State University, Ph.D (1983) Middle Tennessee State University, with post-doctoral studies at Harvard University. Professor Mitchell is the author of *Thy Loyal Children Make Their Way: A History of Fisk University Since 1866* and of 12 entries in 1998's *Tennessee Encyclopedia of History and Culture*. Pro-fessor Mitchell has written several historical monographs and published nu-merous articles in journals, magazines, and newspapers.

Roland Mitchell, Assistant Professor of Higher Education Administration, Louisiana State University. B.A. (1994) Fisk University, M.Ed. (1996) Van-derbilt University, Ph.D. (2005), University of Alabama. Current research in-terests include theorizing the impact of historical and communal knowledge on pedagogy, and an exploration of the understandings that allow educators to provide service to students from different cultural, ethnic, and social back-grounds.

Beverly Moran, Professor of Law and Sociology, Vanderbilt University Law School, A.B. (1977) Vassar College, J.D. (1981) University of Pennsylvania Law School, L.L.M. (1986) New York University. Professor Moran writes and speaks on issues related to public finance, taxation, race, gender, African and comparative law. She has published three books, numerous articles and essays and has lectured on four continents.

Sheila Peters, Interim Associate Provost, Interim Director of the Race Rela-tions Institute, Associate Professor of Psychology, Fisk University. B.A. (1981) University of North Carolina, M.S. (1984) and Ph.D. (1989) from Vanderbilt University. Research interests include the gender-specific pro-gramming within the juvenile justice system, foster care, vulnerable children and adolescents, the African Diaspora and health disparities. Professor Peters is a past President of the Nashville Branch of the NAACP, a former commis-sioner and chair of the Metro Human Relations Commission of Nashville, and a former commissioner with the Tennessee Commission on Children and Youth; she is a licensed clinical psychologist who specializes in working with vulnerable children and youth, and she is a national consultant on juvenile justice.

James A. Quirin, Professor, Department of History, Fisk University, B.A. (1965) and M.A. (1971), University of Oregon, Ph.D. (1977) University of Minnesota. Professor Quirin's research interests are in Ethiopian Studies, particularly, Ethiopian Jewish Studies. He has published a book on that topic and more than fourteen articles, chapters and proceedings as well as eight book reviews.

Jason Stansbury is a doctoral student at the Owen Graduate School of Management at Vanderbilt University. His research interests are concentrated in business ethics and human resources, particularly in how organizational ethics programs can promote ethical business behavior. Before coming to Vanderbilt, he worked as a management consultant in the automotive industry and studied economics at the University of Michigan.

Cecelia Tichi, William R. Kenan, Jr., Professor of English, Vanderbilt University, B.A. (1964) Pennsylvania State University, M.A. (1965) Johns Hopkins University, Ph.D. (1968) University of California-Davis. Professor Tichi writes cultural issues ranging from American television to country music to early American Literature. She is the author of five books, including "High Lonesome: The American Culture of Country Music," "Electronic Hearth: Creating an American television Culture," "Shifting Gears: Technology, Literature, Culture in Modernist America." and "Embodiment of a Nation: Human Form in American Places." She also has edited three books and written three novels in addition to 21 articles.

Stephanie M. Wildman serves as Professor of Law and Director of the Santa Clara University School of Law Center for Social Justice and Public Service. She is the author of Privilege Revealed: How Invisible Preference Undermines America (with contributions by Margalynne Armstrong, Adrienne D. Davis, & Trina Grillo), Race and Races: Cases and Resources for a Diverse America (with Richard Delgado, Angela A. Harris, and Juan F. Perea) (2000) and Social Justice: Professionals Communities and Law (with Martha R. Mahoney and John O. Calmore) (2003). She is past Co-President of the Society of American Law Teachers, and she currently serves on the Association of American Law Schools Executive Committee.

Kenneth K. Wong, The Walter and Leonore Annenberg Professor in Education Policy, Brown University, B.A. (1977), M.A. 1980, and Ph.D. (1983) University of Chicago. Professor Wong's research interests include Urban School Reform, State Finance, and Educational Policies, Intergovernmental Relations, and Federal Educational Policies (such as Title I in high poverty schools). Professor Wong has published three books. He has also edited nine books and written more than fifty-five articles and nine book reviews.